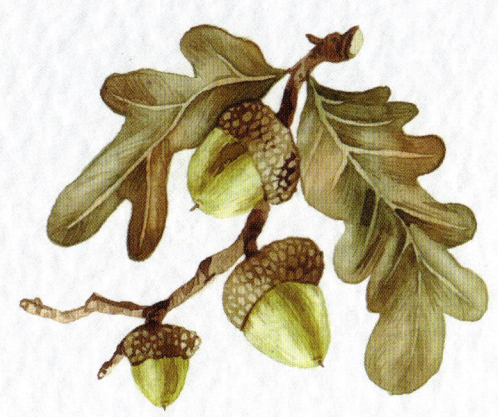

Painting Woodland Watercolors

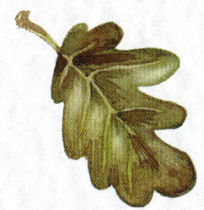

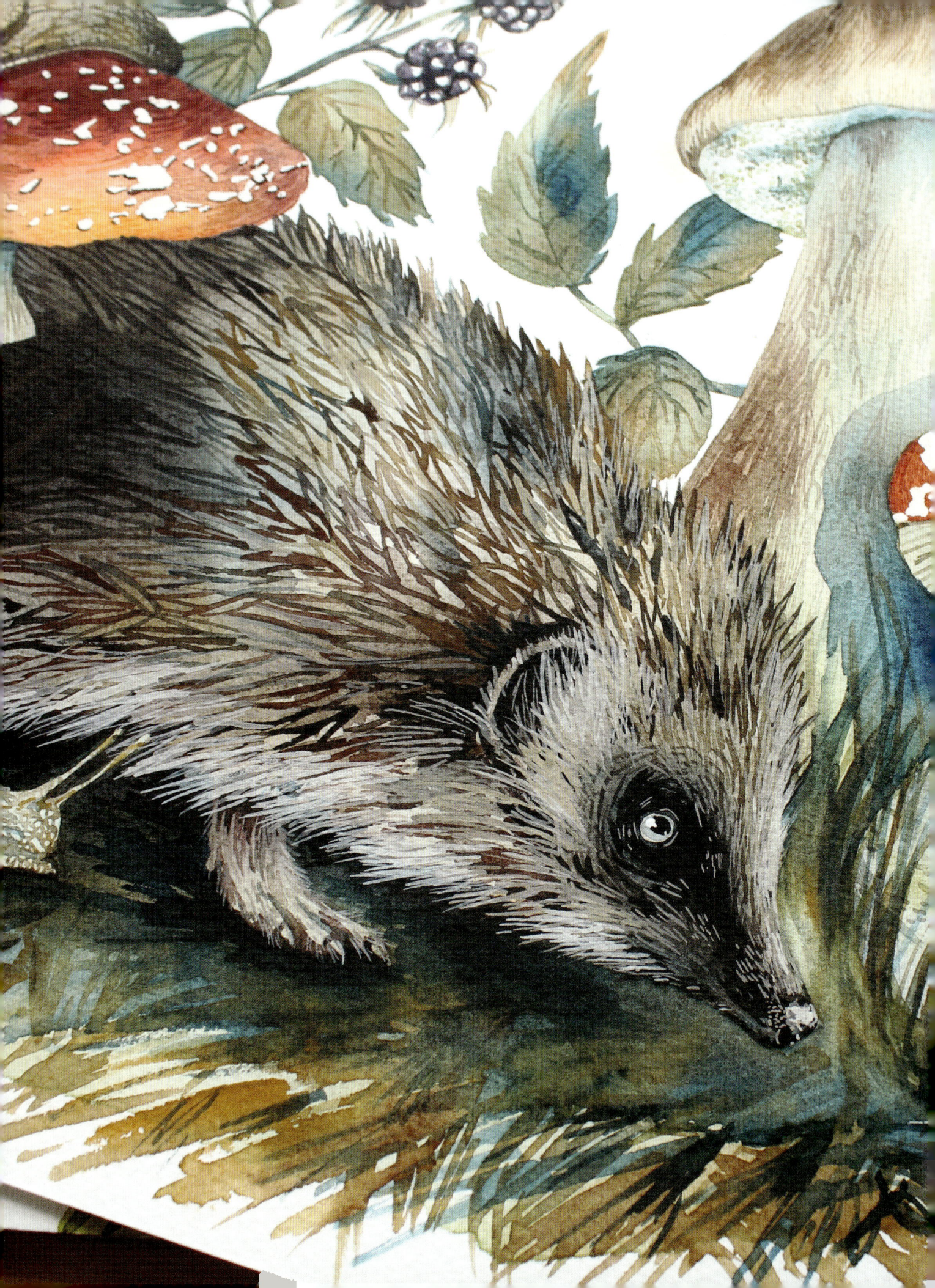

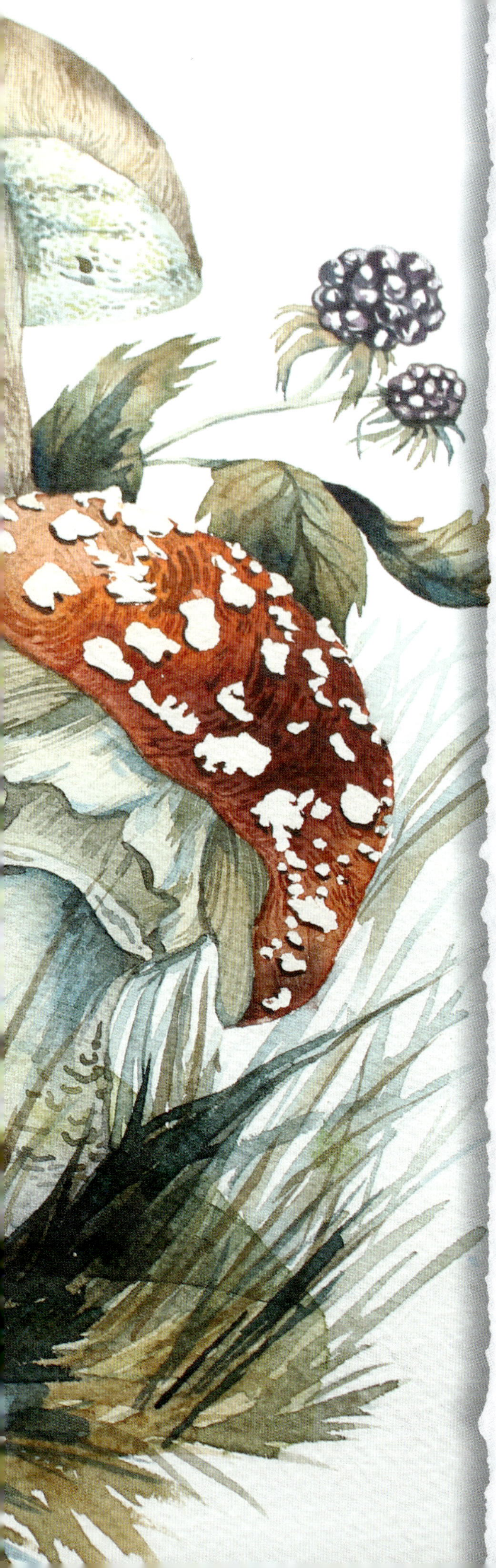

Painting Woodland Watercolors

Learn to Paint Beautiful Mushrooms, Animals, Insects, and Other Forest Wonders

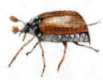

Rita Gould

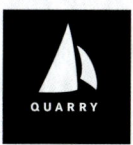

Quarto.com

© 2025 Quarto Publishing
Text, Photos, Illustrations © 2025 Margarita Galkina

First Published in 2025 by Quarry Books, an imprint of The Quarto Group,
100 Cummings Center, Suite 265-D, Beverly, MA 01915, USA.
T (978) 282-9590 F (978) 283-2742

EEA Representation, WTS Tax d.o.o.,
Žanova ulica 3, 4000 Kranj, Slovenia.
www.wts-tax.si

Quarry Books titles are also available at discount for retail, wholesale, promotional, and bulk purchase. For details, contact the Special Sales Manager by email at specialsales@quarto.com or by mail at The Quarto Group, Attn: Special Sales Manager, 100 Cummings Center, Suite 265-D, Beverly, MA 01915, USA.

29 28 27 26 25   2 3 4 5

ISBN: 978-0-7603-9767-1

Digital edition published in 2025
eISBN: 978-0-7603-9768-8

Library of Congress Cataloging-in-Publication Data is available.

Design and Page layout: Laura Klynstra

Printed in Illinois, USA VP092025

Dedication

This book is dedicated to my mom, Galina Galkina, for showing me how to see and enjoy beauty in simple things.

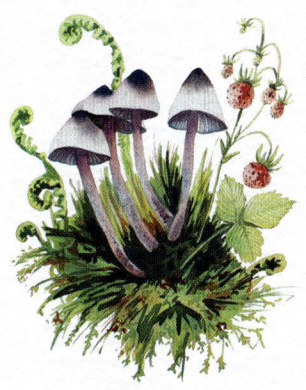

Acknowledgments

I would like to say a huge thank-you to my beloved husband, Chris, for his immense support throughout my art career, helping me with every single step. I would have never gotten this far without you.

I also would like to show gratitude and love to my whole big family in Russia, as well as my friends and their love for animals and the natural world—a mutual interest that has strengthened our relationships.

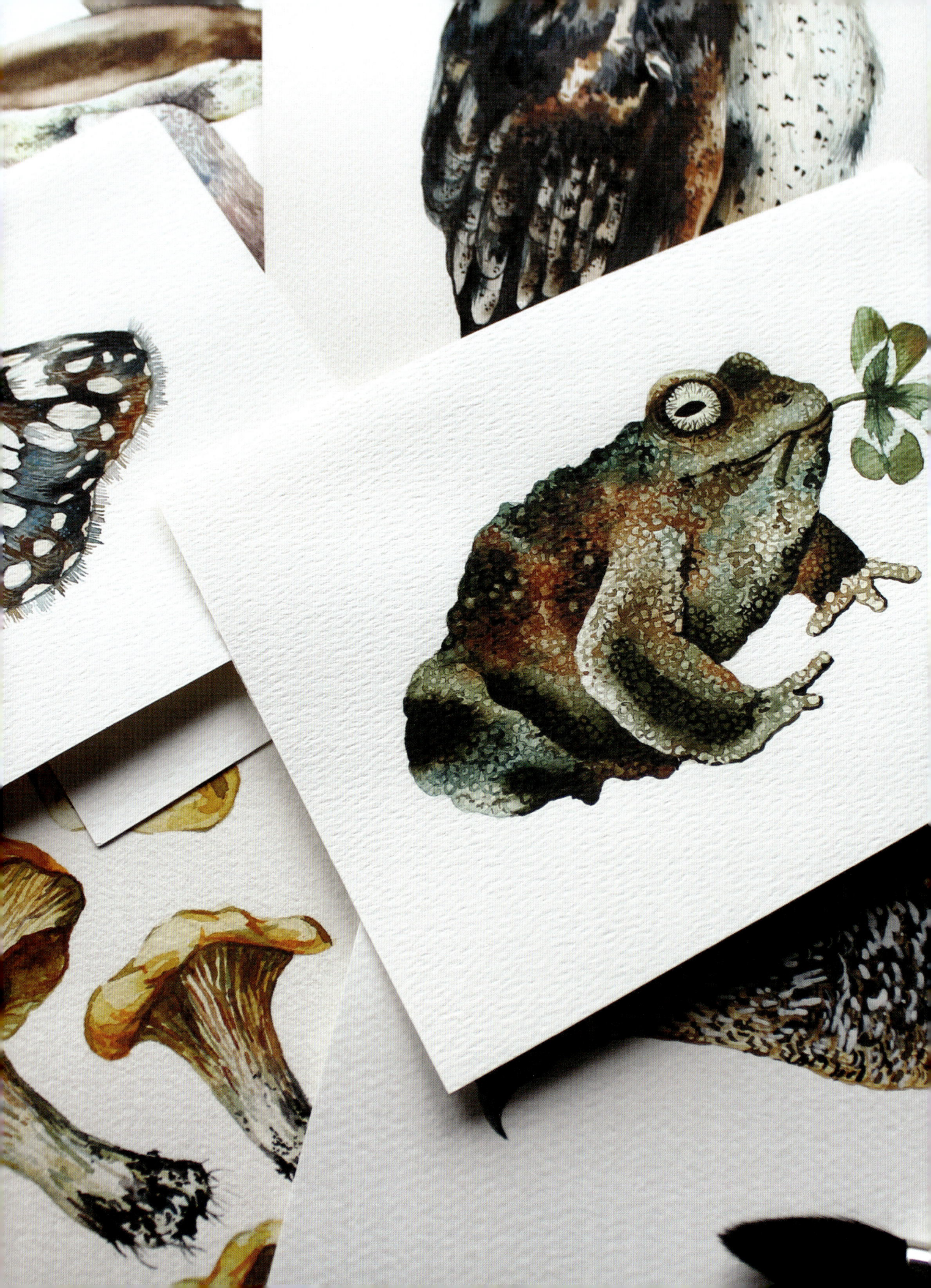

Contents

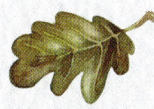

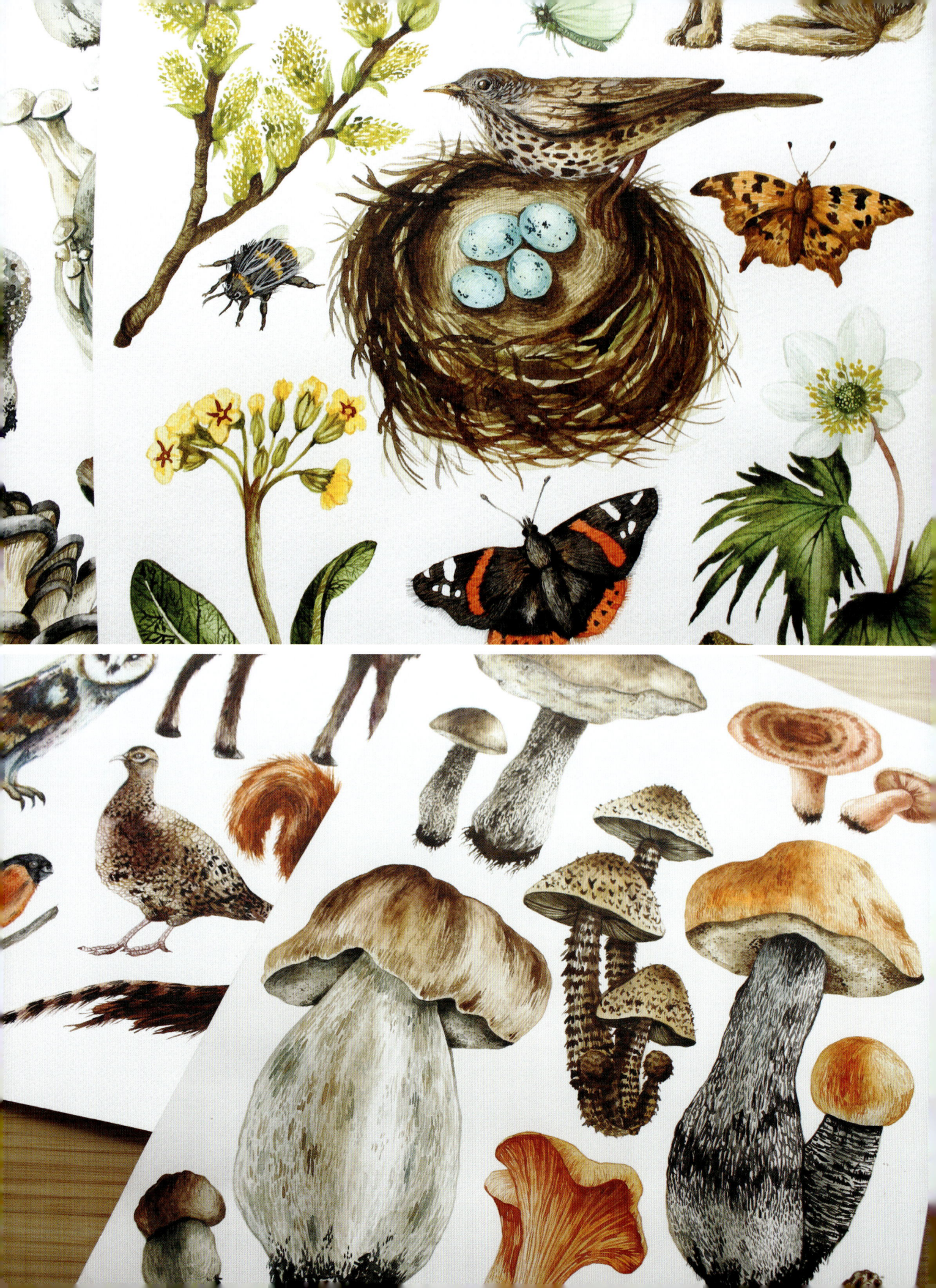

Introduction

This book is a great find for anyone who finds nourishment and joy in nature—those who love spending time in the woods, catching sunlight through the leaves, spotting forest inhabitants, picking berries and pine cones, bird-watching, and finding peace through painting the natural world around them.

I spent my entire childhood on the edge of a forest, where every summer I walked woodland paths, discovering insects, mushrooms, and birds, and encountering wild animals. I was fortunate to experience wildlife in such abundance: listening to endangered frogs sing, watching moths zoom to the nectar of garden flowers, hearing hedgehogs snort as they crossed my path at night, seeing bats swoop over the pond catching midges, watching foxes play with their cubs, and finding wild strawberries ripening in the pine forest. This deeply influenced my lifestyle and career choices, inspiring me to become an artist. I painted nature constantly, as it was so dear to my heart.

I've condensed all my experiences with watercolors—gained through art school and self-education—and I'm excited to share my discoveries and approach to painting nature with watercolors. Teaching watercolor workshops for beginners and more advanced students has shown me that everyone brings a slightly different approach to the medium. Because of this, I've included a lot of practical information in this book to reinforce key aspects of watercolor theory and essential techniques, like how much water to use, how to hold your brush, and why it's better to use pans rather than tubes. These insights are drawn from my direct experience teaching beginners, and they'll help you get a better grasp of the medium.

You'll find that these tips and tricks are often shaped by the artist's personal style, and I'm happy to share the full extent of what I've learned in developing my own. I've always loved the saying, "There is no such thing as talent—just pursued interest," and I believe it's true. Your curiosity and passion for nature, combined with practice and perseverance, will make you a great artist. The key is simply to keep going. Along the way, you'll paint things your way and make mistakes, but the joy of painting wildlife and the satisfaction it brings will help you overcome the fear of failure and perfectionism.

In this book, you'll learn how to set up your workspace, select your art supplies and care for them, work with references, master key watercolor techniques, see and paint values, find inspiration, and fix mistakes. You'll also learn how to prepare for plein air painting and much more.

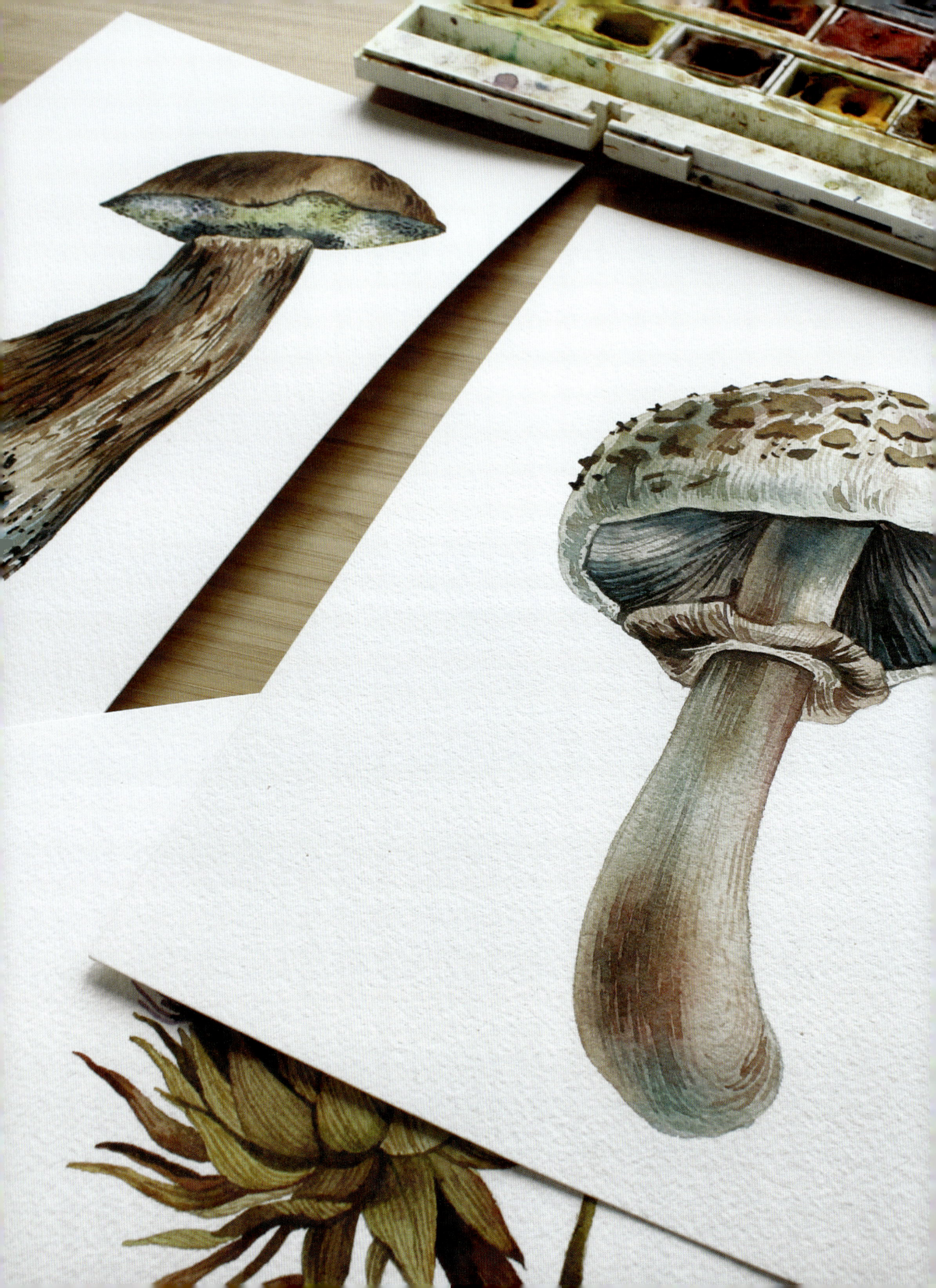

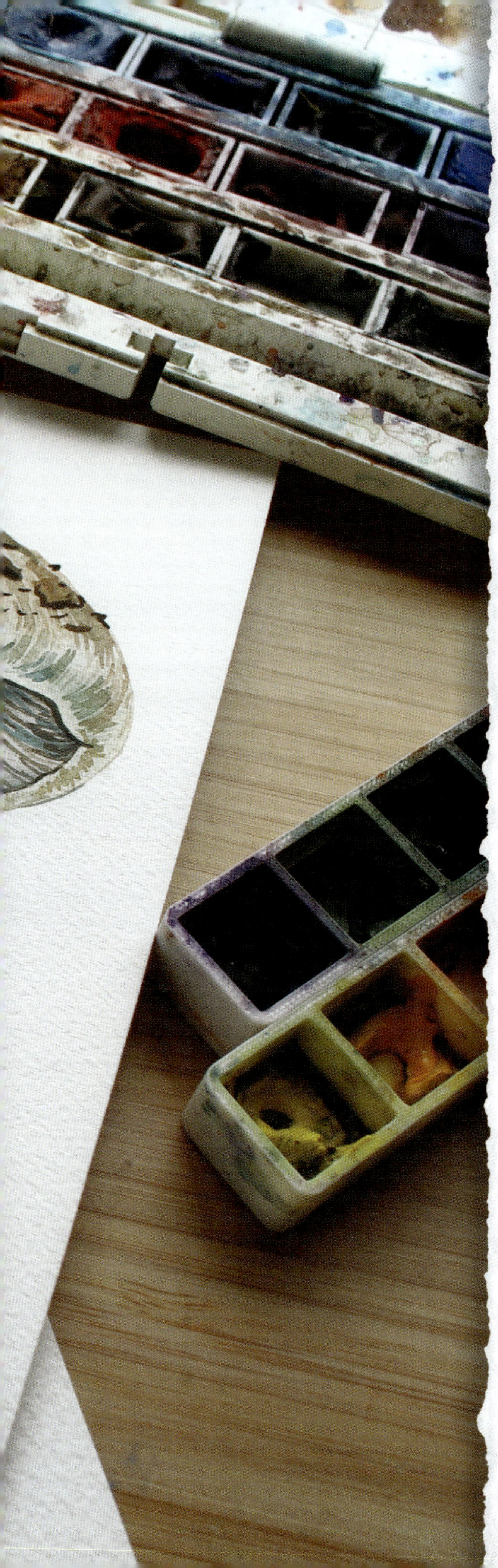

Chapter 1

Essential Supplies and Setup

In this chapter, we'll explore the essential supplies needed to create stunning woodland scenes in watercolor. From the right paper to the best brushes, choosing the right tools can make all the difference in capturing the natural beauty of forests and woodlands. We'll discuss the various types of watercolor paints, their characteristics, and how to select the perfect color palette for your work. Additionally, we'll cover the importance of supporting materials like masking fluid, palettes, and water containers. With the right supplies in hand, you'll be ready to bring the tranquil essence of nature to life on paper.

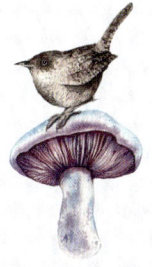

Paints

Choosing and buying paints can be one of the most overwhelming—and fun!—parts of starting to paint with watercolors. While it can seem like there is a mind-boggling number of choices, you really don't need very many to be able to paint just about anything. Here are a few things to keep in mind when choosing watercolors.

Tubes vs. Pans

Watercolor paints come in two main forms: tubes and pans. The paints are the same—the only difference is their consistency. In pans, the paint is solid, whereas the freshly squeezed paint from tubes is wet. Many beginners ask which is the best paint to use. I recommend pans for beginners because they teach the importance of using water and pigments together. People who rush to use tubes often treat them like acrylics or gouache, not adding enough water and using overly saturated colors.

You don't have to buy premade pans; you can create your own pan set by purchasing tubes and squeezing the paints into each section of the palette. Let them dry, and you have your own custom pans. I find this approach very useful for starting with watercolors.

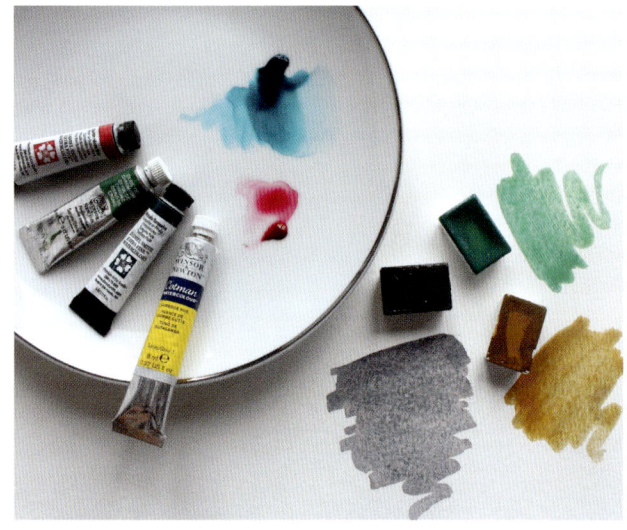

Watercolor paints come in tubes and pans.

Student vs. Artist Grade

Quality is essential when it comes to watercolor paints. Avoid the cheapest paints as you'll likely be disappointed. Instead, start with student-grade ranges, which are more affordable and perform well on paper. Brands I recommend to my students include Winsor & Newton, White Nights, and Paul Rubens.

As you gain experience with watercolors, you'll seek different colors, try new brands, and eventually combine colors from various companies to create unique color combinations. You might move on to professional-grade paints from well-established brands like Rembrandt, Daniel Smith, Sennelier, Schmincke, and Winsor & Newton's professional range.

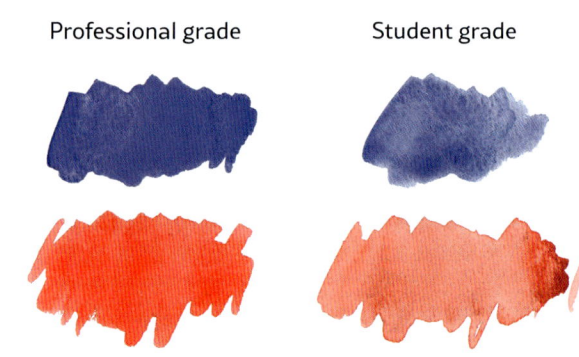

Professional grade   Student grade

Many artists struggle with which range to buy. I certainly recommend starting with student ranges and transitioning to professional ones.

What's the main difference between them?

Student-grade watercolors have less pigment and contain fillers like chalk, making them less intense. Many artists regret not starting with professional-grade paints, which contain pure pigment and gum arabic as a binder. These paints are more vivid, bright, and less likely to fade, though the price reflects their quality. Not everyone can afford professional paints right away, so if you're unsure whether watercolor is your medium, I suggest starting with student-grade paints.

Basic Colors

To get started, you'll need at least six colors. You can mix all the colors you need using just the three primary colors: red, blue, and yellow. Additionally, colors can be warm or cool. Using this principle, we get six primary colors—three warm and three cool:

- Warm Yellow, Cool Yellow
- Warm Red, Cool Red
- Warm blue, cool blue

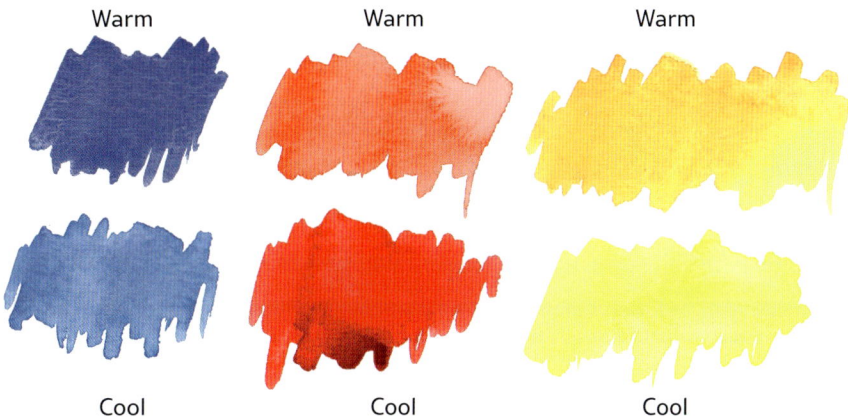

That being said, unlike many teachers, I often suggest trying twelve to twenty-four colors at first to explore the range you'll use and to gain confidence before learning color-mixing basics. Beginners sometimes get frustrated with limited palettes and abandon them due to the unfamiliar results of mixing. After experimenting with colors, make time to study color theory—these exercises are crucial for understanding how colors work together.

My Palette

For my tutorials, I often use the following student-grade paints from Winsor & Newton:

- Lemon Yellow (Cool Yellow)
- Cadmium Yellow Hue (Warm Yellow)
- Raw Sienna
- Cadmium Orange
- Yellow Ochre
- Burnt Sienna
- Cadmium Red Deep Hue (Warm Red)
- Alizarin Crimson (Cool Red)
- Permanent Rose
- Purple Lake
- Light Red

- Burnt Umber
- Sap Green
- Emerald Green
- Hooker's Green
- Cobalt Blue
- French Ultramarine (Warm Blue)
- Cerulean Blue (Cool Blue)
- Dioxazine Purple
- Payne's Gray
- Lamp Black

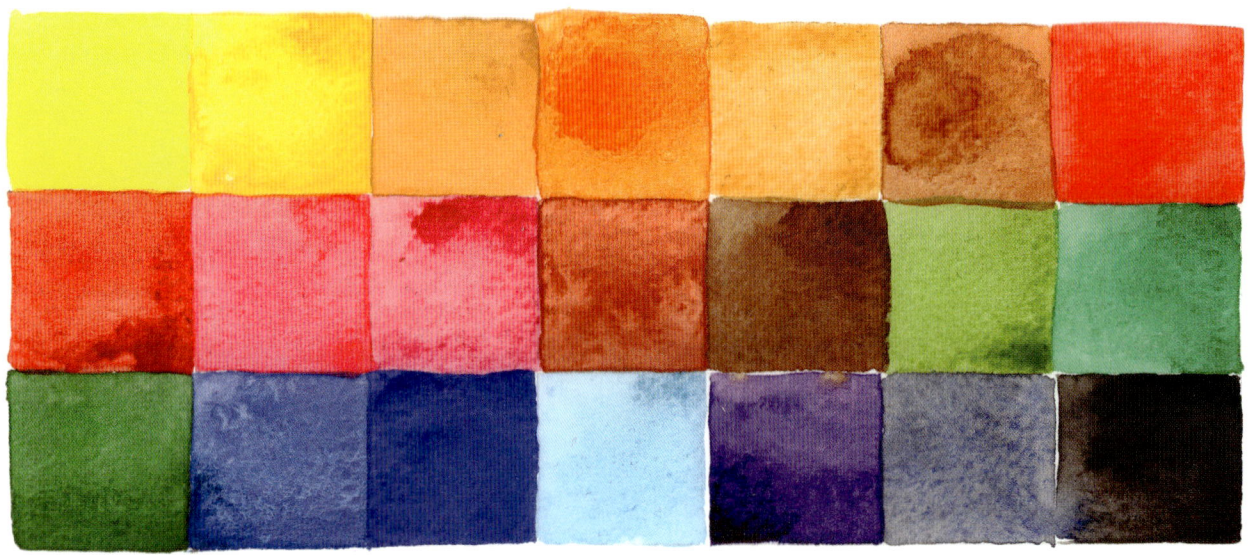

1st line: Lemon Yellow, Cadmium Yellow Hue, Raw Sienna, Cadmium Orange Hue, Yellow Ochre, Burnt Sienna, Cadmium Red Deep Hue

2nd line: Alizarin Crimson, Permanent Rose, Purple Lake, Light Red, Burnt Umber, Sap Green, Emerald Green

3rd line: Hooker's Green, Cobalt Blue, French Ultramarine, Cerulean Blue, Dioxazine Purple, Payne's Gray, Lamp Black

Swatch It!

When you buy new paints, create swatches on watercolor paper and write down the pigment's name. By doing this, you can plan color combinations to achieve harmonious mixes. Store your swatches together in a box.

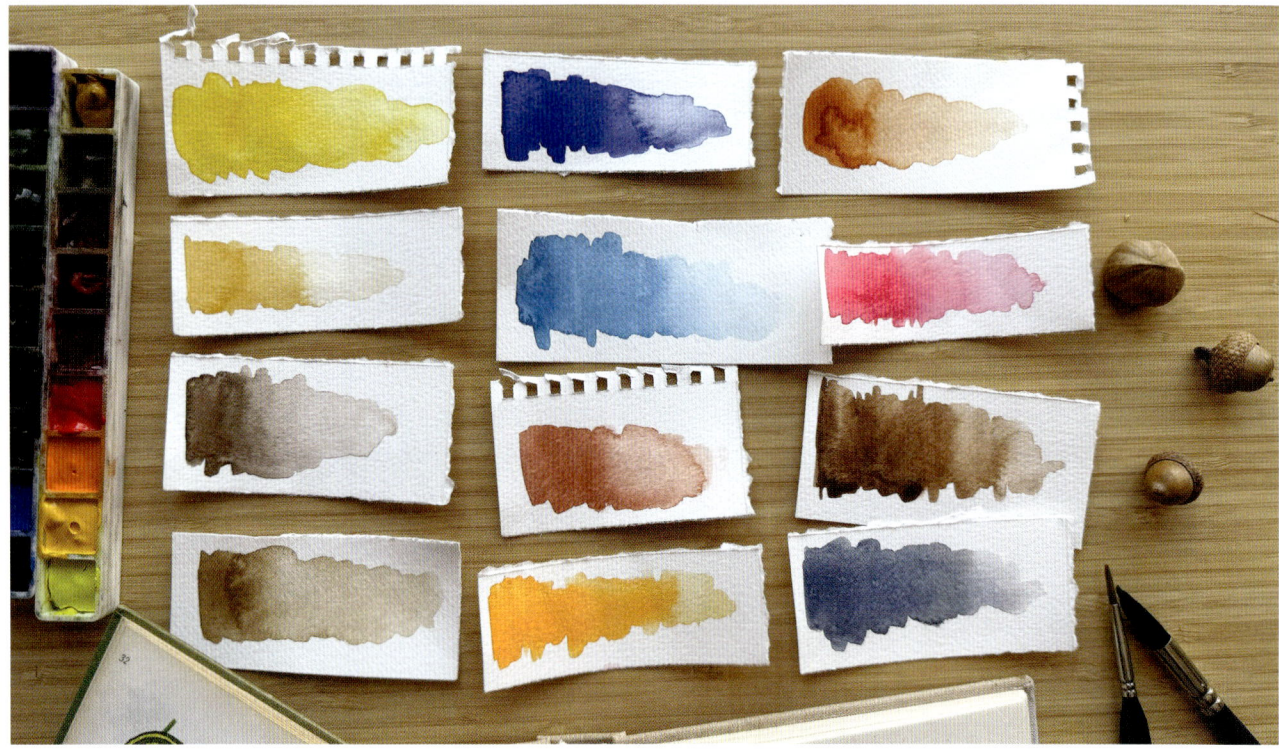

Saving swatches of all your paints and the colors you create by mixing them is a great way to choose colors for a project.

Brushes

Choosing brushes depends on your needs and style, and you'll likely experiment with different types over time. If you're painting botanical art, you won't need a huge brush, but for backgrounds in landscape paintings, a larger brush is useful. In my practice, I use four to six different-sized brushes, from a large mop brush (size 12–16) to a size 2/0 or 000 for details. For most of my work, I use paper that is between 7" x 10" (18 x 26 cm) and 11" x 17" (30 x 42 cm), so I don't require larger brushes.

Synthetic vs. Natural Hair Brushes

You can find good brushes in both synthetic and natural hair options, though buying cheap brushes can lead to disappointment. Invest in a few good brushes to get the best results. Some reputable brush brands include Pro Arte, Winsor & Newton, Panart, Princeton, Escoda, da Vinci, and Kolinsky Sable.

Tip!

Don't force new brush bristles apart, as this can damage the brush. The bristles are coated with water-soluble glue, which will come off easily by rinsing the brush with warm water.

The Three-Brush Rule

For woodland watercolors and insect paintings, I generally use three sizes of round brushes: a large brush (size 6) for the first, watery layer; a middle-size brush (size 3) for the second layer, with more pigment and less water to define shadows; and a size 2/0 brush for details.

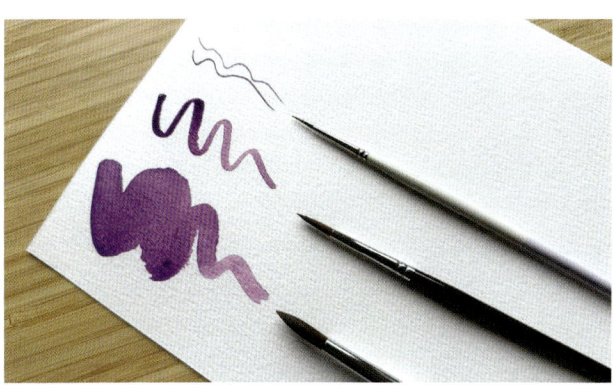

Three round brushes are all you need to create most of the paintings in this book.

	Water	Brush Size	Pigment
1st Layer	💧	8–12 size	💧
2d Layer	💧	3–4 size	💧
3d Layer	💧	0–2/0 size	💧

As you go from the first to the second and third layers of your painting, you will use smaller brushes with less water and more paint.

Palettes

Ceramic palettes are ideal because they allow for even mixing, but you can also use flat white dishes or smaller plates. The white surface helps you see how the colors will appear on paper. Avoid plastic palettes, as the material doesn't let you see color mixtures properly.

Tip!

You don't need to wash your palette after each painting session. You can leave it to dry and then reactivate the colors with a spray bottle when you're ready.

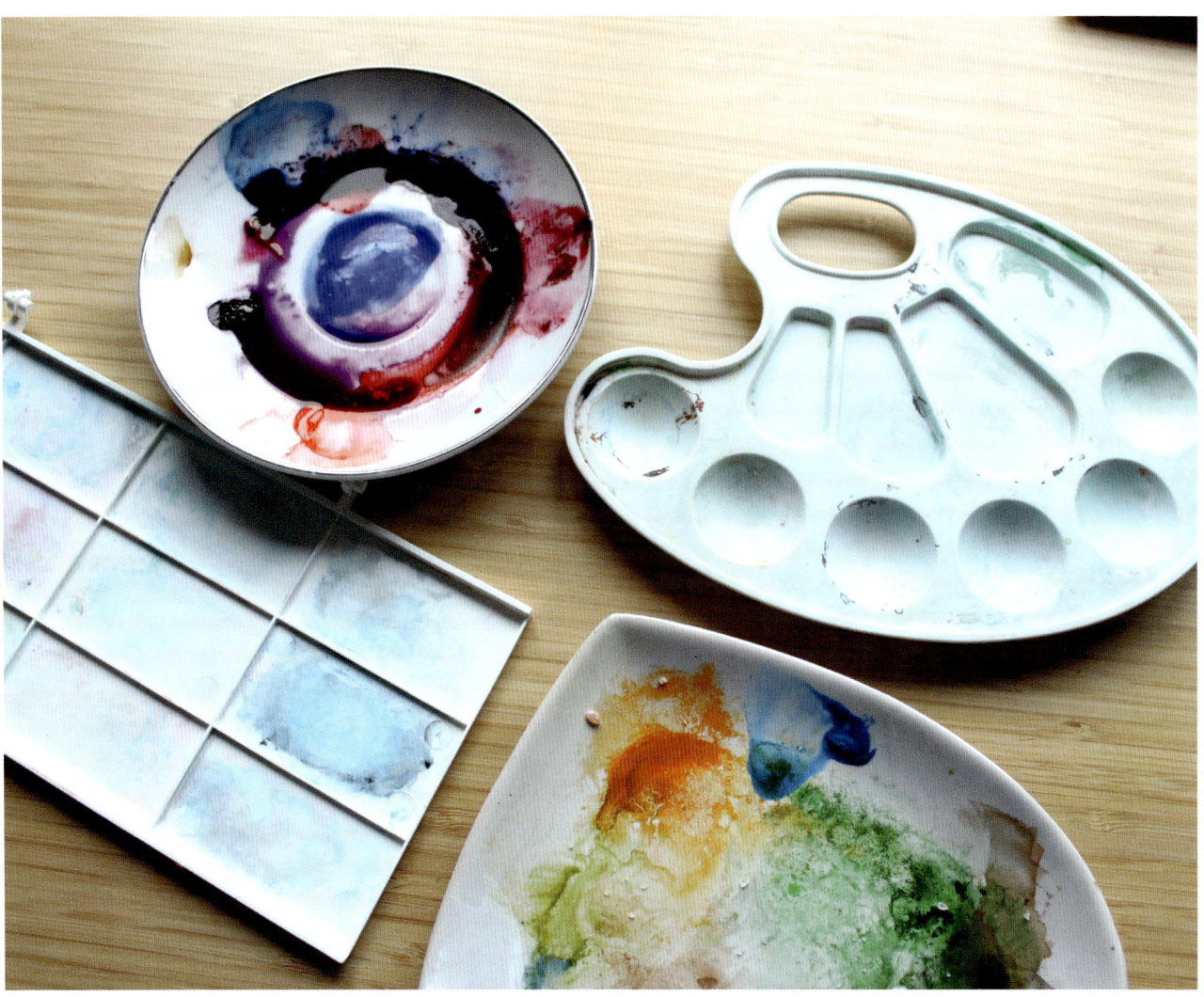

I use a few different types of palettes when painting woodland subjects.

Paper

There are different types of watercolor paper on the market. You can find watercolor paper made of cotton, cellulose, or a mix of both.

Cellulose vs. Cotton

Cellulose is a cheaper watercolor paper, and it's a good option if you want to practice simple things: brushstrokes, bleeds, and main techniques. However, I recommend investing in-100 percent cotton paper as it will give you the best results. It's an amazing choice for wet-on-wet techniques and bleeds, and it holds a lot of water. Once you try it, you will never go back to cellulose.

Types

Watercolor paper comes in three types: hot-pressed (smooth), cold-pressed (more texture), and rough (the most texture). I mostly use cold-pressed paper as it has enough texture to give me more control over how the paint flows but doesn't have so much texture that it affects the image.

Formats

Watercolor paper comes in different formats—pads, blocks, or sheets—and sizes (7" x 10" [18 x 26 cm] and 9" x 12" [23 x 31 cm] are great sizes for a beginner):

- Watercolor pads are bound by a spiral ring or glued on one side, making it easy to peel or rip the paper from the pad and put your artwork on display.

- Watercolor blocks are another good choice, especially if you don't want to stretch your paper: All the sides are glued onto hard cardboard. You can use a palette knife to peel it off. There is just one disadvantage: You can only work on one painting at a time.

- Watercolor sheets are the cheapest and come in big sheets of paper or rolls. You can cut it to the sizes you want.

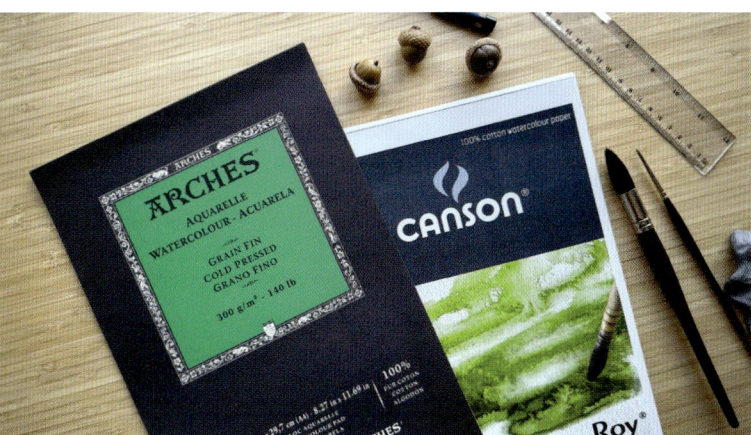

Two of the watercolor papers I use most often.

Additional Tools

Other useful tools for learning watercolor include masking tape, boards, masking fluid, water containers, paper towels, paint additives, white gouache, pencils, and erasers.

Masking Tape

Masking tape is useful for preventing watercolor paper from buckling. Apply it around the edges to secure your paper to a board. I often don't stretch my paper but use tape to minimize buckling. Use a tape made for artwork so it is acid free and will peel off easily.

Tip!

Test masking tape on a small piece of paper with water to see how it interacts. If it leaves residue or tears the paper, you'll know not to use it.

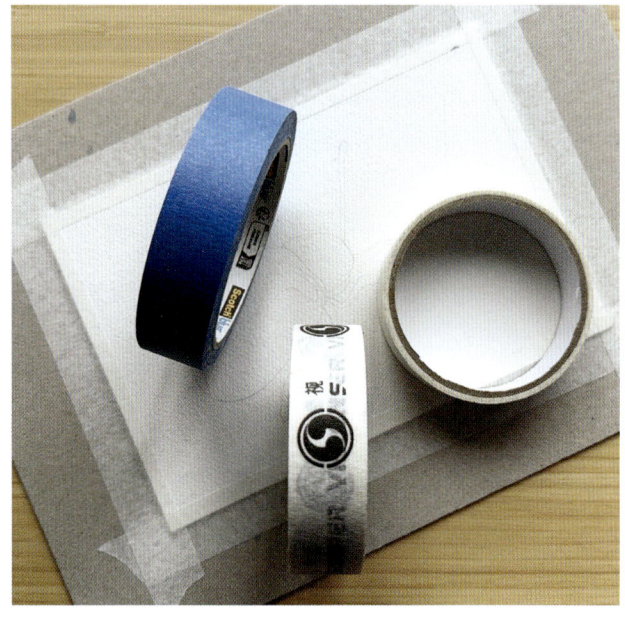

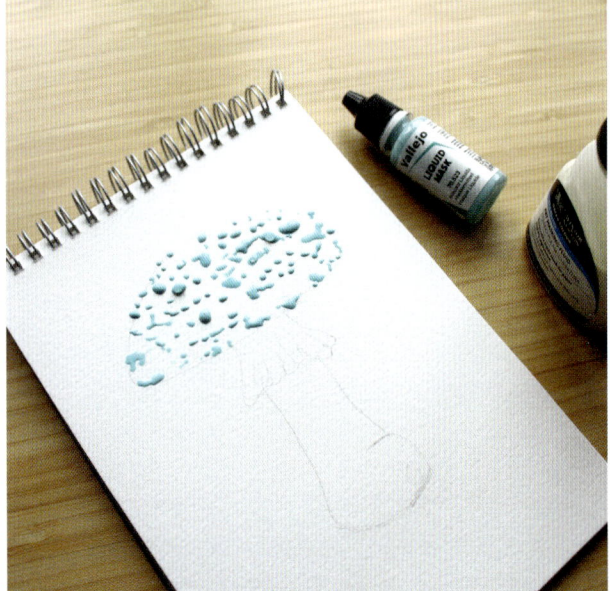

Masking Fluid

Masking fluid helps preserve white areas while you paint over them. It's especially useful for painting delicate white dots on objects like mushrooms. When applying masking fluid, always use an old brush to avoid damaging your good brushes. Several of the projects, such as the Fly Agaric Mushroom on page 60, use masking fluid.

Tip!

Never use your good brushes for masking fluid. Use a disposable brush instead.

Boards

I use cardboard boards for my work, but you can invest in plywood or other wooden boards. The size should be large enough to accommodate the paper and masking tape. These boards can also be used to stretch your paper.

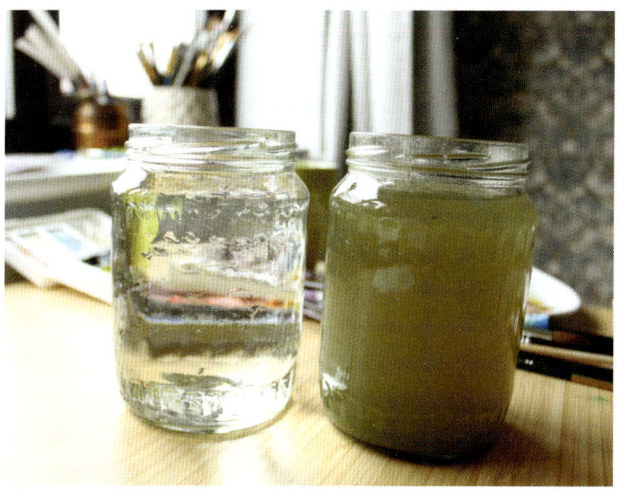

Water Container

A transparent jar is useful for monitoring the color of your water. Many artists use two jars—one for washing brushes and one for mixing water with paints.

Paper and Cotton Towels

Use paper towels or cotton towels to unload your brush and control the amount of pigment and water you use. Always use cotton for the best absorbency.

White Gouache

White gouache is a great addition for adding opaque details, such as fur or small hairs. I prefer it over white watercolor because it's thicker and less transparent. Use it for the last stage of your painting.

Tip!

Apply white gouache with a smaller brush and a tiny amount of water.

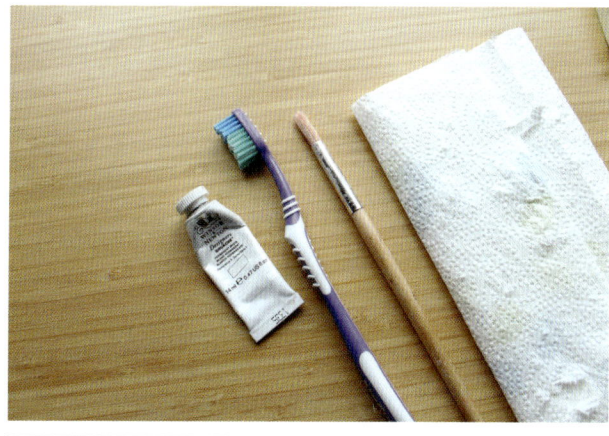

White gouache can be spattered with an old toothbrush to create a speckled effect.

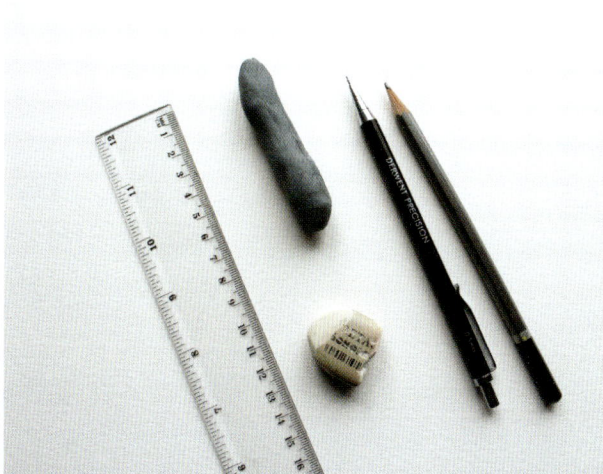

Pencils, Erasers, and Rulers

I prefer mechanical pencils for light sketches and transferring designs. Soft pencils (like 2B and higher) should be used sparingly on watercolor paper to avoid smudging. A kneaded eraser can be used to lighten sketches before applying watercolor. A ruler is helpful for drawing straight lines, which I don't often do when painting woodland subjects.

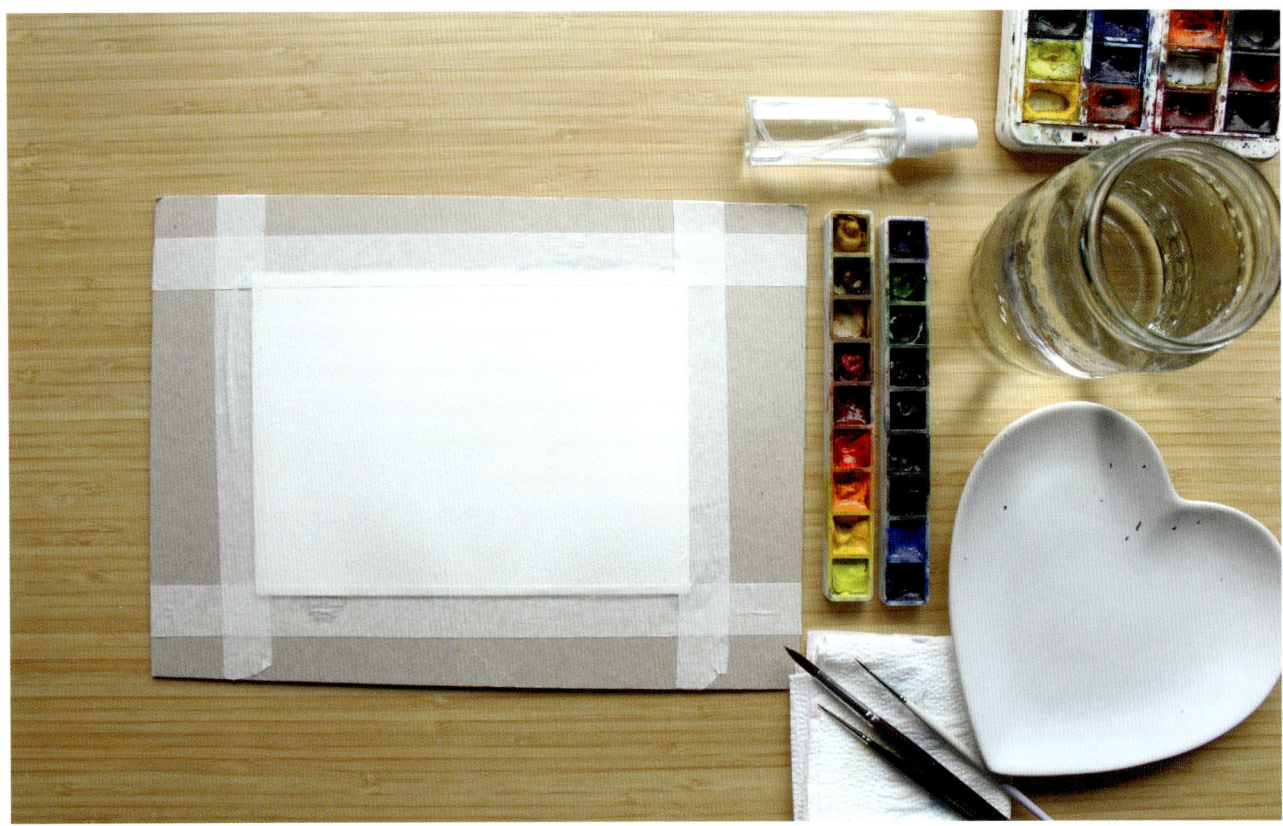

My painting setup.

Setting Up Your Workspace

Find a comfortable spot to practice watercolors where you can relax and see clearly. Ideally, sit by a table with as much natural light as possible.

I work near a window with my table positioned at windowsill height. Natural light is the best choice for watercolor practice as it helps you identify colors clearly and reduces eyestrain. If you can't paint with natural light, invest in a nonflickering natural daylight lamp.

Optional extras, like relaxing music, tea, or candles, can enhance your workspace and create the perfect "me time" atmosphere.

Organizing Your Art Materials

Here's how to set up your materials for a smooth painting session:

1. Place your watercolor paper on a board and secure it with masking tape. You may want to angle the board slightly (around 10 degrees) if you plan to use a lot of water or work quickly.

2. Arrange your materials as follows (for right-handed individuals):

- Paper towel on the bottom right
- Palette above the paper towel

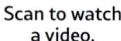

Scan to watch a video.

- Paint pans or a separate palette with squeezed paint above the palette
- Water jar to the far right, away from your paper to avoid spills

This setup helps prevent accidents and keeps your brush away from unwanted paint. If you're left-handed, simply reverse the setup on the left side.

3. Before you start painting, lightly spray your dry paint with a spray bottle then wait for three to five minutes. This helps reactivate the watercolor, making it easier to work with and providing better saturation.

4. Keep a few strips of watercolor paper on hand for color testing during your painting. These can be scrap pieces of the same paper or cheaper alternatives.

Transferring a Sketch to Watercolor Paper

I never sketch directly on my high-quality watercolor paper, as it can damage the surface and leave unwanted marks. Instead, I create a preliminary sketch on regular printer paper and then transfer it to my watercolor paper.

Here are a few methods to transfer your sketches:

- **Light box method:** A light box provides an evenly lit surface that allows you to trace the image onto the watercolor paper. This is the method I use more often.

- **Window method:** Place your sketch under a sheet of good-quality watercolor paper. Hold both sheets up to a well-lit window so that you can see through the paper and lightly sketch over the lines with a pencil.

- **Tablet or screen method:** Set your tablet (such as an iPad) or computer screen to full brightness in a dark room. Place your sketch on the tablet screen, then position the watercolor paper on top and trace over the lines.

- **Tracing paper method:** Place tracing paper over your sketch, trace the lines, then flip the tracing paper and redraw the lines on the other side. This is a popular technique among botanical artists.

Scan to download templates
of all the projects in the book.

Protecting Your Art and Tools

As you learn, it's important to be forgiving with accidental smudges or drops of watercolor on the white areas of your paper. Let go of perfectionism and embrace the playful, enjoyable process of learning. Watercolor is a medium that encourages presence and focus.

I don't aim to predict the outcome of my work because that would make the process too predictable and boring. The unpredictability is what makes watercolor so exciting! That being said, there are steps you can take to prevent unwanted mistakes and damage to your artwork as well as your tools and supplies.

Tips for Preventing Damage to Your Artwork

To prevent damage from smudges, spills, or dust, especially over multiple painting sessions, follow these tips:

Avoid hand cream: Don't use hand creams before painting, as they can make your hands oily, causing the watercolor to slide on the paper instead of soaking in properly.

Use cotton gloves: These gloves keep your hands clean and prevent oils from transferring to your paper. Cut the tips off three fingers to maintain dexterity.

Protect paper while painting: Use tracing paper or printer paper as a protective layer over your watercolor paper to safeguard it from dust, paw prints, or smudges. Attach it with masking tape, leaving a border of about ¾" (2 cm).

Store your artwork: If you have children around, store your artwork flat and out of reach. Once finished and dry, store your paintings in a plastic sleeve.

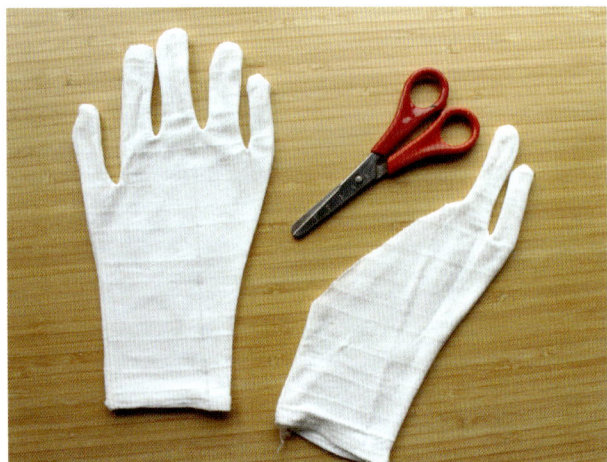 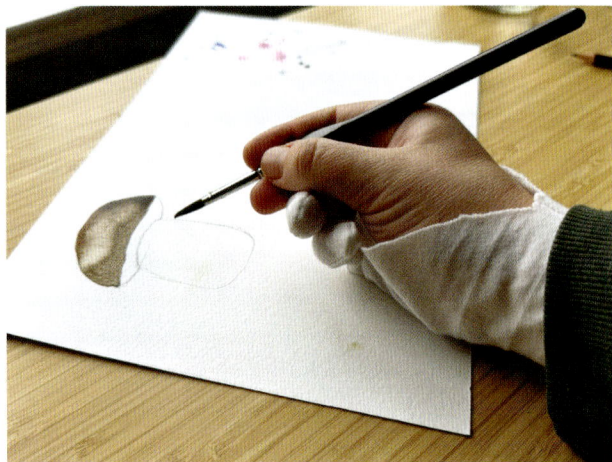

To help protect my paper, I wear a cotton glove with three of the fingers cut off on my painting hand.

Creating a Guard for Your Artwork

If I'm working on a subject that is more labor intensive, I sometimes take the time to create a guard for it out of tracing paper and printer paper. Here's how:

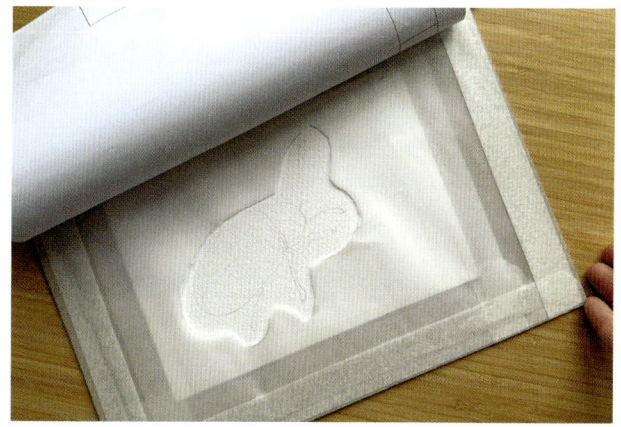

1. Place your watercolor paper on a board and secure it with masking tape on all four sides.

2. Lay the tracing paper over the watercolor paper and use a pencil to outline the area you plan to paint, adding an extra ¾" (2 cm) around the edges for the outline.

3. Cut along the outline with scissors, then place the cut piece back onto the watercolor paper, securing the sides with masking tape.

4. Finally, attach only the top edge of the printer paper to the top of the watercolor paper.

5. The tracing paper will protect the white areas of the watercolor paper, and the printer paper will help cover the finished painting, protecting it from dust, paw prints, and other debris.

Maintaining Your Tools

Taking good care of your art materials will ensure they last longer. Here are some tips that will help you get the most from your supplies.

BRUSHES

- New brushes may have a protective coating on the bristles, which can be dissolved with warm water.
- Clean sable brushes after every session with brush soap or detergent, reshaping the bristles after cleaning.
- Never leave your brush in a jar, as this will bend the bristles.
- Don't use small brushes to mix paints. Instead, use a larger brush to activate watercolor from your palette to prevent damage to the smaller brush.
- If you're traveling, use gum arabic to stiffen the bristles, or attach the brush to a stiff backing card to prevent bending. You can wash off the gum arabic with warm water later.

PALETTES

- Clean ceramic palettes after finishing a painting. If you haven't finished, don't wash the palette right away—this way, you can reuse dried mixes by spraying them with water.
- Protect dried palettes from dust with a tissue.

WATERCOLOR PAINTS

- Always close the lids on your paint pans or tubes after use to keep dust out.

WATER JARS

- Clean your jars regularly, as paint particles can settle at the bottom.
- Change the water frequently during painting.

MASKING FLUID

- Store masking fluid upright and ensure the lid is tightly closed.

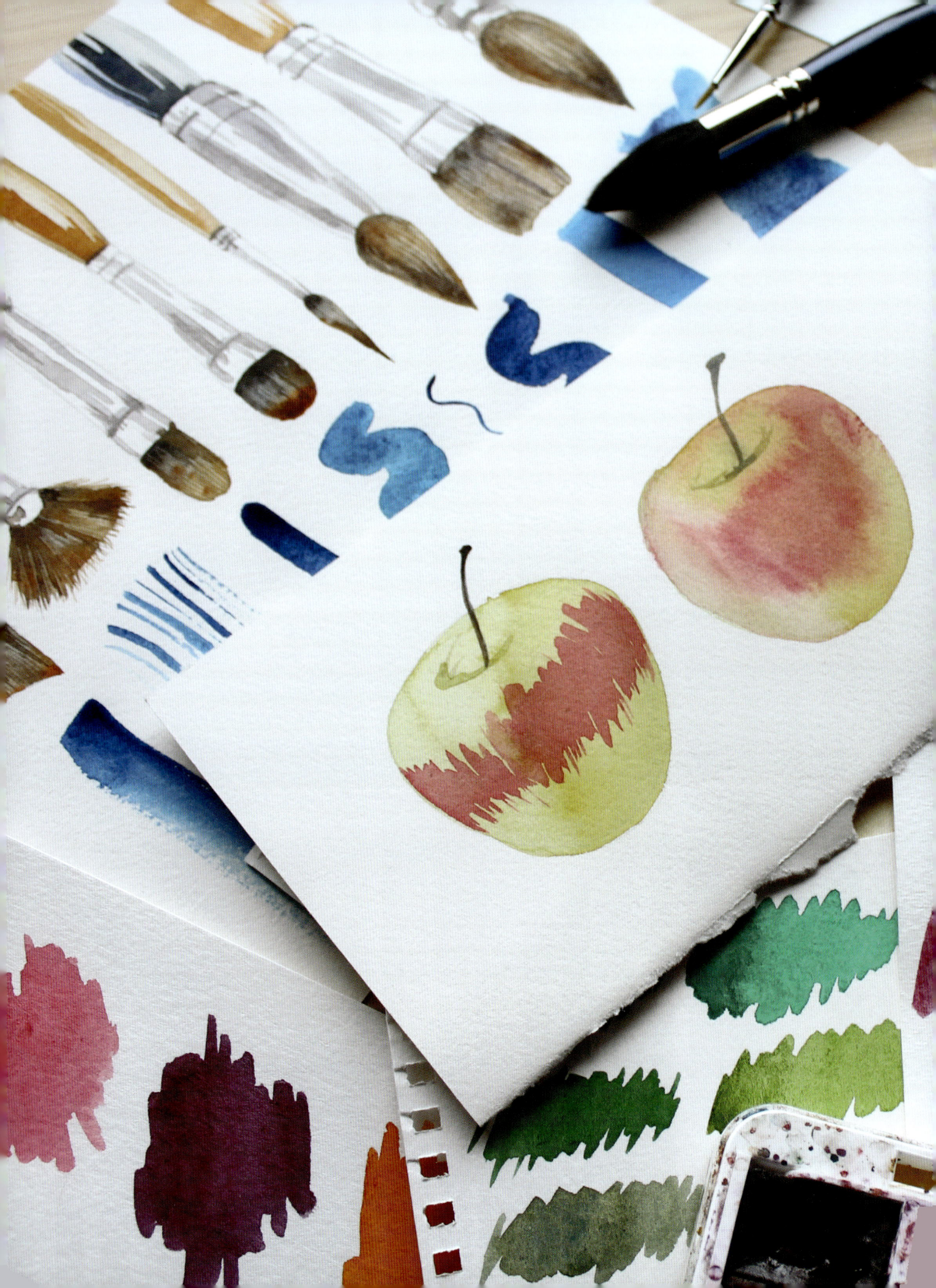

Chapter 2

Watercolor Techniques

In this chapter, we'll explore the essential watercolor techniques that bring woodland scenes to life. Mastering these techniques will help you capture the delicate play of light, texture, and depth found in nature. We'll explore methods such as wet-on-wet for soft, atmospheric backgrounds and drybrushing for fine details. Understanding how to control water flow, manipulate pigment, and create natural effects like fur and bark will elevate your painting skills. By experimenting with these techniques, you'll learn how to translate the beauty of nature onto your canvas.

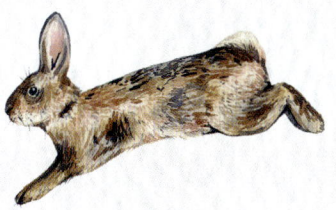

Getting to Know Watercolor

Before you get into the fun part of playing with watercolors and learning new techniques, take a little time to learn about the different consistencies of watercolor you'll be working with, how to hold your brush, and some basic brushstrokes.

Watercolor Consistency: The Tea-to-Butter Method

The right water-to-color ratio helps build correct tonal values and ensures the appropriate consistency for each stage of your watercolor painting.

It can be helpful to think of the consistencies of certain foods and beverages to understand paint consistency:

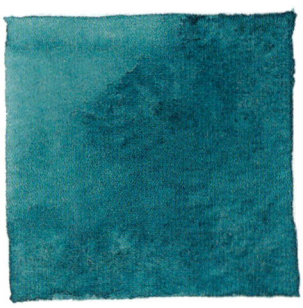

Tea: This is the lightest, with mostly water and a little pigment. Ideal for the first layer for backgrounds, skies, or the lightest areas on an object. The ratio is 80–90 percent water and 10–20 percent pigment.

Scan to watch a video.

Coffee: Thicker than tea but still watery, with 70–80 percent water and 20–30 percent pigment. Suitable for the second layer.

Scan to watch a video.

Milk: The paint is denser and doesn't flow as easily on the palette. The ratio is 50 percent water and 50 percent pigment, ideal for mid-tones or substantial areas.

Scan to watch a video.

Cream: This is thick, with only a little water. The ratio is 20 percent water and 80 percent pigment, suitable for the darkest darks.

Scan to watch a video.

Butter: Sometimes called honey consistency, this is almost pure pigment, with little or no water. It's straight from the tube or a pan.

Scan to watch a video.

Holding the Brush

Most beginners hold their brushes too close to the bristles, like a pen. Ideally, you should hold the brush slightly up, near the middle of the ferrule (the metal part that attaches the bristles to the handle). This allows for smoother, more fluid movements.

The basic rule is to hold your brush lightly by the ferrule. While there is no strict rule for how everyone should hold a brush, certain positions can help achieve better results. For example, when doing detailed brushwork, use a small brush (sizes 1–3) and support your hand by placing the side of your hand on the table, lifting three fingers for full control. When painting backgrounds with large amounts of paint and water, you don't need as much control—just allow the brushwork to flow freely.

Practice with different brushes at varying speeds—slow and fast—and experiment with different brushstroke directions (upward, downward, toward you, or away from you).

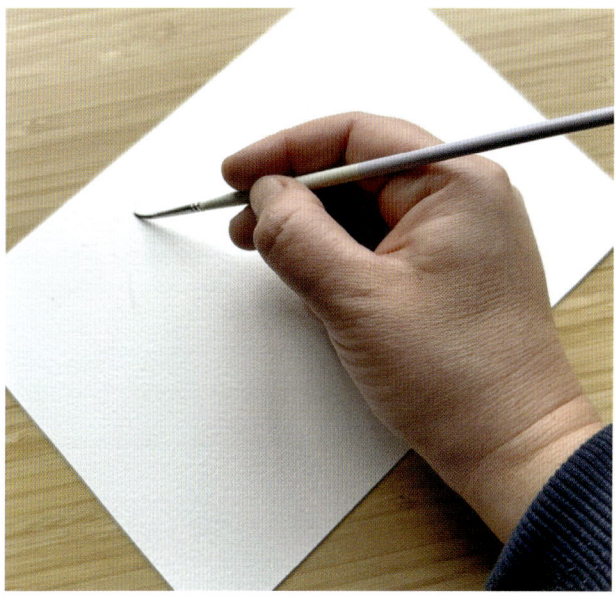

Hand position for detailed brushwork

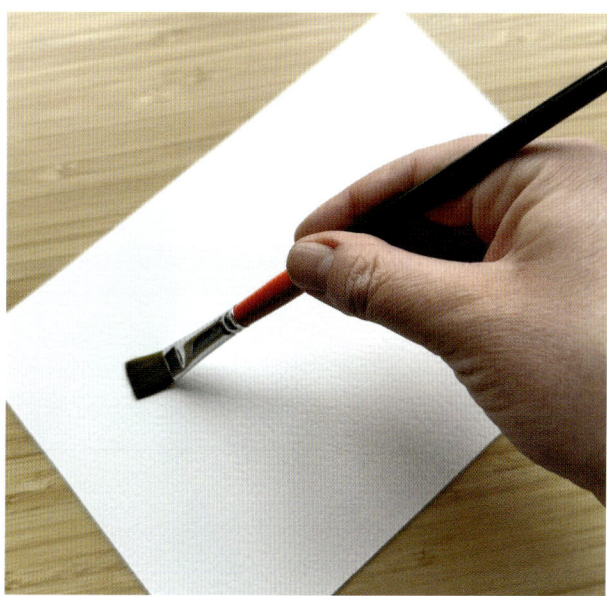

Hand position for painting large areas

Brushstroke Exercises

In the project tutorials in this book, we'll use a range of brushstrokes to create different effects. If you're new to watercolor, it's a good idea to get comfortable making a variety of brushstrokes. Hold your brush lightly and practice painting without pigment or water first. Just focus on the movements. Then load your brush with your favorite paint colors to try these exercises.

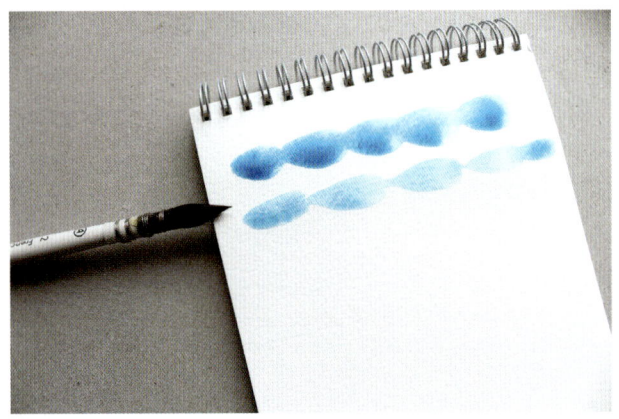

Exercise 1: Thick and Thin

Take your round brush (I recommend size 6–12) and choose a single color to practice with. Load your brush with pigment and press it down onto the paper, allowing the bristles to create a thick mark. Then, reduce the pressure and lift your brush slightly so that only the tip touches the paper. Do not lift your brush completely off the paper. Repeat this several times.

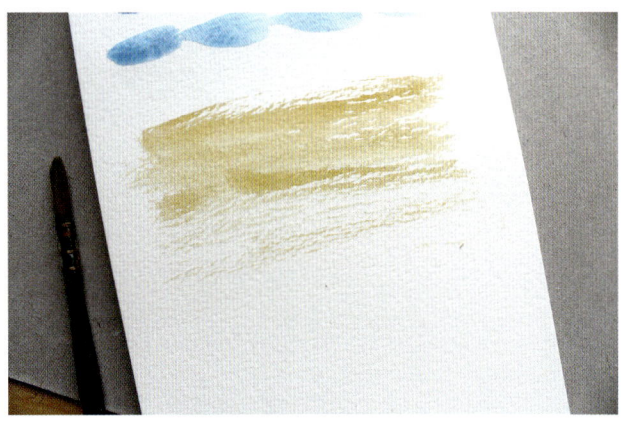

Exercise 2: Dry Brushing

This technique is ideal for creating texture. Hold your brush between your thumb and forefinger, keeping it flat against the paper. Drag your brush lightly to leave some areas unpainted.

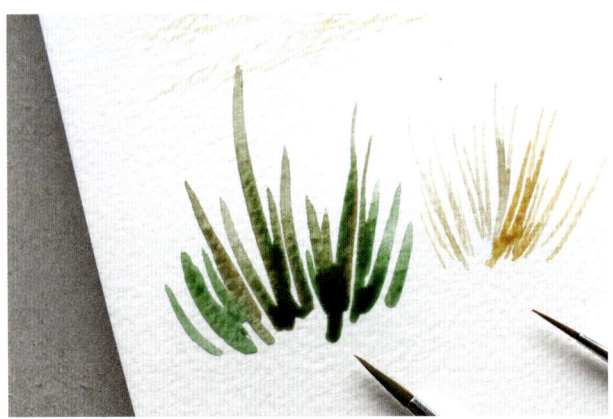

Exercise 3: Painting Grass

Load your brush and try to paint grass by starting with thick strokes. As you finish each stroke, lift your hand slightly so that the end becomes very thin.

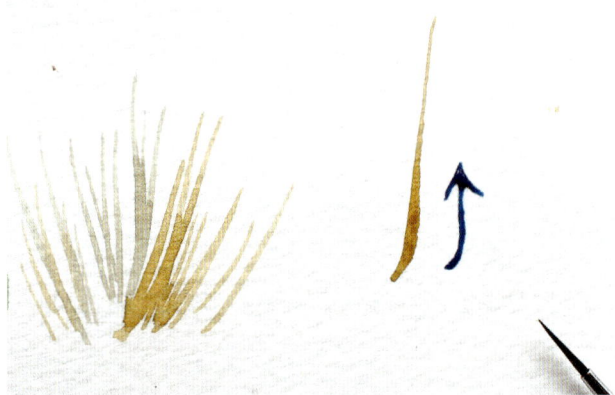

Exercise 4: Painting Fur

Use a fine detail brush and load it with color. Try to paint fur as you would see on an animal, using clusters of brushstrokes placed very close together.

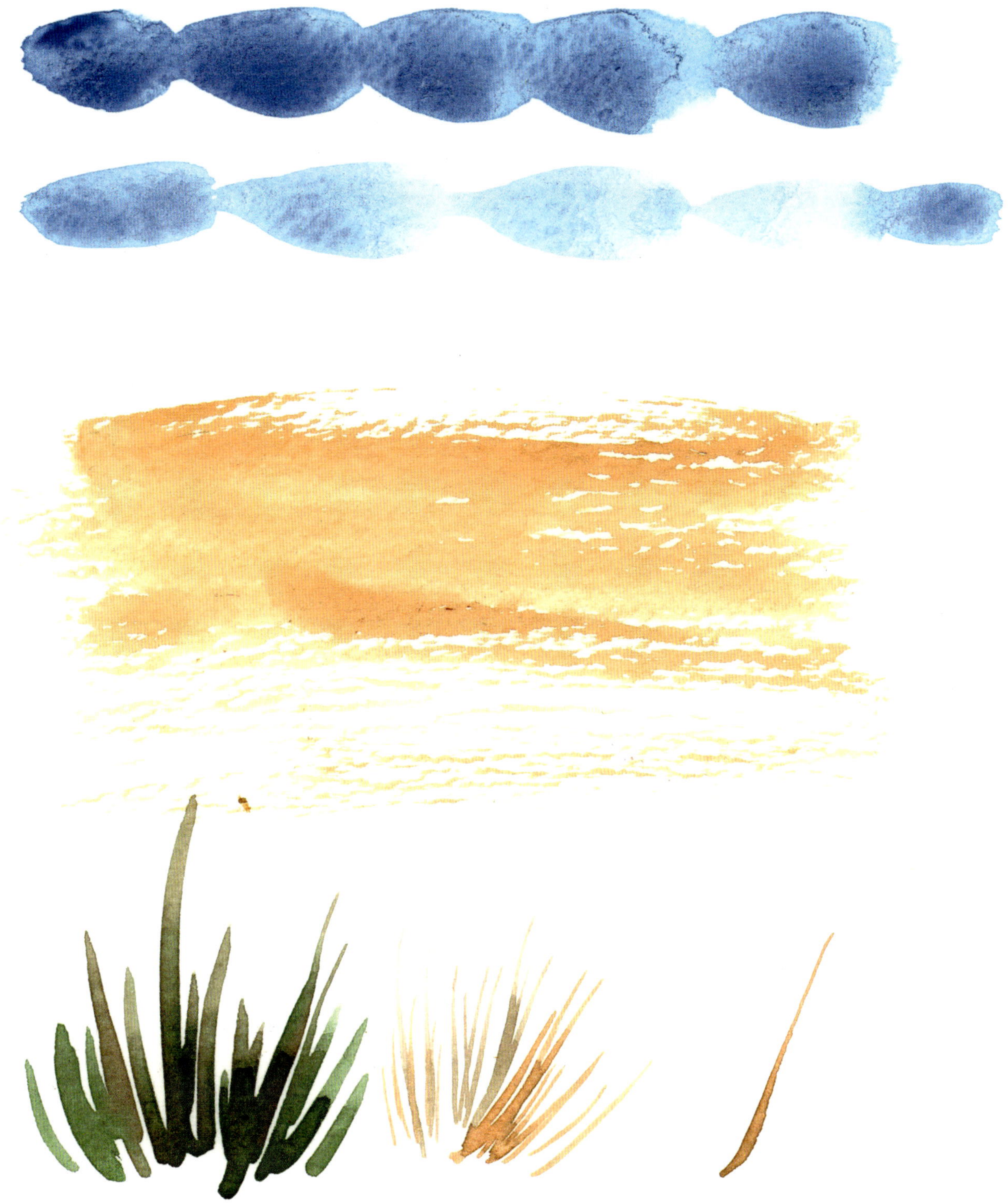

Scan to watch
a video.

Basic Techniques

In the section we'll explore some of the most fundamental watercolor techniques you will use again and again in your paintings.

Wet-on-Wet Technique

The wet-on-wet technique is one of the most common watercolor techniques and involves painting on wet paper with a wet brush. It creates a soft effect.

To paint your first layer wet-on-wet, apply water to the area you are going to paint. The paper should have an even sheen but you want to avoid creating a puddle of water. Drop in paint in a milk consistency. (See "Water Consistency: The Tea-to-Butter Method.) Where the paper is wet, the paint will flow.

You can also add additional colors to the first layer wet-on-wet.

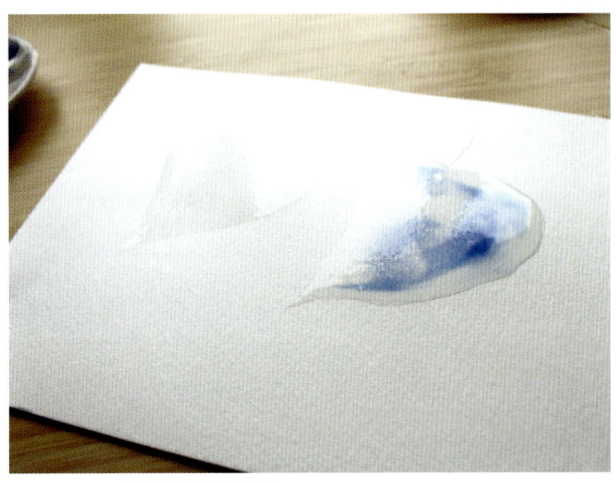

The leaf on the right has too much water.

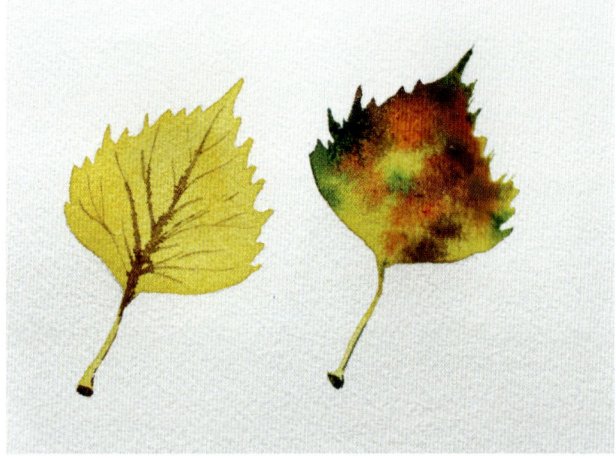

Painting wet-on-wet allows the paint to flow and create softer details like the veins on this leaf (left) or splotches of color (right).

Scan to watch a video.

PINE TREES EXERCISE

1. Secure your watercolor paper to the table or board with masking tape, if desired. Position the paper horizontally (landscape orientation). Divide the paper into 5 sections and label the sections with times, as shown in the picture.

2. Wet the first section of paper, then immediately load your brush with dark green paint (e.g., Hooker's Green) and paint a pine tree, following the example shown in the picture.

3. Wet the second section of paper, but wait for one minute before painting the same pine tree.

4. Repeat the process for the rest of the sections, waiting an additional minute for each section.

5. You should see that the longer you allow the paper to dry, the darker and more controlled the watercolor becomes.

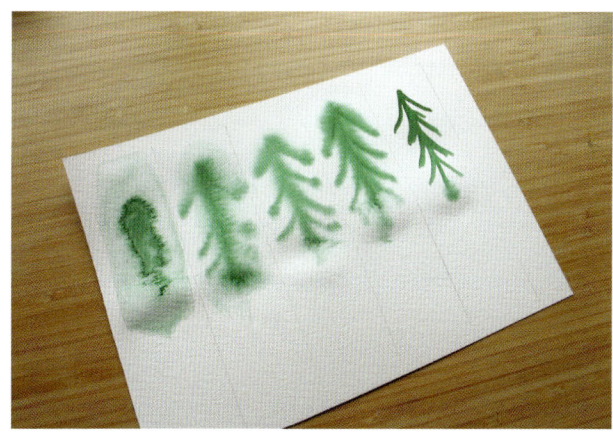

I wet the paper and paint the trees, allowing the paper to dry a little longer for each tree. From left to right: 0 seconds, 50 seconds, 90 seconds, 5 minutes, 10 minutes.

Scan to watch a video.

Wet-on-Dry Technique

With this technique, you paint wet paint onto dry paper or paint. It's often used for adding depth and detail in the second or third layers of your painting.

Mountain exercise: Create a mountain scene using the wet-on-dry technique. Start with a blue tone for the top (farthest away) mountain, then gradually add darker blues for the subsequent layers, allowing each layer to dry completely before adding the next.

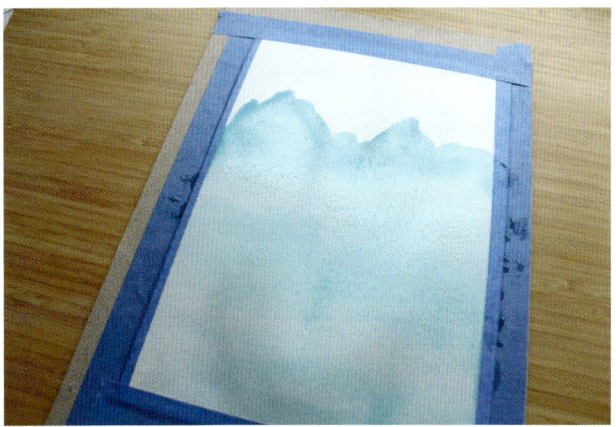

First layer of mountain exercise (left), finished mountains (right).

Scan to watch a video.

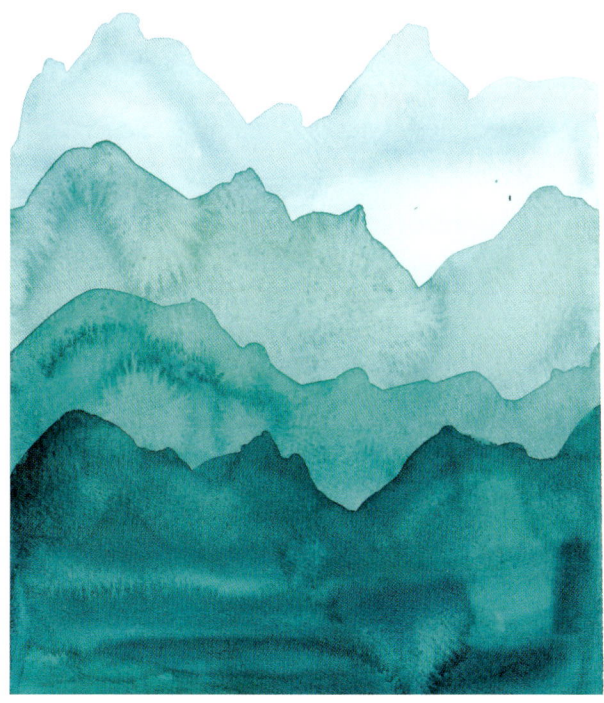

Combining Wet-on-Wet and Wet-on-Dry

For most painting, you will combine wet-on-wet and wet-on-dry techniques. For example, to paint a mushroom:

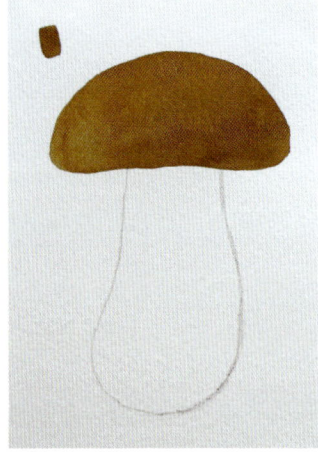

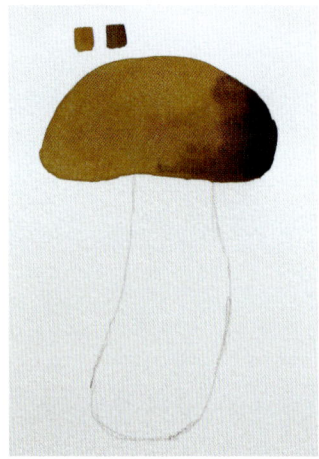

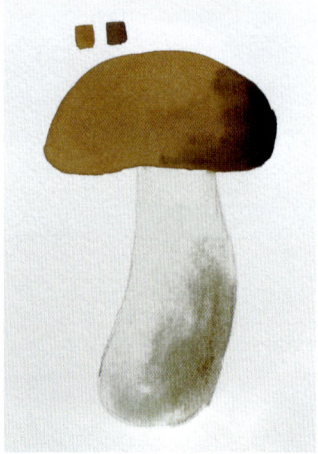

Scan to watch a video.

1. Use Yellow Ochre to paint the cap with a wet-on-dry technique.

2. Add Burnt Umber to the right side of the cap, allowing the paint to bleed into the wet surface.

3. Once dry, use a smaller brush to add details to the stalk using the wet-on-dry technique.

Filling Objects with Color

To fill objects with color, build up the shape slowly, using a brush loaded with plenty of water and pigment. Avoid outlines at the start, as they dry too quickly and will leave visible lines.

Flat Wash

Scan to watch a video.

To fill a large area evenly, use a larger brush (size 12–16) with a 50/50 water-paint mixture. Start painting from the left and work your way to the right, then slightly down, overlapping your brushstrokes to avoid dry spots.

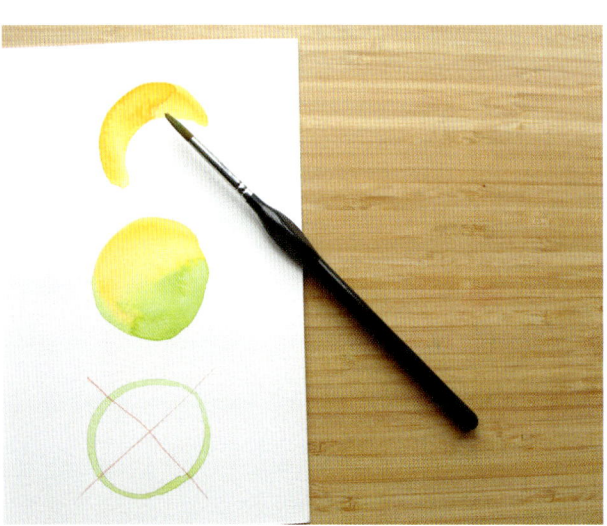

Don't outline your shape first as the line will remain visible after the paint dries.

A flat wash is used to cover a larger area evenly.

To create a graduated wash that is light on top and darker on the bottom, just turn the paper upside down!

Graduated Wash

This technique starts with a strong color at the top and gradually fades as you move downward:

Scan to watch a video.

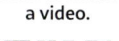

1. Wet the entire paper and make sure it's evenly glistening without puddles.

2. Mix your chosen color with full saturation and apply it at the top.

3. Gradually add more water and work your way down, creating a fade from dark to light.

Drybrushing

We talked about drybrushing when we did the Brushstroke Exercises on page 28. This technique is perfect for textures such as fur, grass, or wood. Use minimal water to create fine, scratchy details.

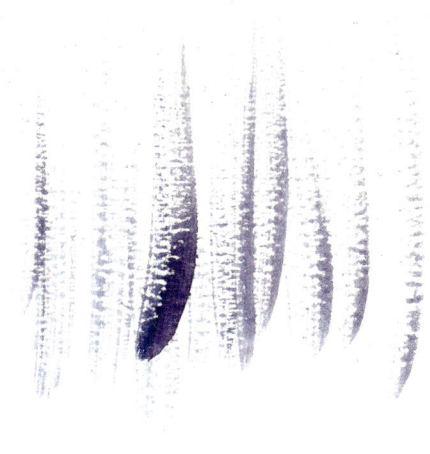

Drybrushing example

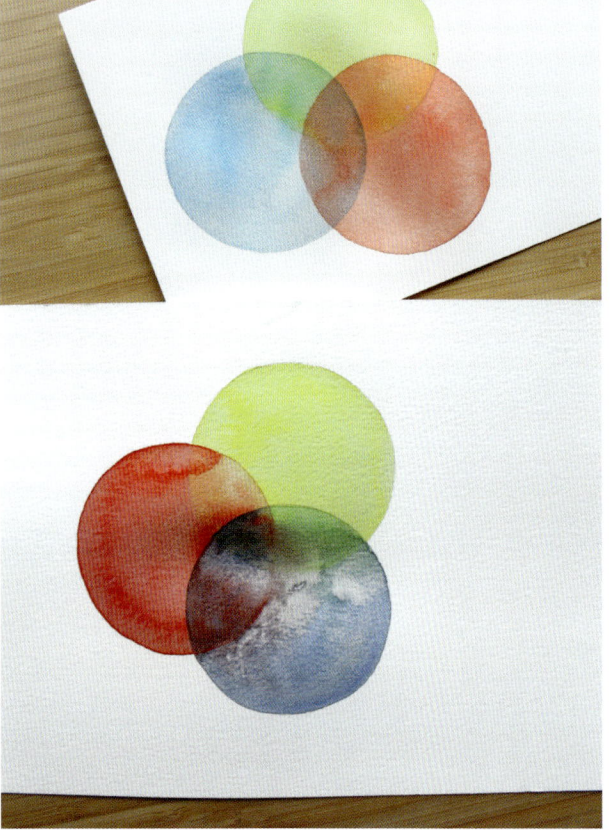

Layering/Glazing

Layering, or glazing, is a wet-on-dry technique that involves applying multiple thin layers of paint, allowing each to dry before adding the next. This technique helps to build depth and control tonal values.

By applying watercolor in thin layers, the previous layers show through, resulting in new colors.

LAYERING/GLAZING EXERCISE:

1. Paint a leaf Lemon Yellow using a size 6 brush, then allow it to dry.

2. Once dry, add a layer of Cadmium Red Deep Hue over it. This will help you learn how glazing can modify colors and values.

Scan to watch a video.

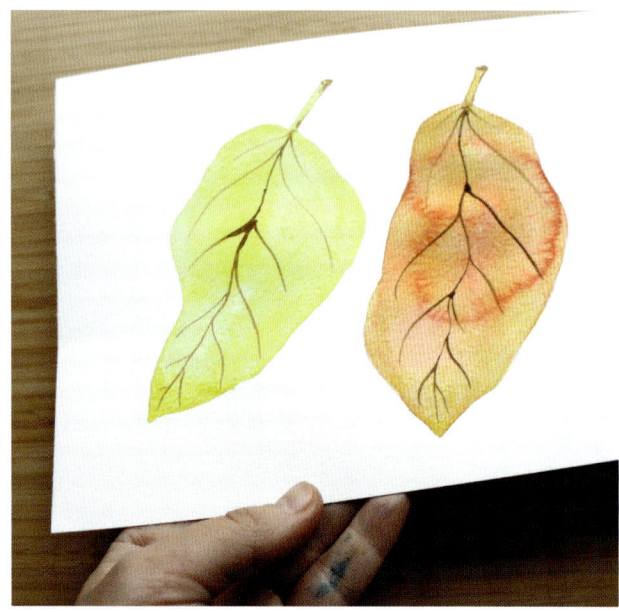

By applying watercolor in thin layers, the previous layers show through, resulting in new colors.

Hard and Soft Edges

To create a hard edge, paint a shape and let it dry before applying a second color on top. For a soft edge, paint one color and then, while still wet, gently blend it with a second color to create a smooth transition.

Scan to watch a video.
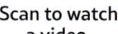

Soft (left) and hard (right edges)

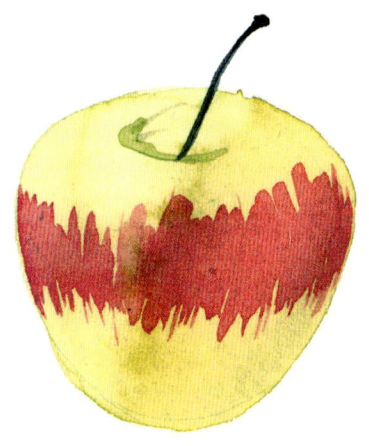
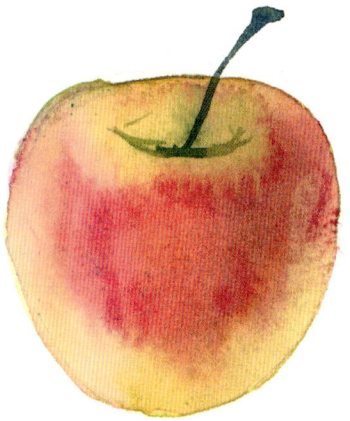

Painting an apple with soft (right) edges creates a more natural look.

Scan to watch a video.

Special Effects

In addition to basic techniques you'll use all the time, such as wet-on-wet, there are other techniques that can be useful from time to time and add interesting elements to your artwork.

Lifting the Pigment

In traditional watercolor, you don't use white pigment (such as white watercolor or gouache). Instead, you create light areas by either leaving white spaces or lifting pigments in certain areas to make them lighter.

Lifting the pigment means simply removing color from an area you're already painted. You will struggle more to lift off pigment when it becomes dry, so try to do it while the paper remains wet.

I use the lifting technique all the time to control how my watercolor bleeds and moves on the paper or to create volume, highlights, and points of interest for the viewer's eye.

Here are two methods for lifting pigment:

With a paper towel: Press on the wet area with a paper towel. The towel will absorb the pigment, leaving a lighter area.

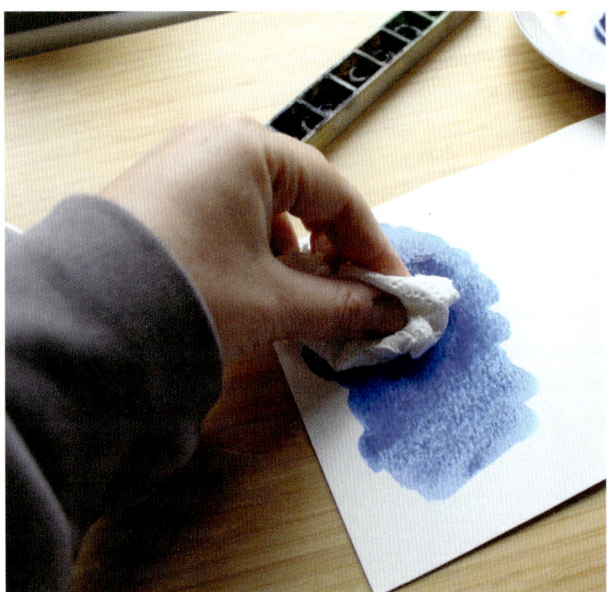 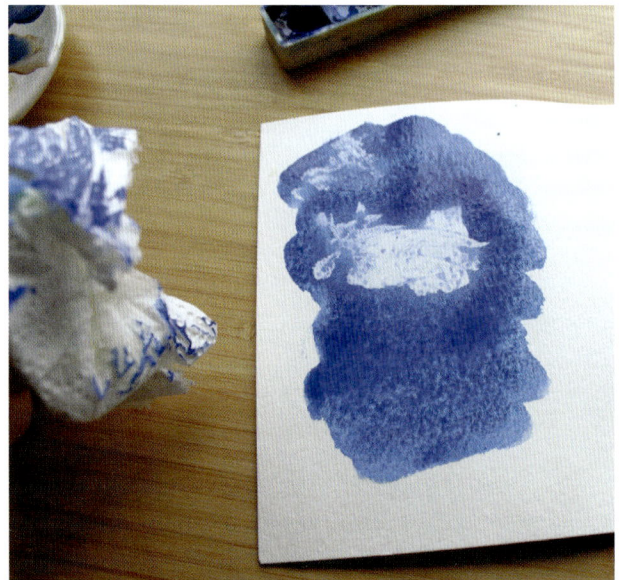

With a brush: Take a size 6 round brush and paint a circle using any color. Wait 50 seconds, then wash your brush in a jar and dab it on a paper towel until all excess water is removed. While the surface of the circle is still wet, apply the brush, putting all the bristles on the paper. Lightly press and move your brush downward, then lift it. This is a very controlled, swiping motion. Wash your brush, dab it on a towel, and repeat the process if necessary.

Scan to watch a video.

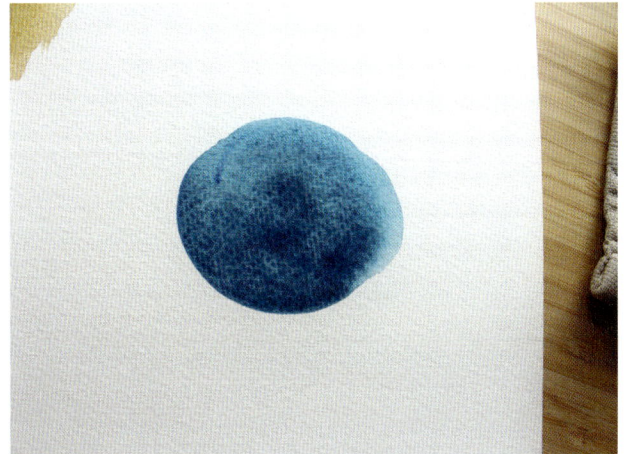

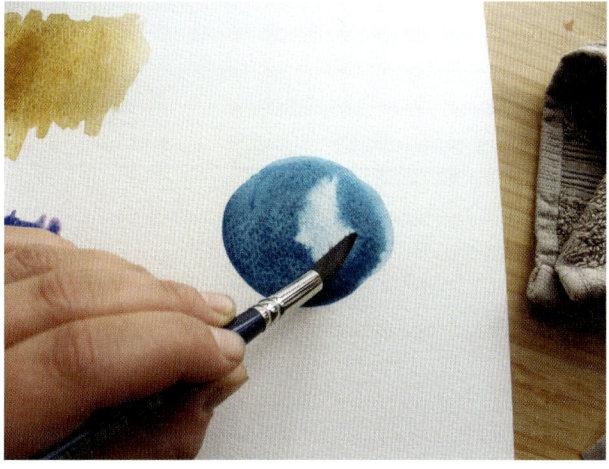

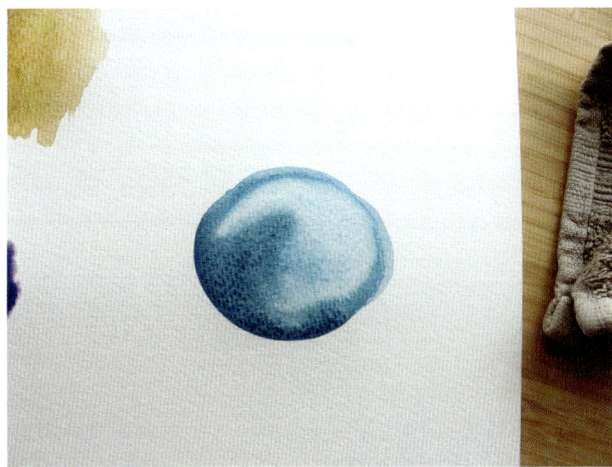

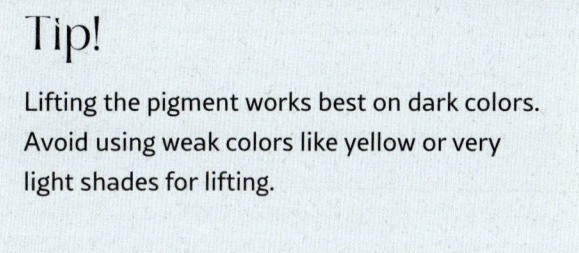

Tip!

Lifting the pigment works best on dark colors. Avoid using weak colors like yellow or very light shades for lifting.

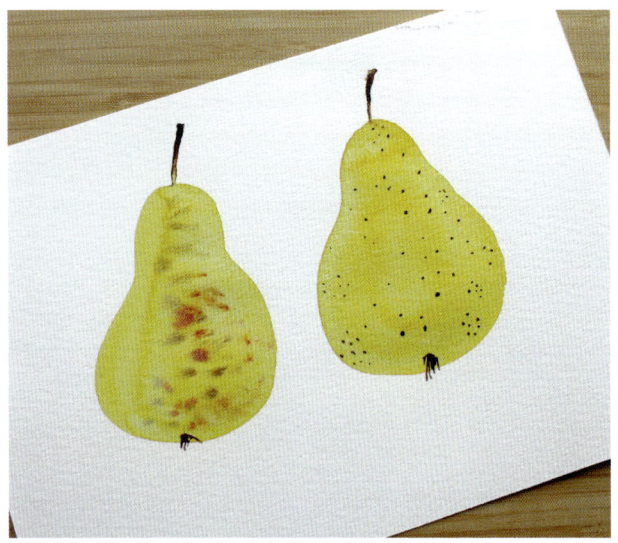

The dots on the pear on the left were painted while the pear was wet; the dots on the right were added to dry paint.

Dotting

Scan to watch a video.

This technique is used to add details and is typically done with a wet-on-dry method. It can be applied in the middle of your painting (two or three layers) to add texture or at the final stage to add bold details. Dotting can also be applied with the wet-on-wet technique.

Let's paint two yellow pears with a warm yellow color using a size 6 round brush.

1. For the first pear, use a dark brown color and a small size 2/0 brush to apply dots while the pear is still wet.

2. For the second pear, wait until it's dry before applying the dots.

Water Drops

Scan to watch a video.

Water drops are a fantastic technique for adding interest and style to your artwork. Using a size 6 round brush, you can apply drops of clean water (or colored water) to a damp or wet object to create lighter areas. Water drops work best on darker colors, such as blue, dark green, black, and brown.

1. Paint a 2¾"–10"(7–10 cm)-wide circle using dark purple color. Let it dry to a damp stage (a few minutes).

2. Then, load a size 6 brush with water so that a drop of water hangs from the bristles. Lightly apply the drop to the circle. Don't press hard; just let the water fall.

3. Return to the water jar, reload your brush, and repeat for more drops. You can use different colors in the drops if you prefer. The key is to combine the paper's wetness and the amount of water in the drop.

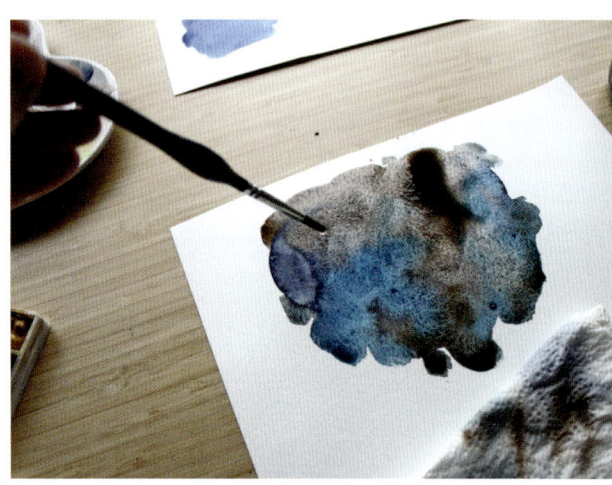

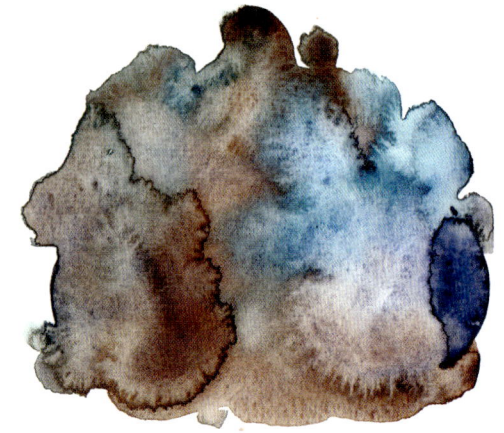

Charging

Charging is a wet-on-wet technique where you drop one wet color into another wet color. This allows you to mix colors directly on the paper rather than on the palette, creating fantastic results.

Scan to watch a video.

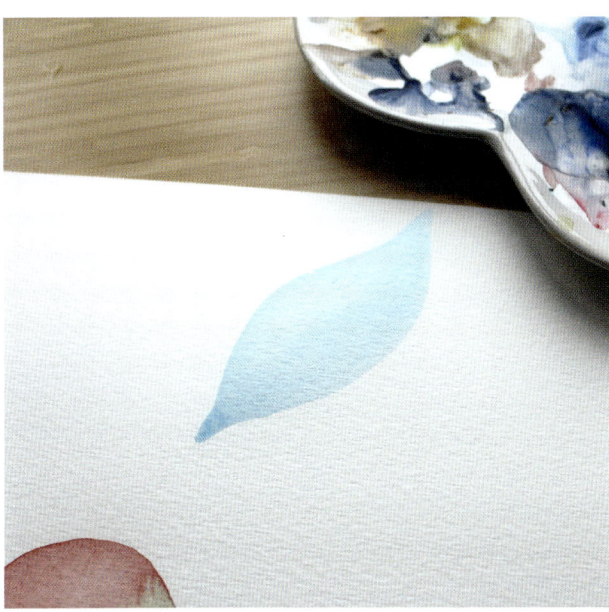

1. Paint a simple leaf using a size 6 round brush and a light color.

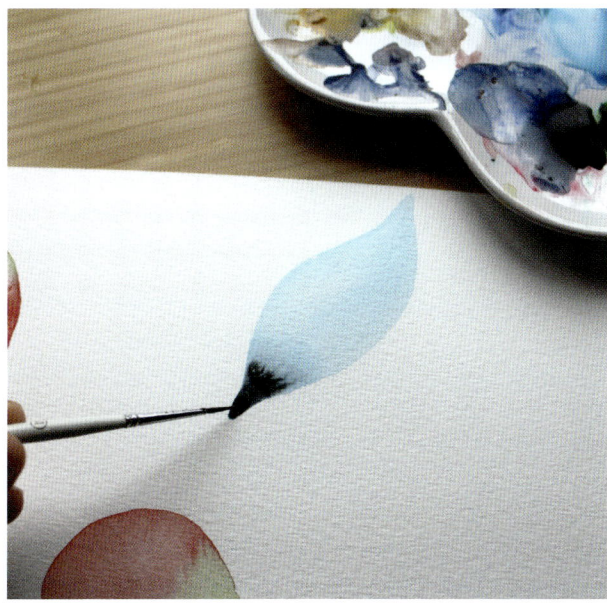

2. While the first paint is wet, take a size 2/0 brush and load it with a darker color. Apply the color by dabbing and lightly pressing to release the pigment.

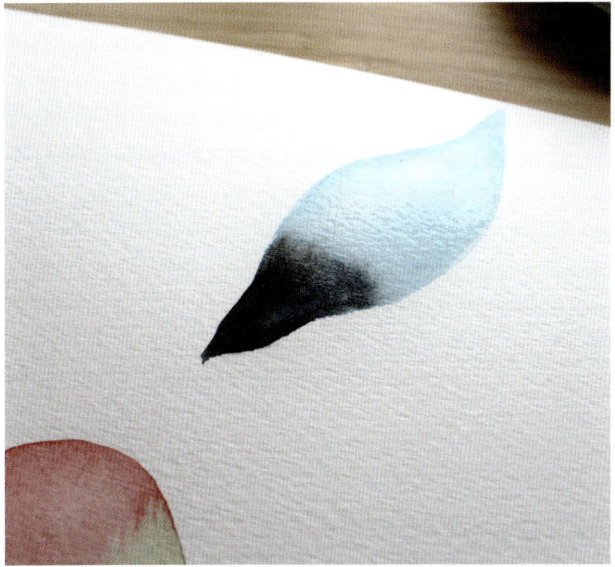

3. If desired, repeat Step 2 with the same or a different color. You can charge the paint in the same area or other areas in the painting.

Negative Painting

Negative painting is a technique where you paint around the subject, rather than on it, adding depth and dimension to your artwork. Instead of painting the subject first (the positive space), you paint the background color around the object.

Though the traditional approach is to paint light to dark, negative painting flips that process. Instead of filling in the silhouette first, focus on painting the darker areas around the subject.

Scan to watch a video.

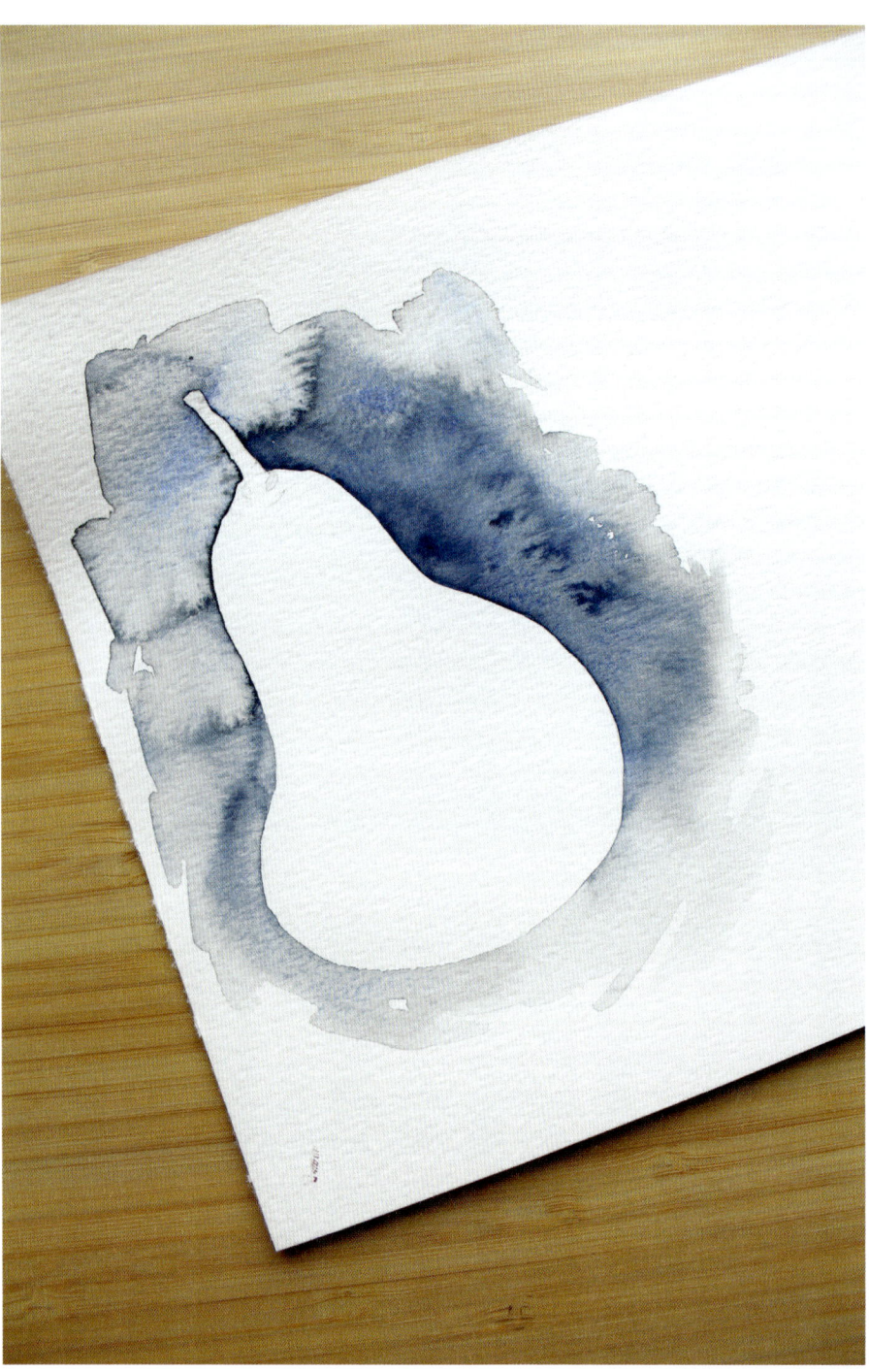

Here I painted with water around the pear, then dropped paint into the water to create a negative painting.

Fixing Mistakes in Watercolor

Watercolor often presents challenges, and many beginners struggle with mistakes. Here are some tips for fixing common issues:

Dropped paint: If you drop paint onto a white area, immediately place a clean tissue on it to absorb the excess. You can then use a wet brush to gently press on the stain and remove it, repeating as necessary. The faster you act, the less likely the stain will set.

Pigments that stain: Some pigments are harder to remove due to their staining properties. Examples include Phthalo colors, Alizarin Crimson, the Cadmiums, Prussian Blue, and others. With good-quality watercolor paper, you may be able to lift stains while they are still wet.

Dried paint: For small, dry spots of watercolor, you can use a razor blade to gently scrape off the top layer of paper. This is risky and should be done only with thick, high-quality watercolor paper.

Other mistakes: If you paint over a pencil line, you can either enlarge the shape or make it darker to conceal the mistake. If a stain has dried and can't be removed, consider painting something over it—such as a fly or a leaf—or darkening the background.

Remember, your work isn't ruined until you've tried everything to fix it.

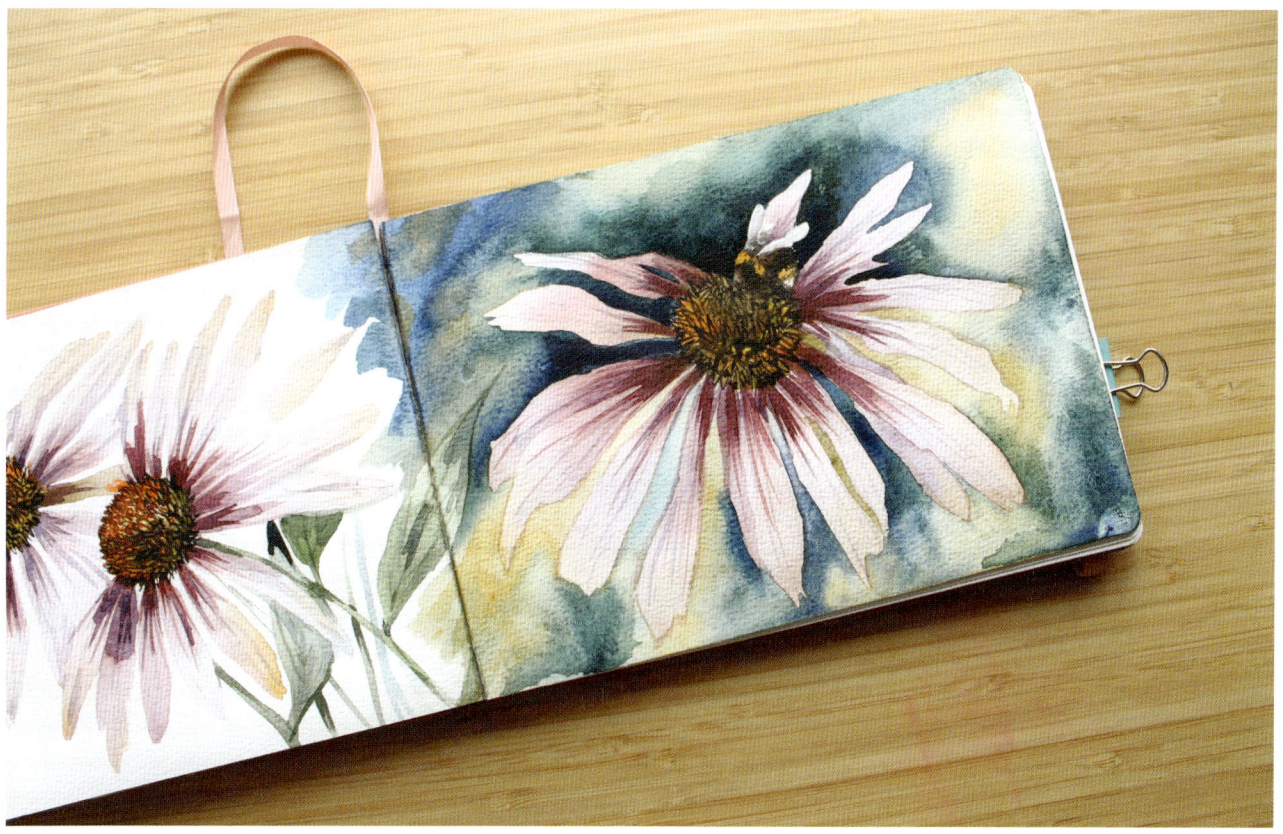

A sketchbook is a wonderful place to experiment and not stress about making mistakes.

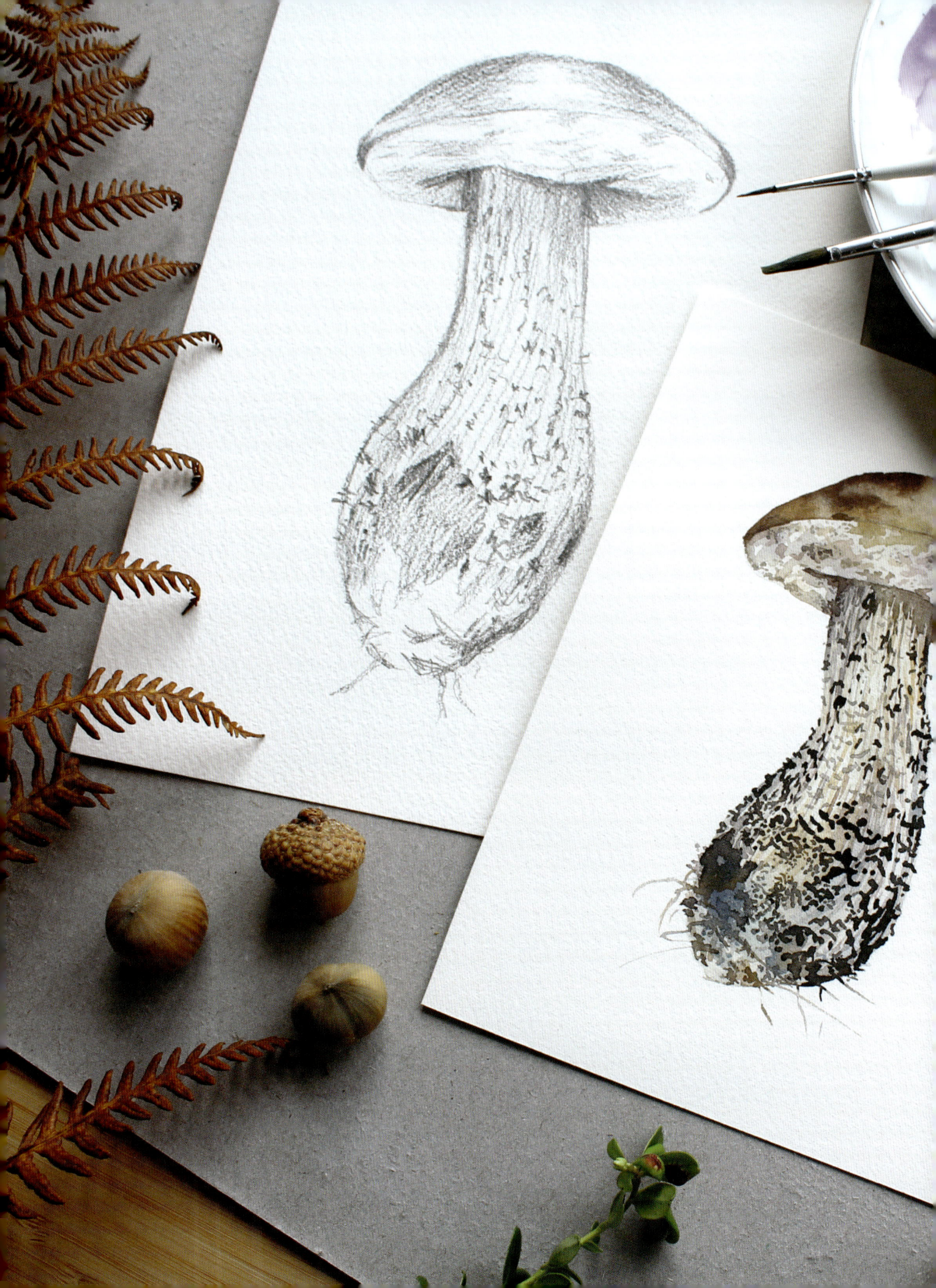

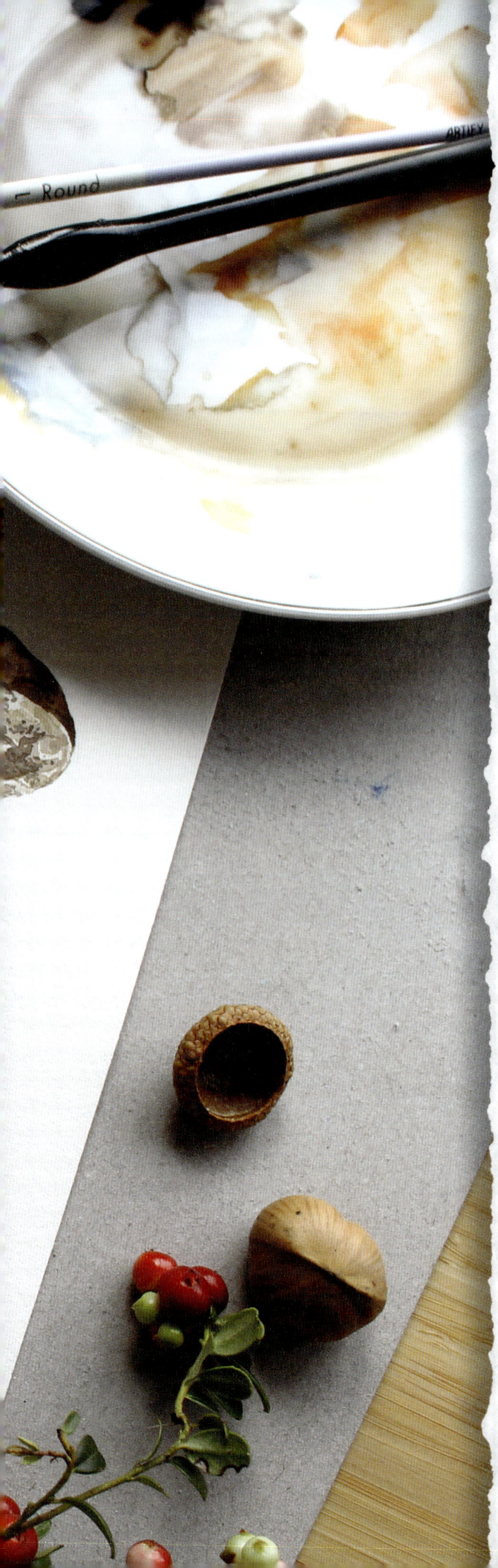

Chapter 3

Working with Your Idea

In this chapter, we'll explore how to draw inspiration from the natural world and use references to enhance your woodland paintings. Whether you're working from photographs, sketches, or plein air studies, understanding how to interpret and adapt your references is key to creating compelling compositions. We'll also delve into color theory, learning how to create harmonious color palettes that reflect the true essence of the forest. By applying principles of color harmony and thoughtful composition, you'll be able to create balanced, dynamic paintings that capture the beauty and tranquility of woodlands, both in the studio and on location.

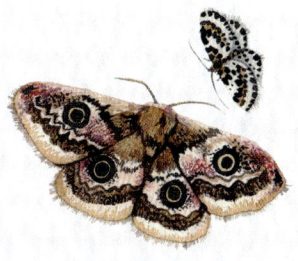

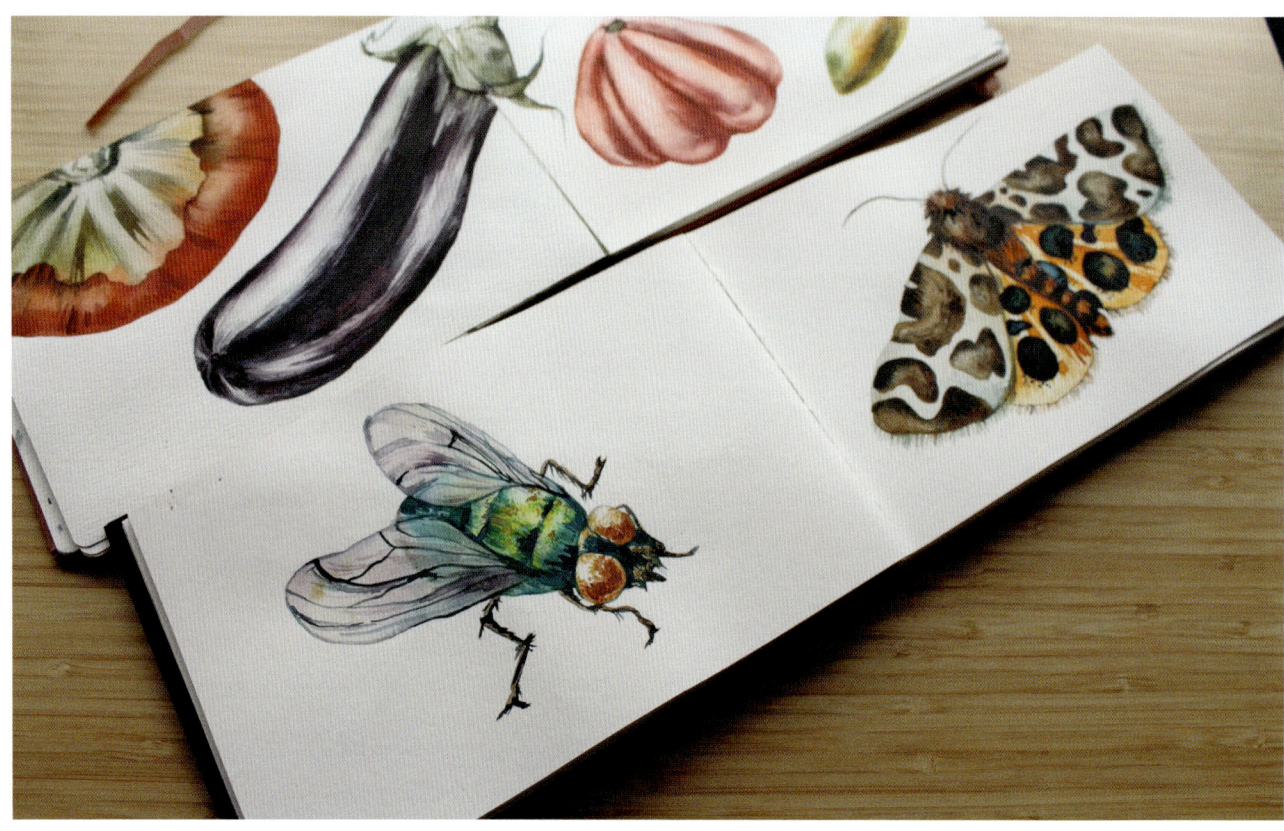

I fill my sketchbooks with subjects that capture my interest, painting either from life or from references.

References and Inspiration

Inspiration drives an artist to create. It's fueled by passion and curiosity, not by fear of difficult subjects. It's about exploring your own interests—whether that's capturing light, obsessing over moths, or experimenting with color combinations. It's never about saying, "I can't paint"; it's about asking, "What if?" and "Should I try this?"

For me, finding inspiration is easy because I'm always excited to paint many things. One of the best ways to develop your watercolor skills and find your style is to focus on a subject you're passionate about. For me, it's moths and butterflies—I've painted more than two hundred species, experimenting with style and media. Nature, old architecture, folklore, sunsets, and color combinations have also inspired me.

Get Inspired

- Make a list of things that interest you—subjects, themes, colors, techniques, styles.

- Explore how other artists paint similar subjects.

- Visit libraries to see how others have painted the same things.

- Look at magazines, museums, social media, Pinterest, and people around you for ideas.

Make Lists

Create categories like these:

- **Themes:** woodland, cottage houses, fields, tropics
- **Subjects:** mushrooms, insects, animals, plants
- **Places:** rivers, forests, small villages
- **Colors:** Burnt Sienna, Sap Green, Prussian Blue
- **Techniques:** wet-on-wet, detailed brushstrokes
- **Styles:** botanical, vintage, whimsical

Next, study artists whose work aligns with your list. Notice what you like in their art and save your favorite pieces. Watching artists work through videos can be highly educational.

You can even try copying your favorite artist's work. This is a great way to learn techniques and break free from traditional art school rules, like using only certain pigments or working light to dark.

Use References

I personally find it difficult to paint without a reference. A good reference photo can elevate your skills. A reference helps you observe details, identify colors, and mix precise combinations. The key phrase for artists is "paint what you see."

TIPS FOR TAKING GOOD REFERENCE PHOTOS

- Ensure good lighting (no nighttime or dusk photos).
- Use contrast to make the subject stand out.
- Keep the photo simple, avoiding too many details.
- Capture the whole object in the shot.

REFERENCE BOOKS

If you're drawn to nature but unsure how to paint certain animals or plants, consider buying reference books. These can often be found online, in thrift stores, or in secondhand shops. They're valuable for learning about color choices and techniques used by past artists.

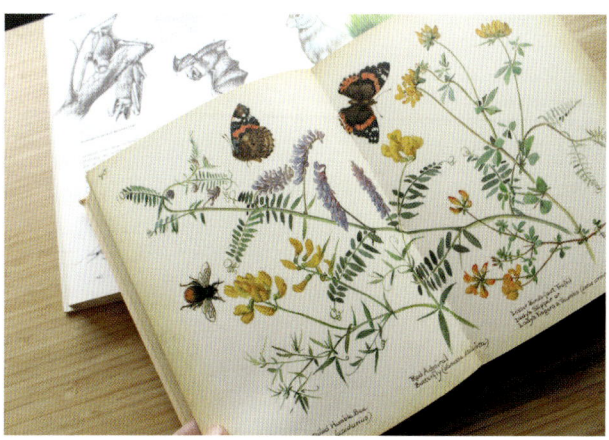

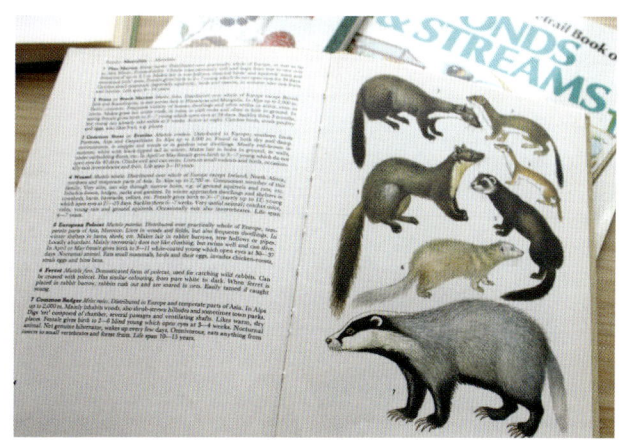

I have a large collection of beautiful old books I use to find painting inspiration.

Tonal Values

Understanding tonal value—how light or dark a color is—is essential in watercolor. To create depth and volume, it's important to use contrasting values: light highlights, dark shadows, and intermediate tones. Watercolors are semitranslucent, so adding water lightens the tone.

Tonal Value Exercise

To practice tonal values, choose a single color and create a gradient from dark to light. Paint six or seven concentric squares, starting with a thick, dark mixture and gradually adding more water to lighten each square. This helps you develop an understanding of how to manipulate tonal values.

Using Tonal Values in Your Painting

When painting realistic objects like pinecones, animals, or plants, understanding light and shadow is crucial. Decide where the light source is and apply corresponding values to areas of the object. A monochrome exercise—painting an object with just one color—can help you focus on values before adding color.

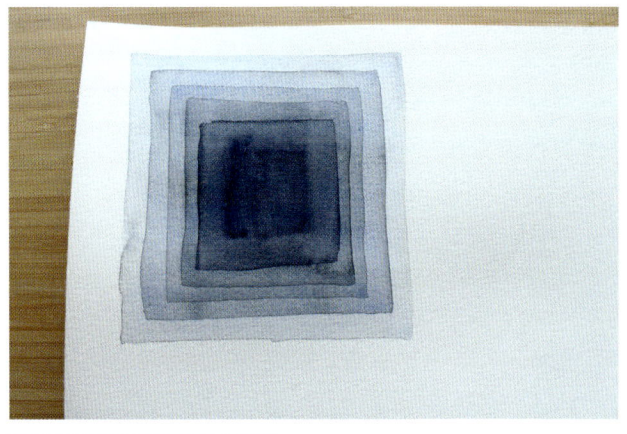

Here I used Prussian blue for my tonal value exercise. It helps to use a color that is dark enough to have a range of values. Very light colors, like yellow, won't work as well.

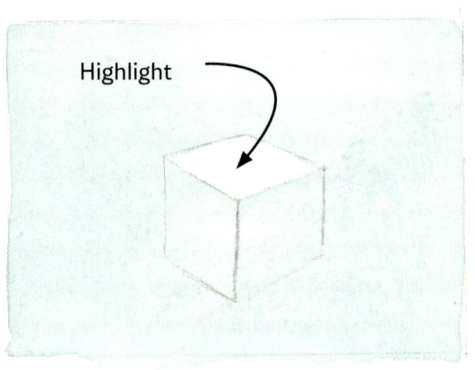

Highlight

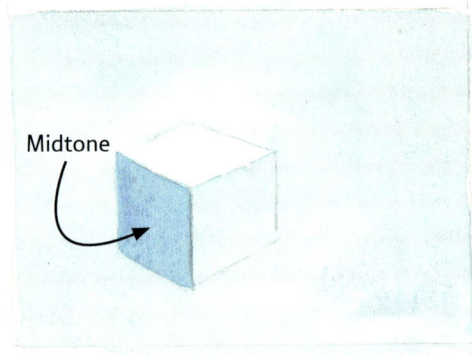

Midtone

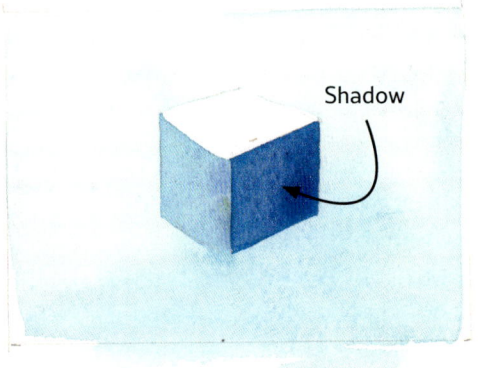

Shadow

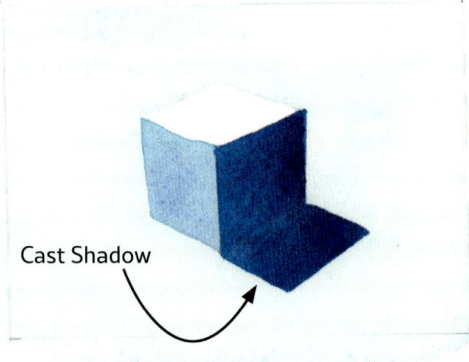

Cast Shadow

Using a range of tonal values creates the illusion of three dimensions in a cube. Start with the lightest tones and gradually darken them.

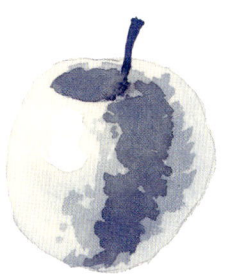
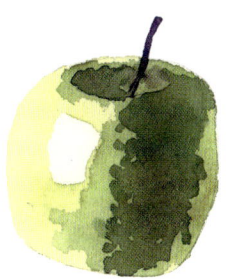

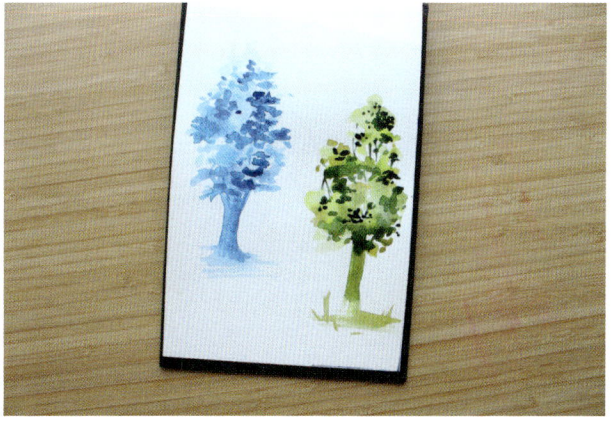

You can create a monochromatic (single color) painting using different tonal values.

Tonal studies, like these trees, are a good way to get familiar with a subject before painting it in a variety of colors.

Seeing Value in Color

To see tonal values in color images, try squinting your eyes to reduce light and enhance contrast. Alternatively, use a red filter to block out color and focus on light and dark areas. Converting a reference photo to black and white can also help you identify values more easily.

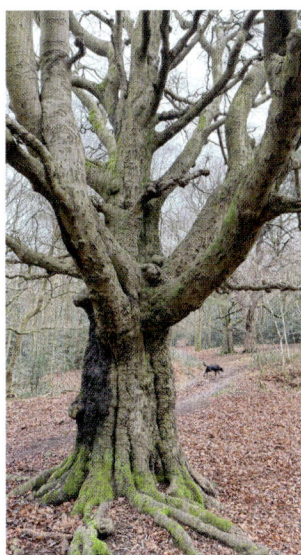
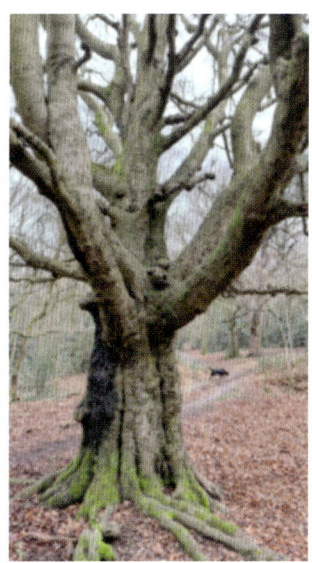
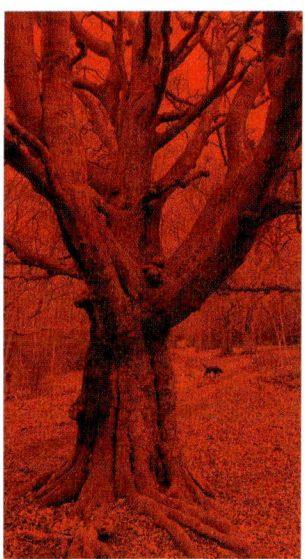
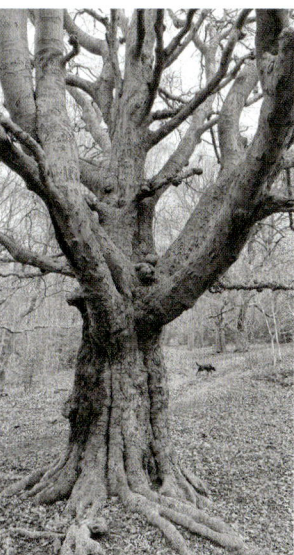

From left to right: Original photo, with squinted eyes, through a red filter, and black-and-white version.

Color Theory

In the first chapter, I briefly touched on color theory, explaining how you can mix nearly every color using six primary colors—three warm and three cool. In this section, we'll go deeper into color theory, which is essential for mastering color mixing.

Understanding the relationships between colors is fundamental. It helps you grasp the basics of mixing and how color relationships work. Learning how to mix colors confidently is one of the key factors for successful and enjoyable painting.

Primary Colors

Primary colors are the foundation of all other colors. These are:

1. Yellow
2. Red
3. Blue

Primary colors cannot be created by mixing other colors, but they can be combined in various ways to create other colors. They are the building blocks of color mixing.

Secondary Colors

Secondary colors are made by mixing two primary colors together:

1. Yellow + red = orange
2. Red + blue = purple
3. Blue + yellow = green

These secondary colors expand your palette and allow you to create a broader range of hues.

Tertiary Colors

Tertiary colors are achieved by mixing a primary color with a secondary color that's adjacent to it on the color wheel. These are the more nuanced, often subtle colors that appear between primary and secondary colors. The six tertiary colors are:

1. Yellow + orange = yellow-orange
2. Red + orange = red-orange
3. Red + purple = red-purple
4. Blue + purple = blue-purple
5. Blue + green = blue-green
6. Yellow + green = yellow-green

Tertiary colors allow you to create even more variety in your paintings and help add depth and richness to your color choices.

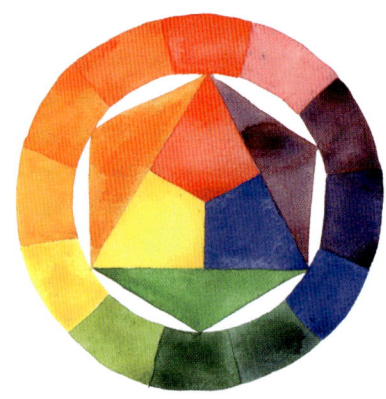

A color wheel is a visual arrangement of the primary, secondary, and tertiary colors.

Warm and Cool Colors

Colors can be classified as warm or cool.

Warm colors: These colors are on one side of the color wheel and include yellow, orange, and red. They tend to evoke warmth, energy, and excitement.

Cool colors: These colors are on the opposite side of the color wheel and include purple, blue, and green. They typically convey calm, tranquility, and coolness.

Any color can have a warm or cool bias. For example, a green closer to yellow is a warmer green, while one closer to blue is cooler.

Color Harmony

Harmony in color refers to a pleasing arrangement of colors that work well together. Harmony engages the viewer and creates a balanced, visually satisfying experience. When colors are not harmonious, the artwork can be either boring or chaotic.

You can also use factors like value (lightness or darkness) and saturation (intensity of color) to create contrast and balance within your composition. Temperature (warm versus cool colors) is another critical element in creating harmony, as it can convey different moods and emotions.

Here are some popular color harmony formulas:

Complementary colors: These are colors that are directly opposite each other on the color wheel. For example:

Yellow + purple
Red + green
Blue + orange

These combinations create maximum contrast and stability. When mixed, complementary colors neutralize each other, often resulting in a grayscale color.

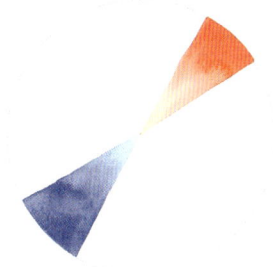

Complementary color harmony

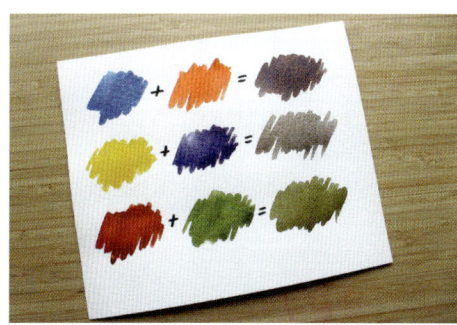

Combing a color and its complement creates a neutral color.

Analogous colors: These are colors that sit next to each other on the color wheel. For example:

Yellow-Green, Yellow, Yellow-Orange

Typically, one of the three colors dominates, while the others serve as supporting colors.

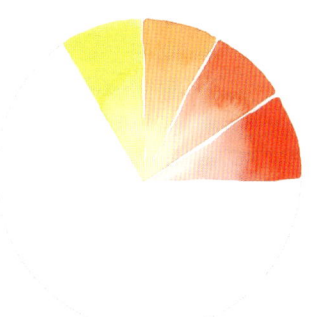

Analogous color harmony.

Split-complementary colors: This involves a base color and the two colors adjacent to its complementary color. For example, if your base color is yellow, the split-complementary colors would be yellow-green and yellow-orange.

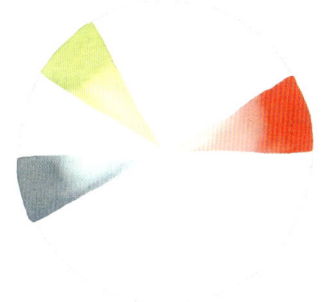

Split-complementary color harmony

Other popular color harmonies include primary triads (all three primary colors) and secondary triads (all three secondary colors).

Tip!

If you want to go into even more depth with color theory, there are many books dedicated to color.

More Color Tips

Mix gradually: Add colors slowly when mixing to avoid oversaturation. It's easy to add more paint, but harder to adjust if you've gone too far. Gradually push the mix toward your desired hue.

Start with concentrated paint: Begin with concentrated paint and add water as needed to adjust the tone. If your mix becomes too watery too quickly, you'll have to start over.

Rinse well: When rinsing your brush, be sure to squeeze out excess water to avoid diluting your mix.

Avoid pan contamination: When mixing two colors, add one color to your mixing area at a time to avoid contamination if you're using pan paints.

Create a swatch library: The swatch library should include the names of pigments and their brands, and successful color combinations. This will help you match real-life objects with your mixes.

Limit your palette: Limiting the number of colors you use can improve harmony and prevent your palette from becoming too busy.

Stick to your palette: Once you've chosen your colors, avoid adding others. Many color schemes fail because artists start adding extra colors halfway through.

Choose a dominant color: Pick one color to dominate the piece and incorporate it throughout the painting to maintain unity.

How to Paint White in Watercolors

Many beginners search for white paint in their watercolor palettes, but traditionally, white is achieved in watercolor by leaving parts of the paper untouched or using very light tones. Some artists do use white watercolor for pastel effects, but this compromises transparency. Instead, using white gouache for highlights and details is a better option.

Use it sparingly: White gouache has a different consistency and opacity compared with watercolor. Apply it toward the end of your painting process to avoid disrupting transparency.

Mix in carefully: When mixing gouache with watercolor, keep the consistency thick. Gouache should be like cream or butter, and it's best to mix a small amount at a time.

Other methods to paint white in watercolor include masking fluid (to protect areas of paper), white gel pens, and white acrylics. Experimenting with these techniques can help you decide what works best for your style.

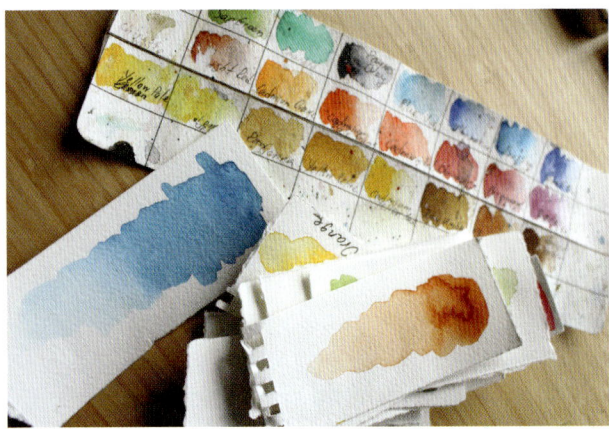

Swatches of paints and color mixes are a great resources when choosing colors for a painting.

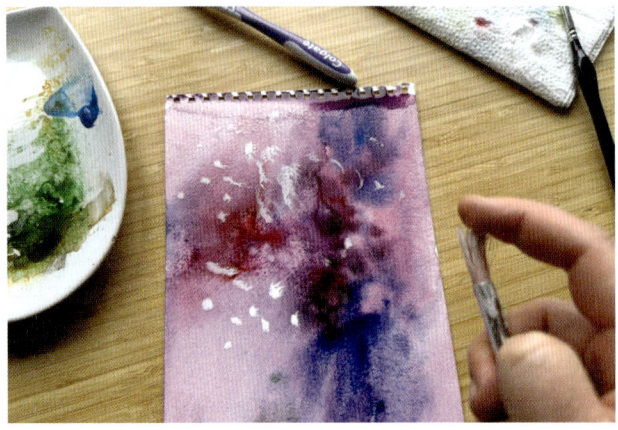

White gouache can be either painted on or even sprayed on with an old paintbrush or toothbrush.

Composition in Art

Composition in art refers to how you arrange the elements within a piece. In watercolor, this means organizing visual elements to create a harmonious balance that conveys a message, mood, or feeling.

Good composition can make your painting more engaging and professional-looking. Even if you don't memorize every composition rule, knowing the basics can make a huge difference in the impact of your artwork.

Composition Tips

- **Focus on the most important element:** Identify the most important part of your scene and make sure your composition highlights it.

- **Experiment with reference images:** Print your reference images and cut them out. Arrange them on your paper to see what composition works best before starting your painting.

- **Vertical versus horizontal format:** Decide whether your canvas will be vertical or horizontal, and think about what format suits your subject matter best.

Types of Compositions

There are many ways you can arrange a composition. Here are a few of the most popular and effective.

- **Rule of thirds:** Divide your canvas into thirds (both horizontally and vertically) and place important elements where the lines intersect. This creates a more dynamic composition, as the viewer's eye is naturally drawn to these areas.

- **Golden ratio:** The golden ratio (approximately 1.618) is another way to divide space in a balanced, pleasing way. This ratio is often used in nature and is thought to be aesthetically pleasing to the human eye.

- **Golden triangle:** Imagine a diagonal line that goes from one corner of the page to the opposite corner and two lines from the other two corners that meet that line at a 90-degree angle. Arrange your elements at one of the intersections or along one of the paths. This can make your composition feel more dynamic and balanced, especially for compositions with diagonal elements.

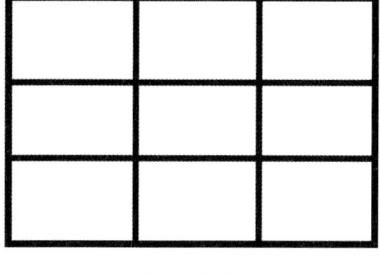

Rule of thirds

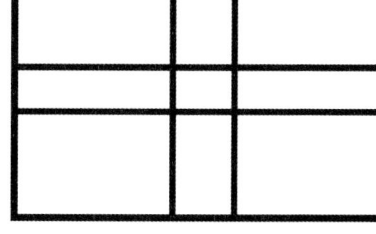

Golden ratio

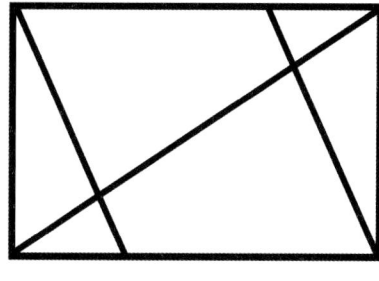

Golden triangle

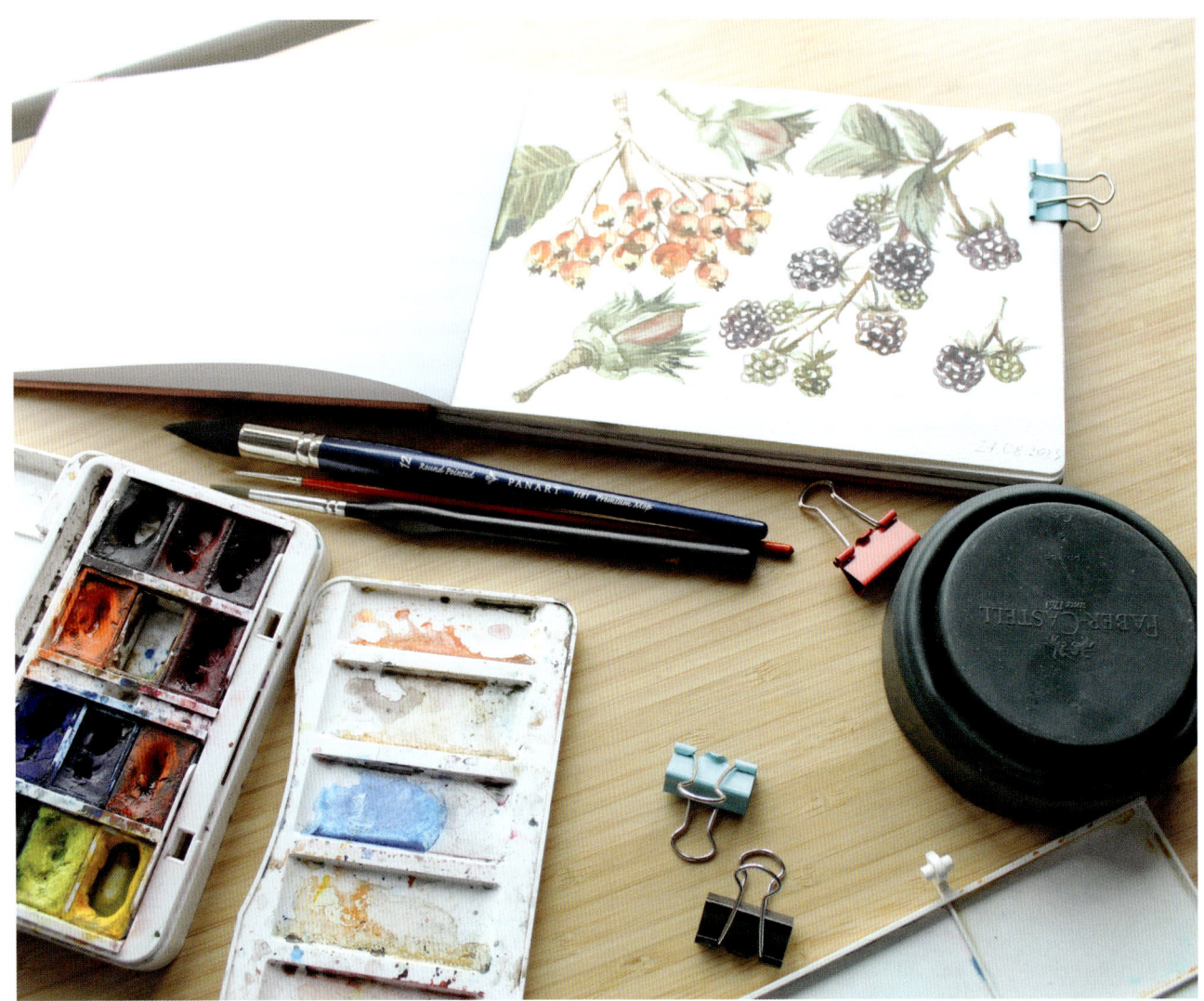

Sketching Outdoors

Outdoor painting, also known as plein air painting, is a great way to practice creativity. You get to work directly with nature, taking in the sights, sounds, and smells around you. It's a challenge but offers incredible rewards.

Why Paint Outdoors?

More details and colors: Painting from real life gives you a richer sense of color and texture than photographs can capture.

Freedom from perfectionism: The goal of plein air painting isn't perfection—it's about capturing the feel of the moment.

Color experimentation: Painting outdoors encourages you to try unusual color combinations. For instance, a pine cone might look brown in your head, but in the light, it could reveal unexpected hues like red or black.

Plein Air Painting Tips

Check the weather: Make sure to plan for the conditions you'll be working in.

Prepare your supplies: Keep your kit simple at first. A small sketchbook, a portable watercolor palette, and a couple of brushes should be enough.

Start with simpler subjects: Pick an object or scene that won't overwhelm you.

Find a quiet spot: Look for a peaceful place to paint where you can relax and concentrate.

Essential Plein Air Supplies

Sketchbook: A portable, lightweight sketchbook.

Watercolors: A small portable set for travel or a plastic or metal container with a lid filled with your favorite colors.

Palette: A plastic palette or small ceramic plate to mix colors.

Brushes: A small selection (sizes 12, 6, 3, and 2/0).

Water container: Collapsible containers, which are ideal for painting outdoors.

Blotting paper: A roll of kitchen paper to help keep your brushes clean.

Foldable chair: To sit comfortably while painting.

Clamps: To secure your paper in windy conditions.

Snacks and water: For staying hydrated and energized.

Sun protection: A hat and sunscreen for long sessions.

Insect repellent: To keep away pesky distractions.

Whether you're working on understanding color theory, refining your composition, or venturing outside to paint, every part of the process adds to your development as an artist. Embrace each challenge and remember to enjoy the creative journey.

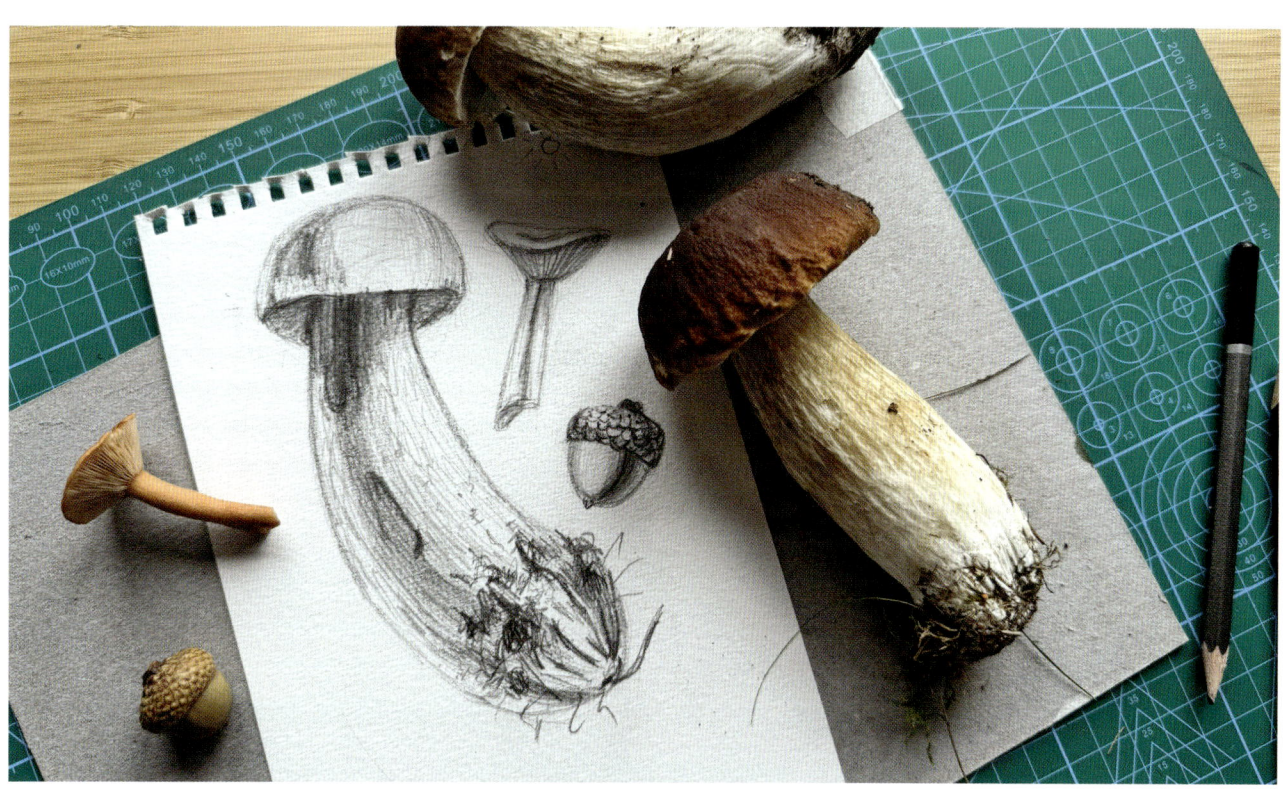

If you can't get outdoors to paint, collecting specimens and sketching and painting from them is also a valuable practice.

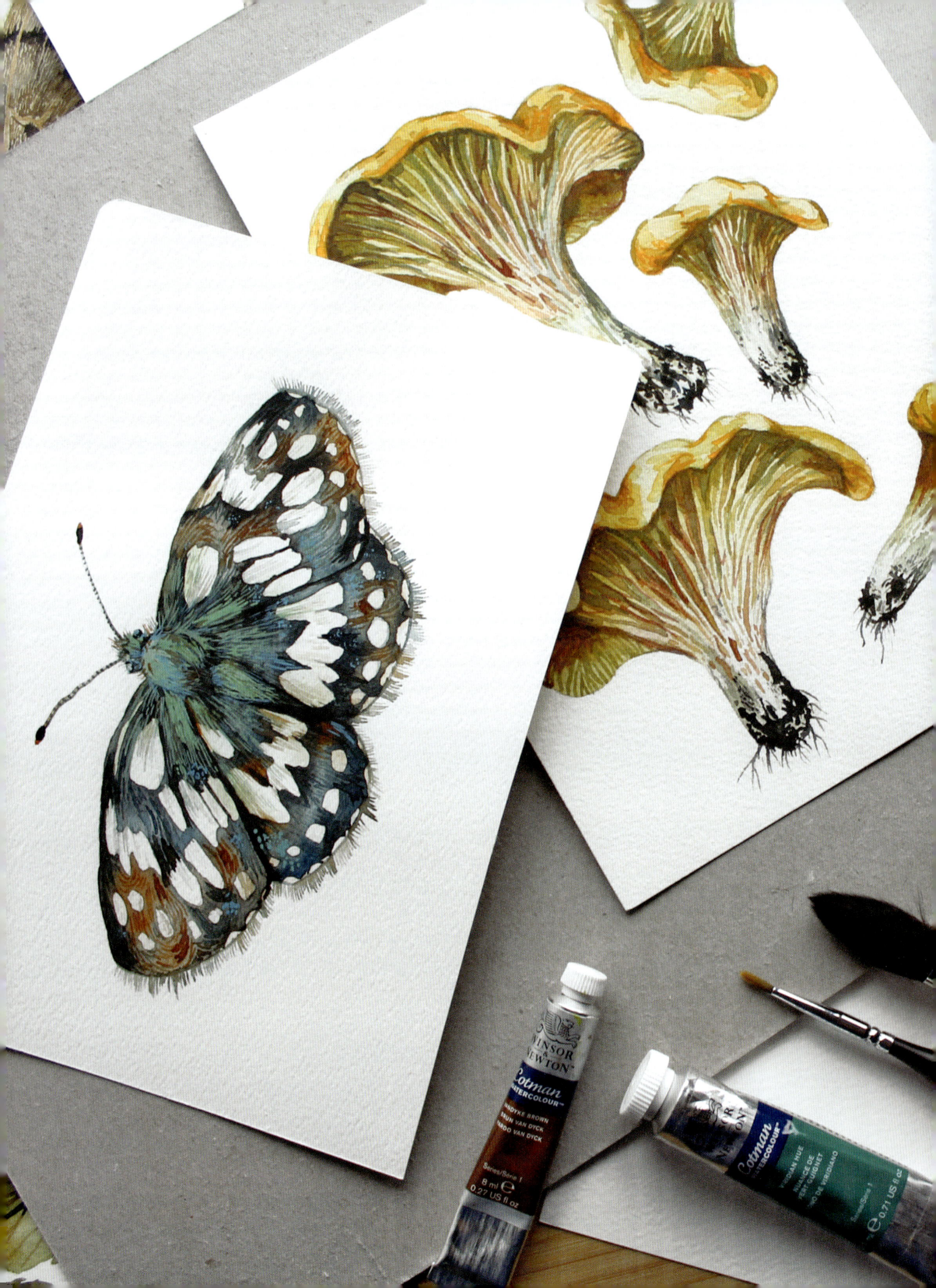

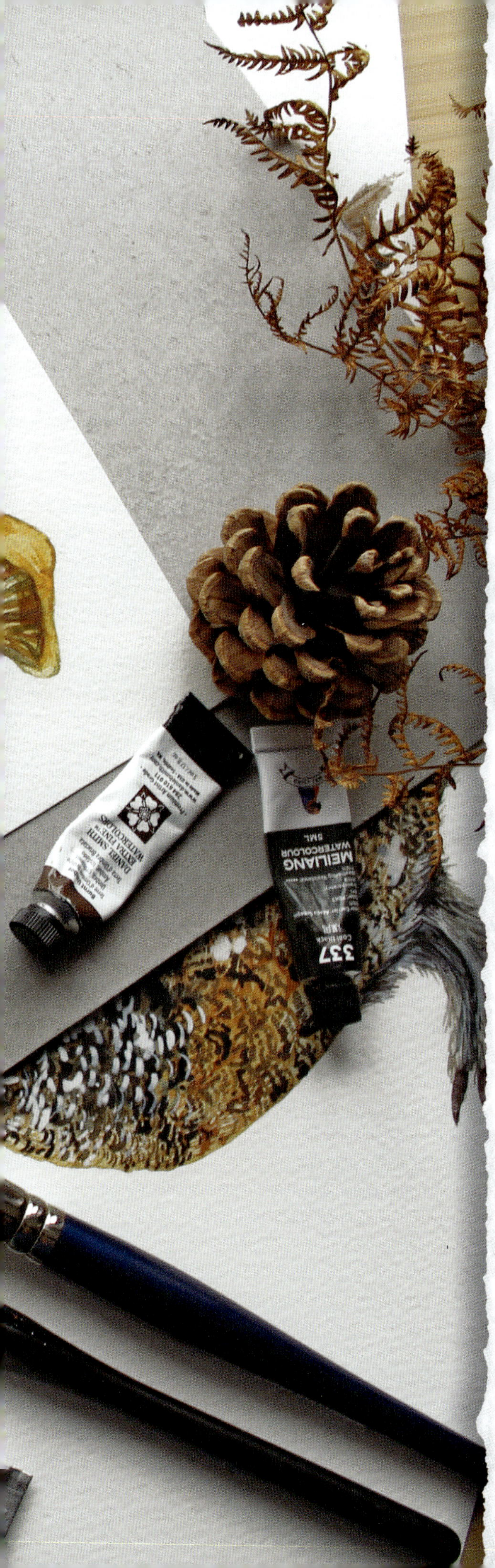

Chapter 4

The Projects

The best way to learn a specific painting style is to copy it—not to claim it as your own but to explore whether you enjoy that style while also honing your observation skills. Completing tutorials from various artists can greatly benefit you by improving your techniques, helping you find your unique style, and encouraging you to experiment with new art supplies.

I've created twenty comprehensive step-by-step watercolor tutorials focused on woodland themes, such as delicate mushrooms, adorable animals, fascinating insects, and colorful plants. I encourage you to try my approach, and I hope you find it enjoyable!

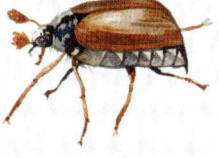

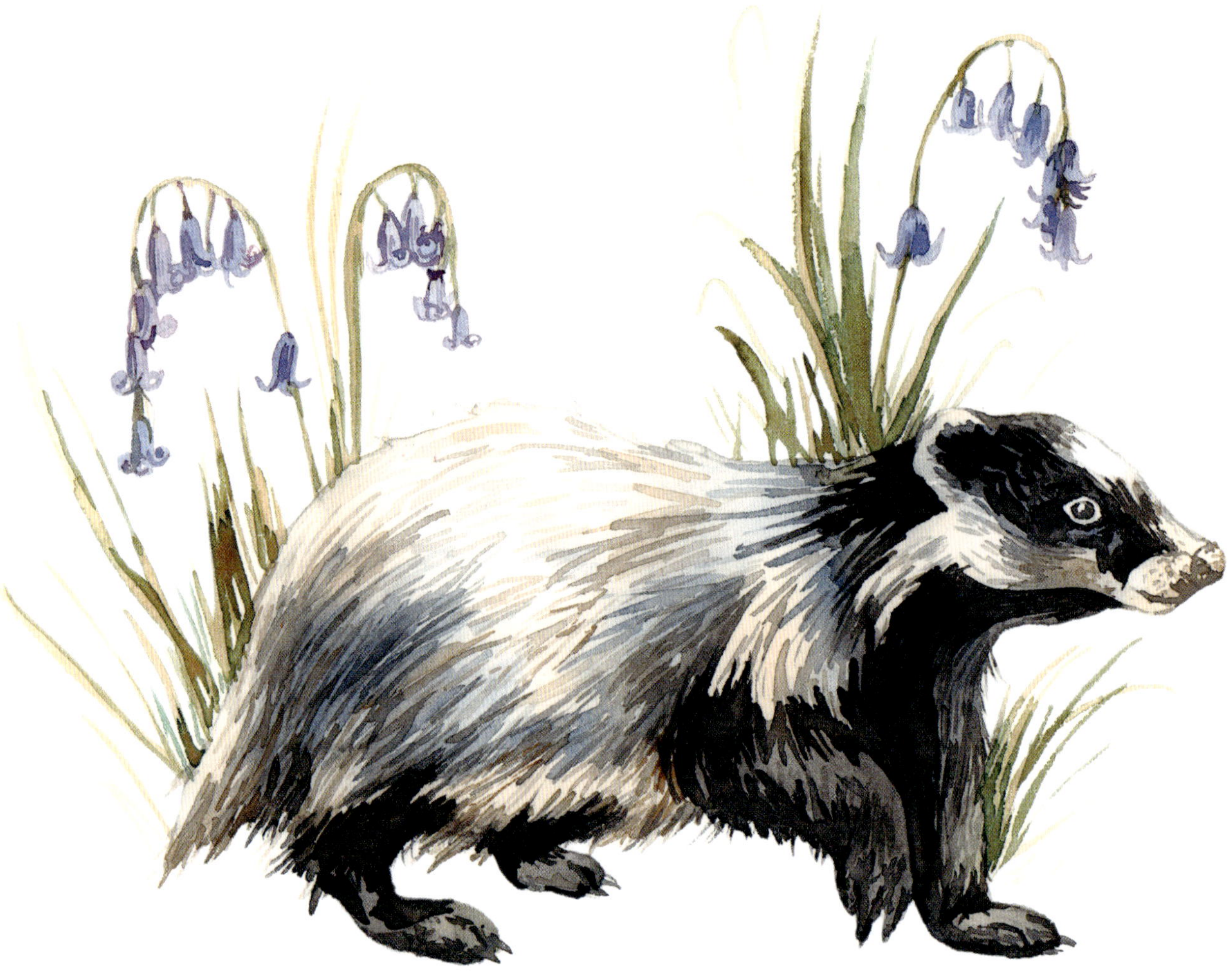

Badger with Bluebells

What could be sweeter than a badger nestled among bluebells? The soft, vibrant hues of the bluebells contrast beautifully with the badger's earthy tones. In this project, you'll learn how to use different strokes to create all the various textures in the painting, from the stems of the bluebells to the badger's fur.

Colors

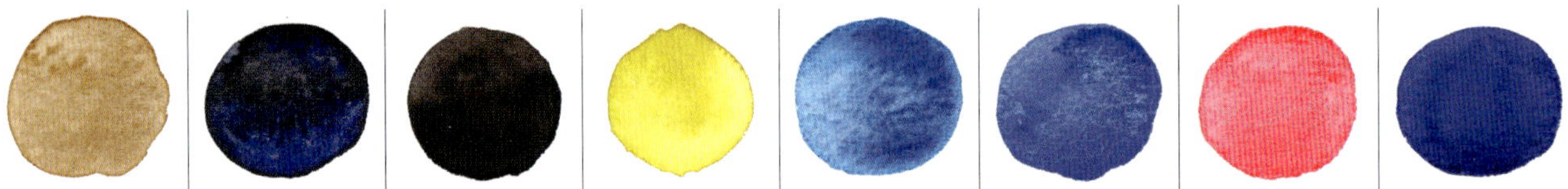

	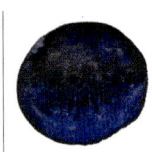		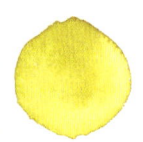	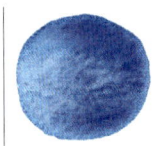		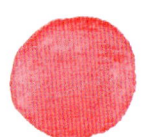	
RAW UMBER	PAYNE'S GRAY	IVORY BLACK	OLIVE GREEN	PRUSSIAN BLUE	COBALT BLUE	PERMANENT ROSE	ULTRAMARINE BLUE

Brushes

Size 6 round

Size 3 round

Size 2/0 round for details

Paper

300 gsm cold-pressed

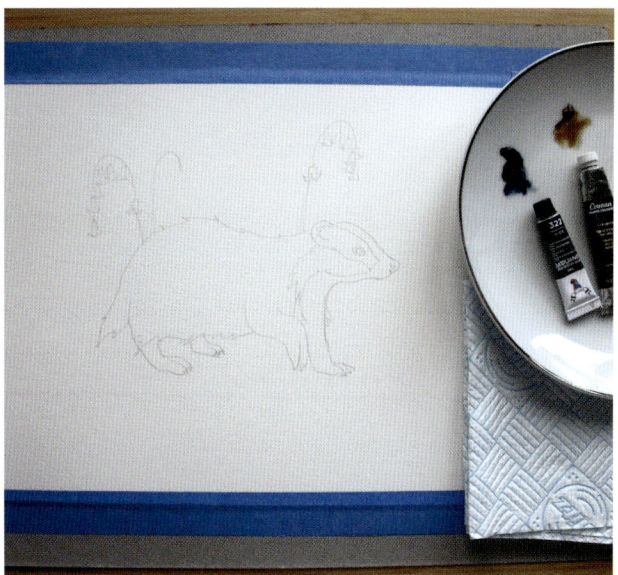

1. Draw or transfer the sketch onto the paper. Attach the watercolor paper to a board or your table using masking tape.

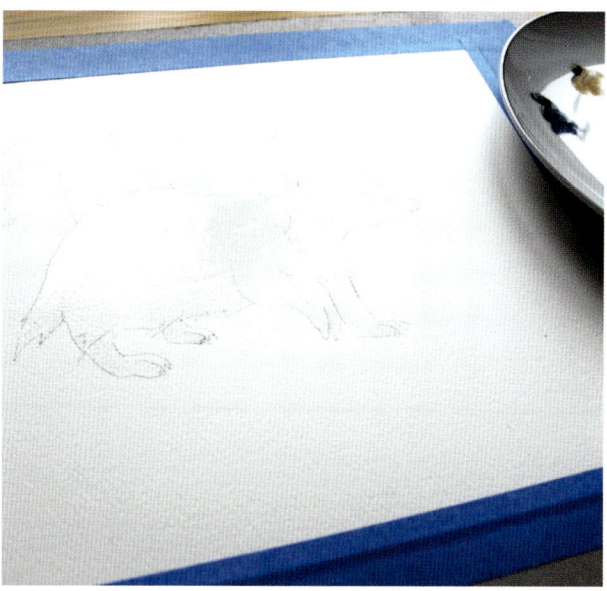

2. Using a size 6 brush, apply a thick layer of water to the entire area with the badger. Try not to go over the edge, and avoid leaving dry areas. To check if you applied the water evenly, tilt your paper. If the area is glossy and reflects light, you did it correctly. If you see dry patches, simply add more water there.

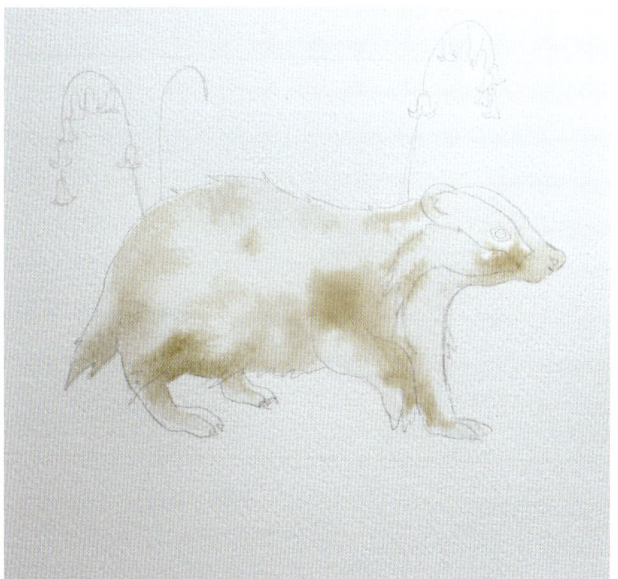

3. Apply Raw Umber (tea consistency) wet-on-wet to the badger's belly and legs, leaving some white areas.

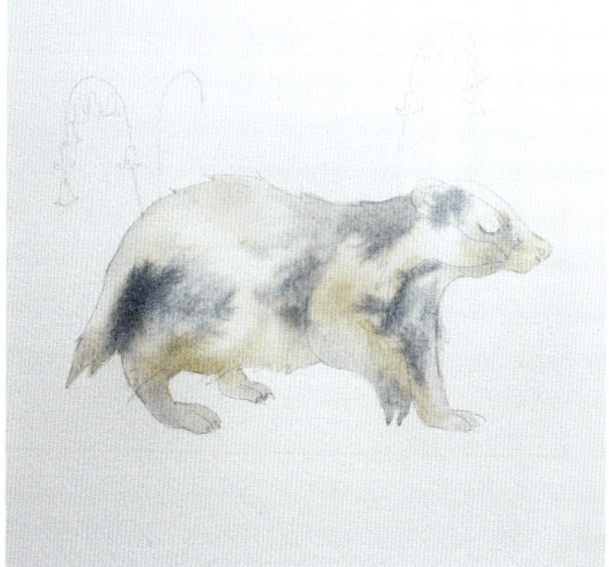

4. Immediately after applying the Raw Umber, while the surface is still wet, apply Payne's Gray (tea consistency). Let it dry completely.

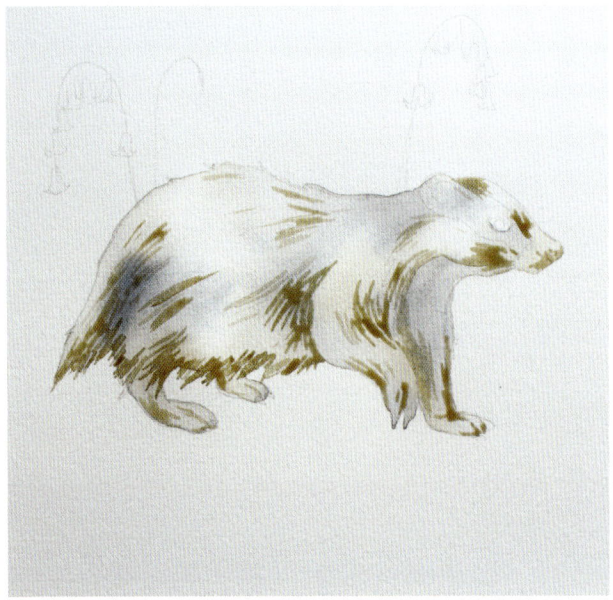

5. Switch to a size 3 brush and apply Raw Umber (tea consistency) to the dry badger, using brushstrokes to mimic fur.

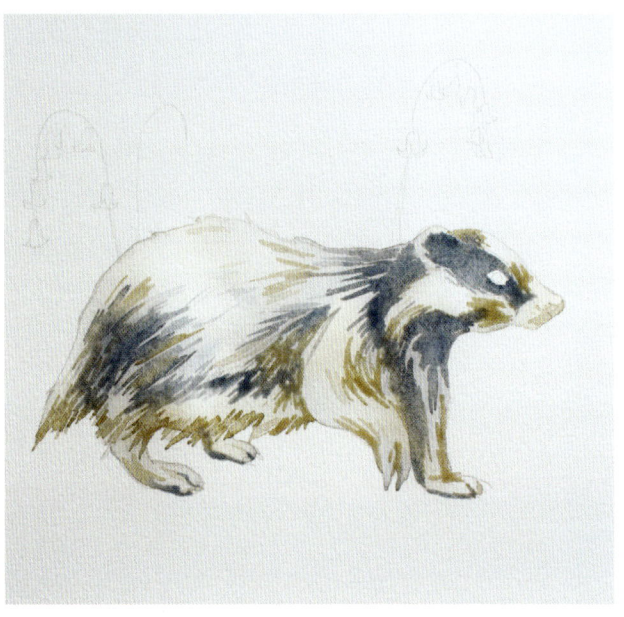

6. Use Payne's Gray to work on fine details, painting the fur, and applying this color to the black areas on the badger.

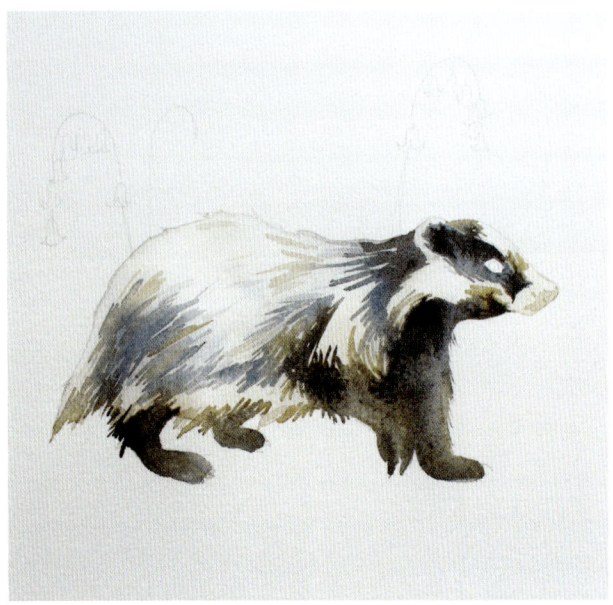

7. Now use Ivory Black and apply it to the black patches on the badger, leaving some areas for the previous color to shine through. Paint the legs and chest, then let it dry.

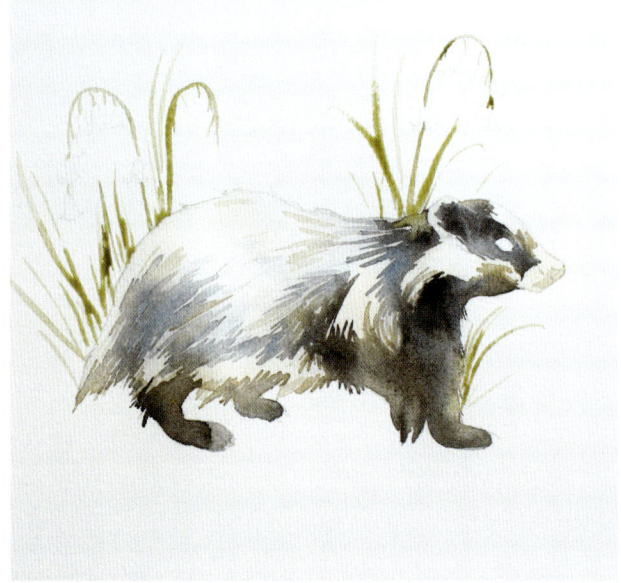

8. Apply Olive Green wet-on-dry using a size 6 brush to paint the bluebell stems.

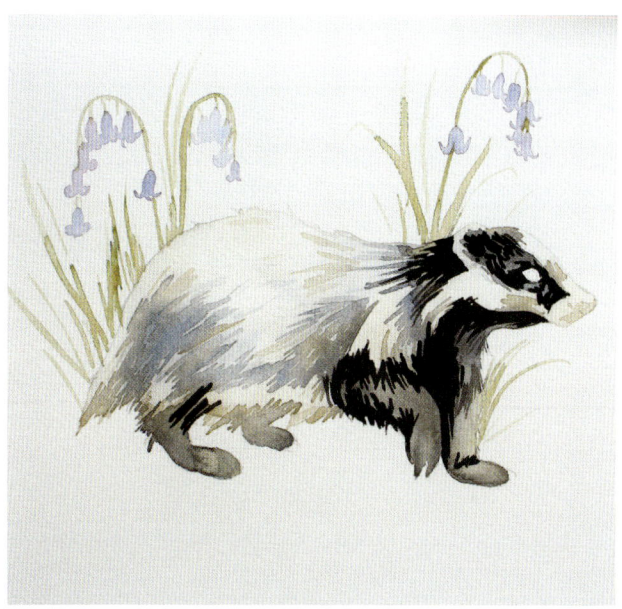

9. Apply a mix of Cobalt Blue and Permanent Rose (tea consistency) wet-on-dry using a size 3 brush to paint the first layer on the bluebells.

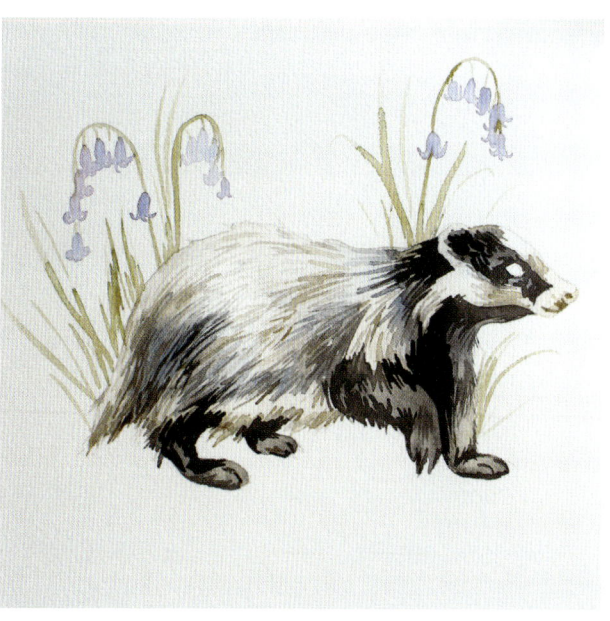

10. Apply Ivory Black using a size 2/0 brush to add fine details to the badger, painting the fur and focusing on the darkest tonal values. Follow the natural curves of the badger to create shapes and volume in the fur.

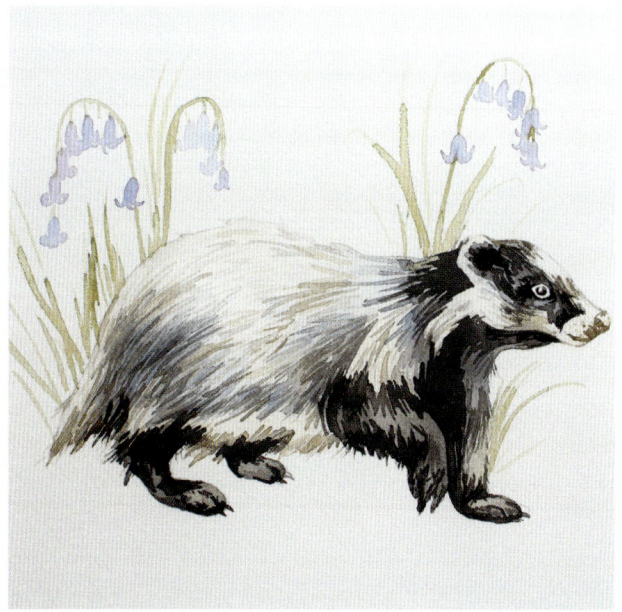

11. Use a mix of Raw Umber and Ivory Black to define the nose by painting a few dots. Work on the eye, filling it in with Ivory Black and leaving a white area for a highlight, as well as a bit of space around the eye.

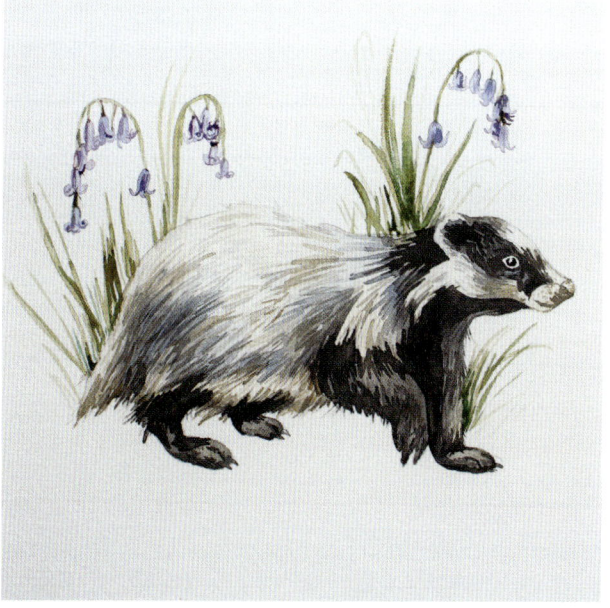

12. Combine Olive Green and Prussian Blue to create a cooler shade of green. Apply this color to paint a few blades of grass around the bluebells and add shadows to the bluebell leaves. Use a mix of Ultramarine Blue and Permanent Rose (coffee consistency) to add more shadows and add a few brushstrokes to the flowers using a size 2/0 brush.

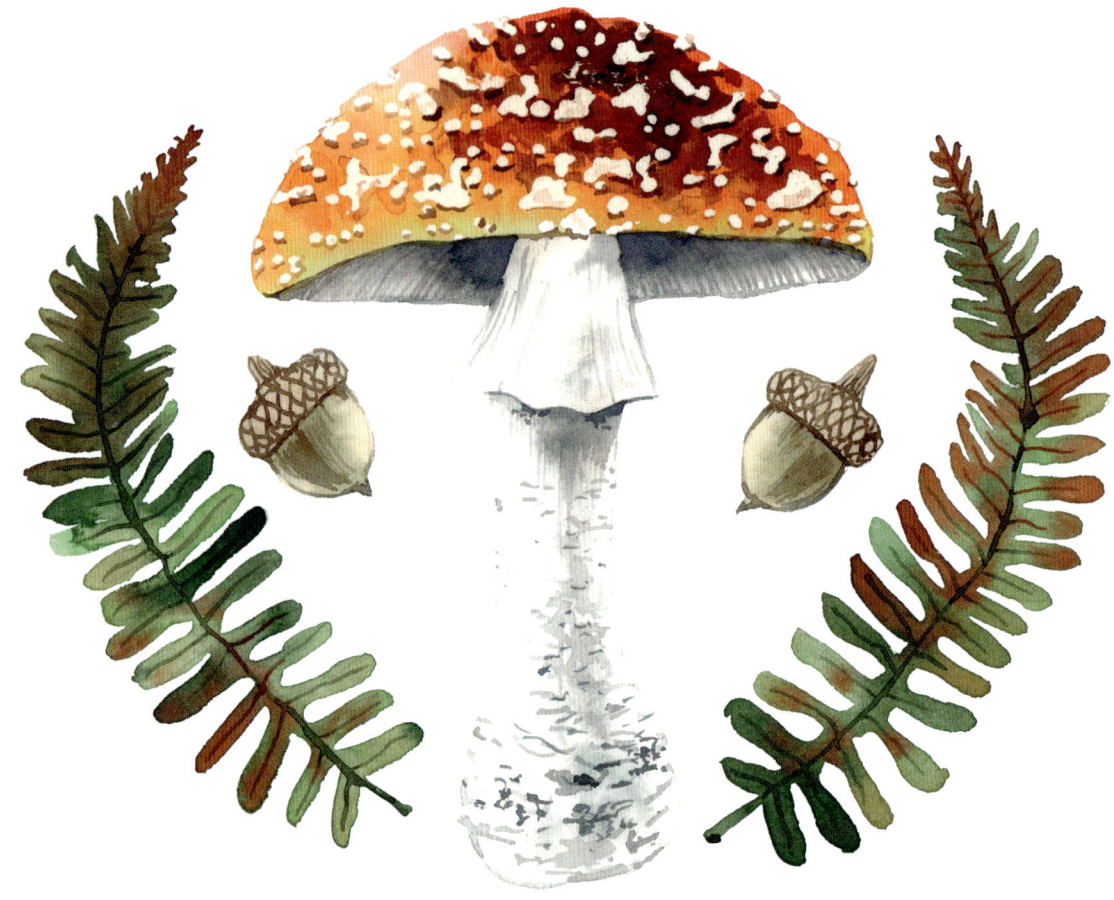

Fly Agaric Mushroom with Ferns and Acorns

This is the classic red polka-dotted mushroom. The Fly Agaric mushroom (*Amanita muscaria*) is a beautiful sight that brightens any gray day. In this lesson, you'll practice using masking fluid to block out white dots and experience the satisfying moment of removing them!

Colors

 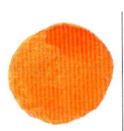 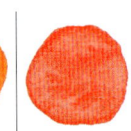 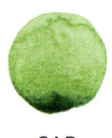 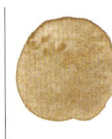  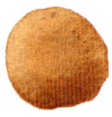  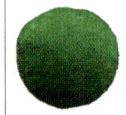  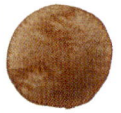

| CADMIUM YELLOW HUE | CADMIUM ORANGE HUE | CADMIUM RED DEEP HUE | SAP GREEN | RAW UMBER | BURNT SIENNA | YELLOW OCHRE | HOOKER'S GREEN | PAYNE'S GRAY | BURNT UMBER |

Brushes
Size 6 round brush

Size 3 round brush

Size 2/0 round brush for details

Old brush for masking fluid

Paper
300 gsm cold-pressed

Other
Masking fluid

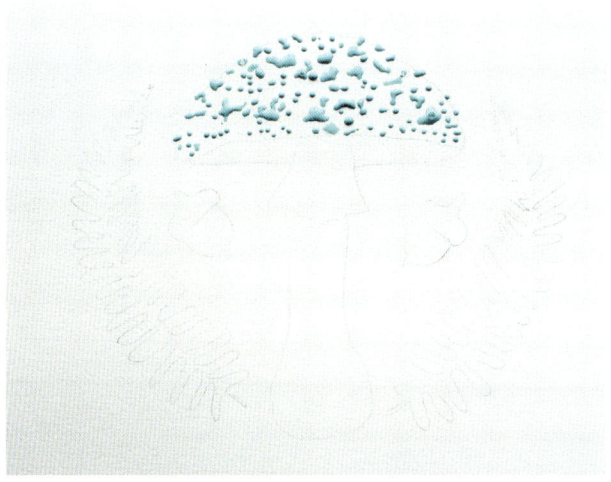

1. Apply masking fluid to the cap of the mushroom using an old unneeded brush or a dropper. Cover the white dots on top of the mushroom. Leave it to dry completely.

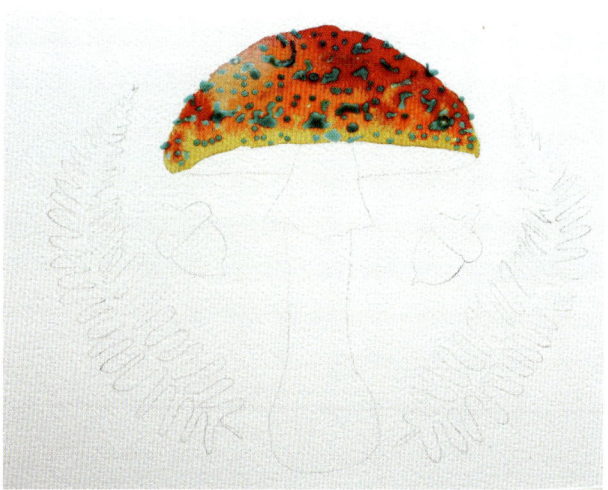

2. Prepare these three colors (milk consistency): Cadmium Yellow Hue, Cadmium Orange Hue, and Cadmium Red Deep Hue. Use a size 6 brush to create three puddles on a ceramic palette. Start applying Cadmium Yellow Hue to the bottom of the cap, then Cadmium Orange Hue in the middle, and finally Cadmium Red Deep Hue on the top. Leave it to dry.

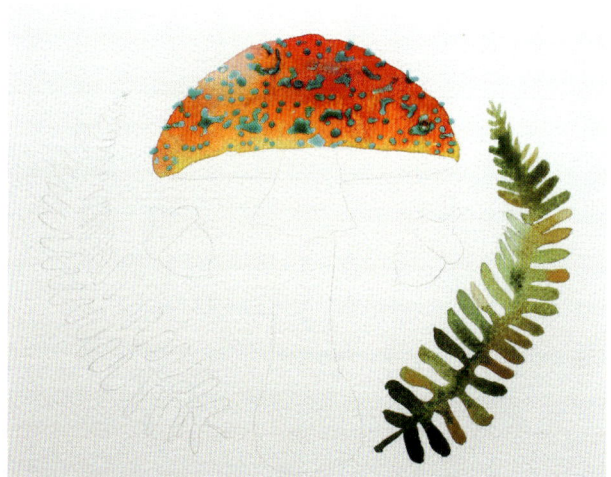

3. To paint the ferns, you will need a mix of Sap Green and Raw Umber, as well as Burnt Sienna, Yellow Ochre, and Hooker's Green. Start by filling the middle of the fern with the Sap Green and Raw Umber mix (tea consistency) using a size 3–6 brush. While it's still wet, wash your brush and apply Burnt Sienna (cream consistency) wet-on-wet on top of the fern and the edges of the leaves. Then, use Yellow Ochre (cream consistency), followed by Hooker's Green (cream consistency).

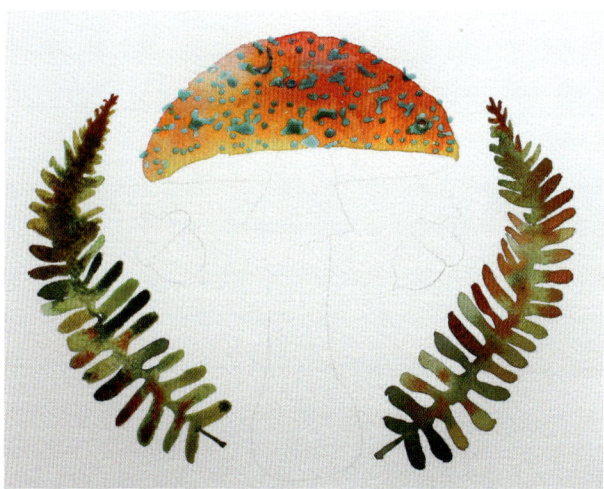

4. Repeat the same for the other fern, slightly changing where the colors should be, making it look different from the fern on the right. Leave it to dry.

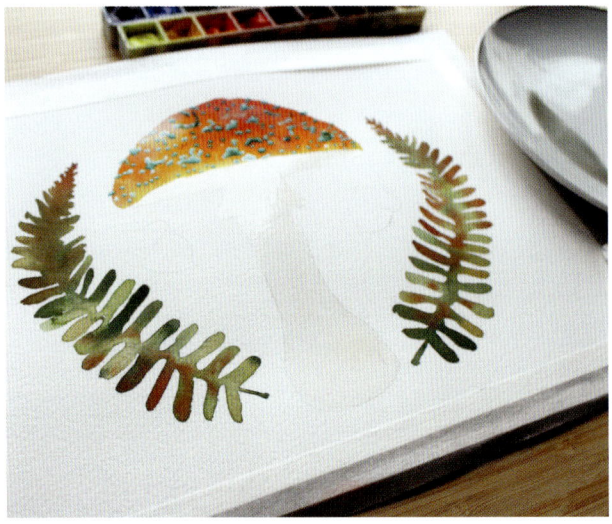

5. Apply an even, thick layer of water to the mushroom's stalk using a clean size 6 brush.

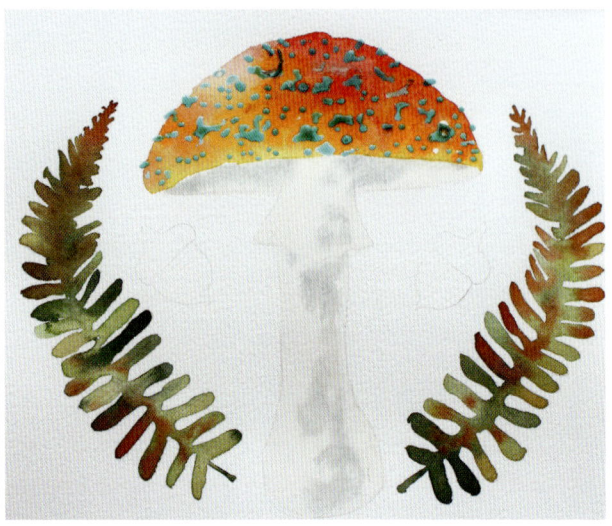

6. Apply Payne's Gray (tea consistency) wet-on-wet to the right-hand side of the stalk using a size 3 brush.

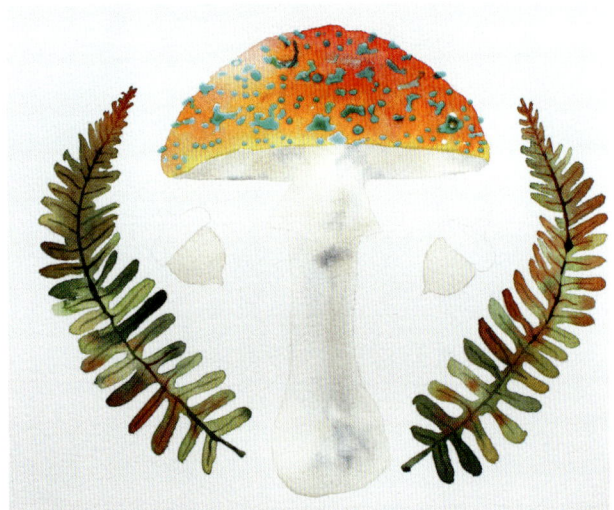

7. Use Raw Umber and the same brush to apply some color on the wet stalk. Paint acorns with Raw Umber (tea consistency).

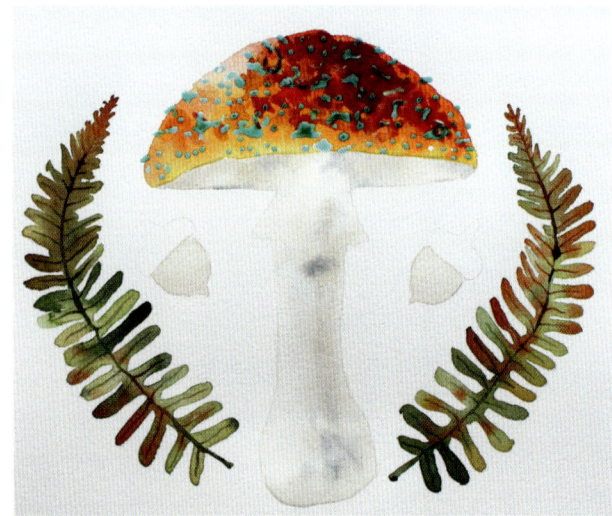

8. Apply a mix of Hooker's Green and Burnt Umber (cream consistency) wet-on-dry to paint veins on the ferns. Use Burnt Sienna (cream consistency) to paint a few veins as well. Apply a mix of Cadmium Red Deep Hue and Burnt Umber wet-on-dry to the top of the cap using a size 6 brush and make more transparent to add some texture. Leave it to dry.

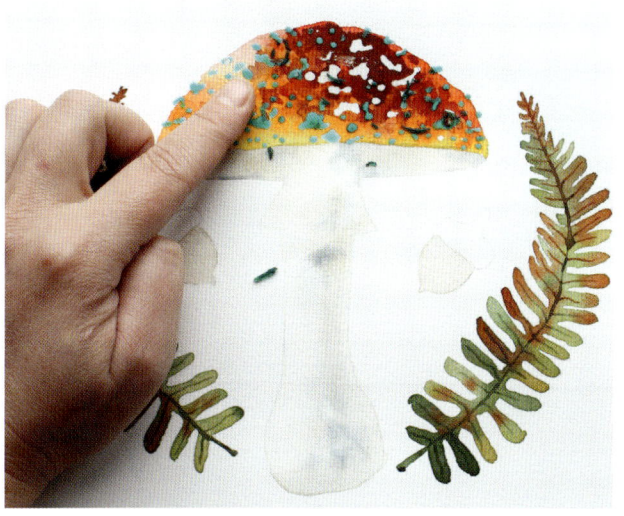

9. Peel off the masking fluid.

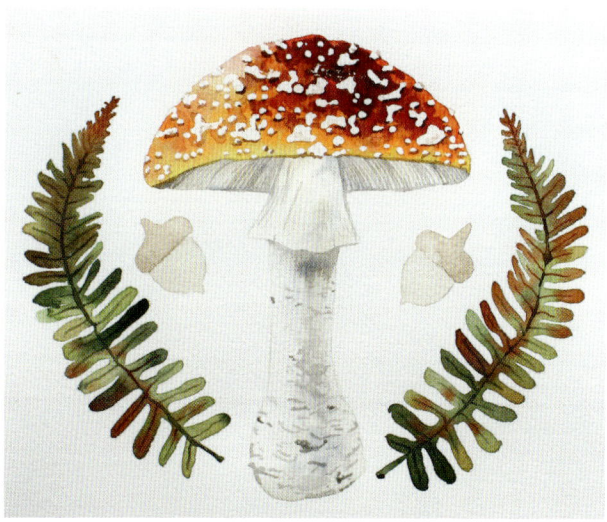

10. Paint shadows using a mix of Cadmium Red Deep Hue and Burnt Umber wet-on-dry with a size 3 brush. Prepare a mix of Payne's Gray and Burnt Umber (tea consistency) and paint details under the cap, and on the skirt and stalk. Use two or three values to combine. Paint a cap on the acorns using a mix of Raw Umber and Burnt Umber (tea consistency) wet-on-dry using a size 3 brush. Let it dry.

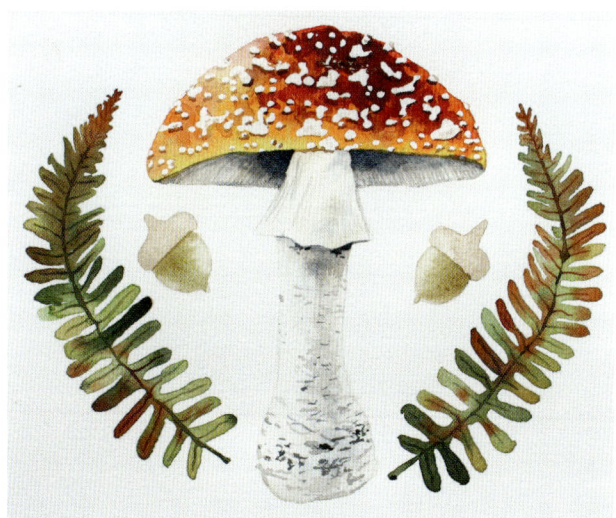

11. Mix more Payne's Gray (milk consistency) and apply to paint darker values (shadows). Use a mix of Raw Umber and Sap Green and paint acorns, leaving one side lighter. Let it dry.

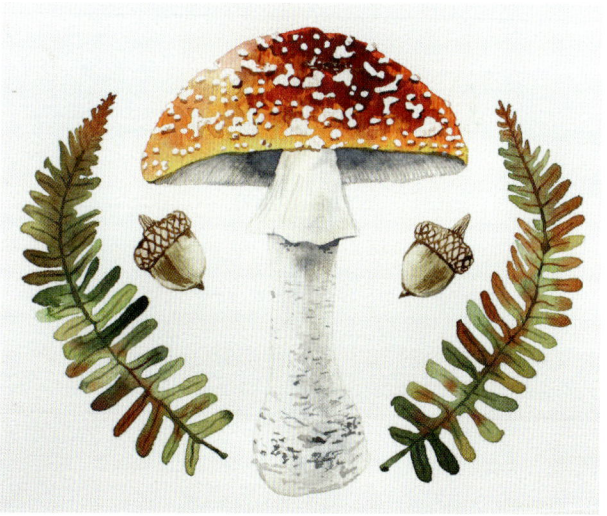

12. Apply a mix of Burnt Umber and Raw Umber wet-on-dry to paint details on the cap of the mushroom using a size 2/0 brush. Then, paint a few curved brushstrokes on the acorn to create a shadow area.

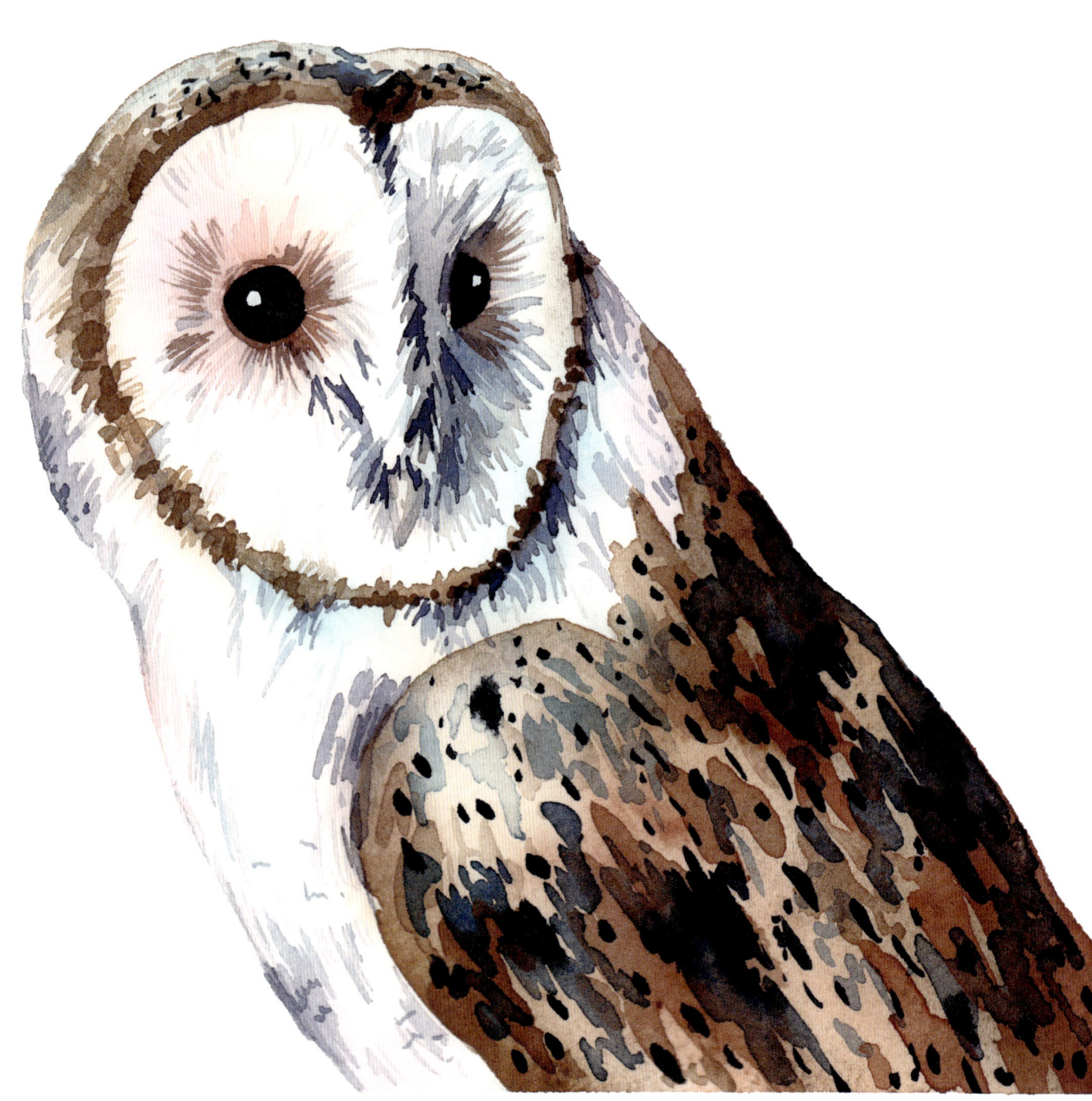

Barn Owl

Owls are magnificent woodland creatures! In this lesson, you'll work in three or four layers, practicing wet-on-wet techniques. With each layer, you'll build essential tonal values, which are crucial for creating a successful watercolor painting.

Colors

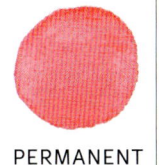 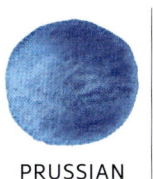  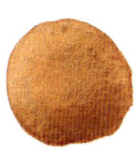 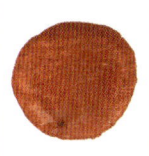 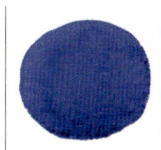 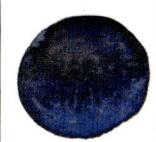 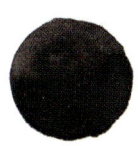

PERMANENT ROSE	PRUSSIAN BLUE	RAW UMBER	BURNT SIENNA	LIGHT RED	ULTRAMARINE BLUE	PAYNE'S GRAY	LAMP BLACK

Brushes

Size 6 round brush

Size 3 round brush

Size 2/0 round brush for details

Paper

300 gsm cold-pressed

1. Apply a thick layer of water using a size 6 brush to the whole area of the owl, evenly spreading water and going into all corners up to the pencil marks. The surface must be watered evenly.

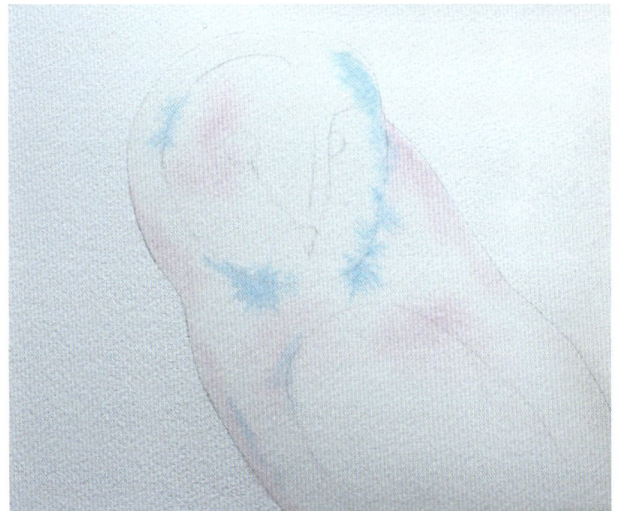

2. Straightaway, prepare the colors on a ceramic palette in this order: Permanent Rose, Prussian Blue, Raw Umber, and Burnt Sienna (tea consistency). Apply the colors wet-on-wet using a size 3 brush so that you can get soft edges.

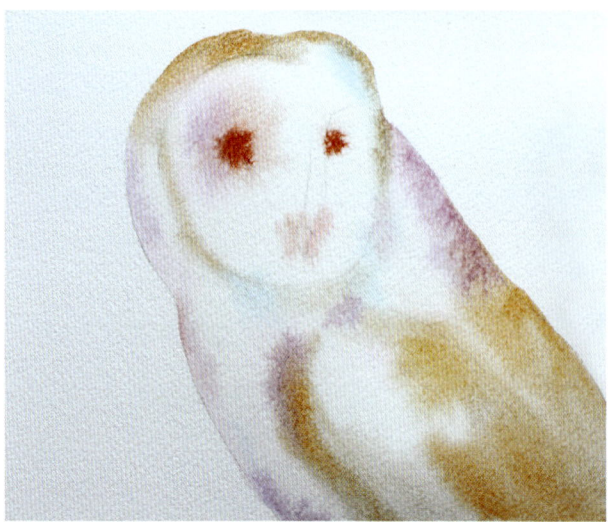

3. Prepare Light Red (cream consistency) and Burnt Sienna (cream consistency). Apply Burnt Sienna to the wings and back, then apply Light Red wet-on-wet to the eye area, using a size 3 brush. Use a clean, damp size 6 brush to define lighter areas if the colors traveled too far by using the lifting the pigment technique. Let it dry.

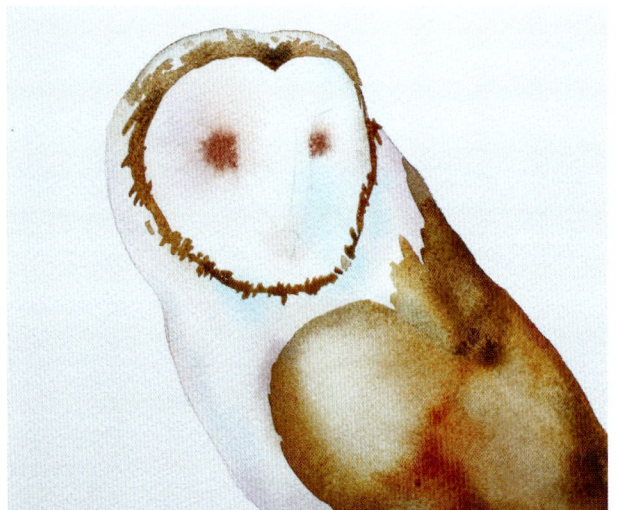

4. Use Raw Umber and Burnt Sienna (milk consistency) separately to apply colors wet-on-dry on the back and wings of the owl using a size 6 brush. Use a size 3 brush to apply the same colors around the face of the owl. Let it dry.

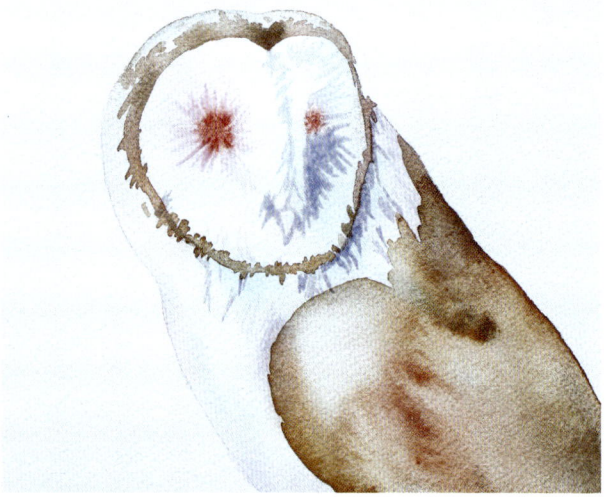

5. Prepare two color mixes (tea consistency)—Permanent Rose and Raw Umber, and Ultramarine Blue and Light Red—and apply them wet-on-dry using a size 2/0 brush. Apply the Ultramarine Blue and Light Red mix around the right eye, then use that color mix to add more definition to the feathers. Then use the Permanent Rose and Raw Umber mix with the same brush to add details to areas where there was pink color in the previous layer.

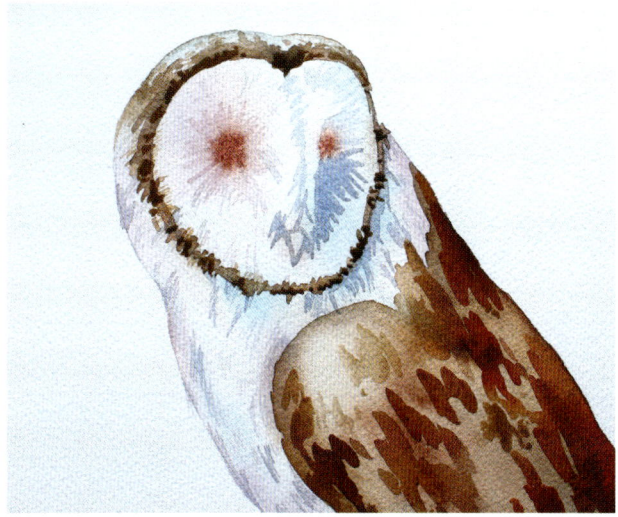

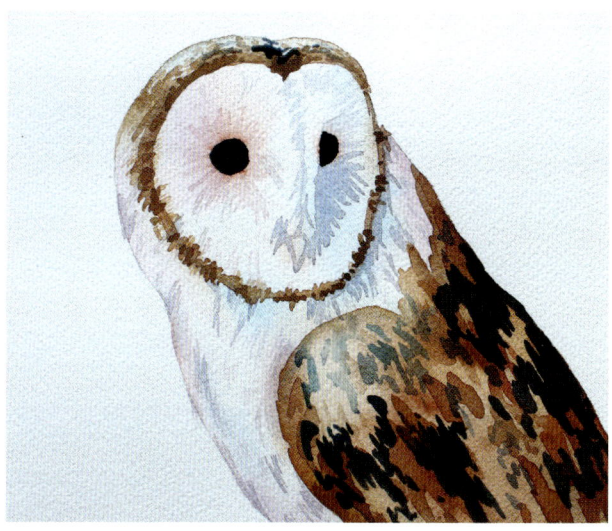

6. In the same way, apply thicker patches of Raw Umber and Burnt Sienna (milk consistency) on the wings and around the face wet-on-dry using a size 6 brush. Let it dry.

7. Mix Payne's Gray on your palette. You will first need a tea consistency to add a highlight on the wing wet-on-dry using a size 3 brush. Then prepare a thicker mix (cream consistency) of Payne's Gray and apply wet-on-dry on the back and wings using a size 6 brush. Use the same color and the size 3 brush to paint the black eyes, leaving a highlight untouched in the center of the eye. Let it dry.

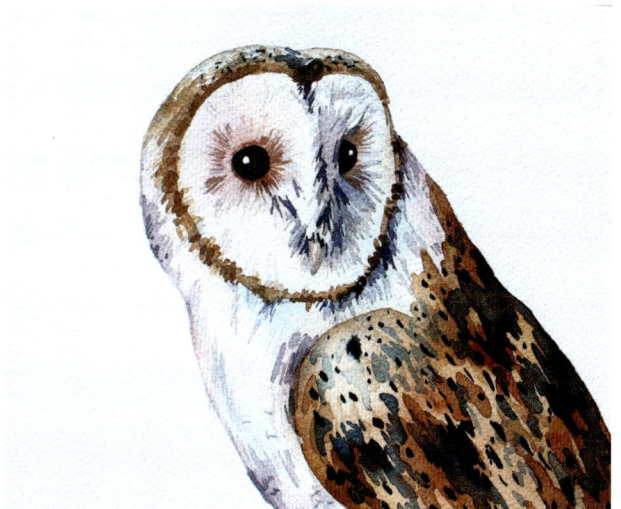

8. Paint black dots on top of the wings and the back of the owl with Lamp Black (cream consistency) using a size 3 brush.

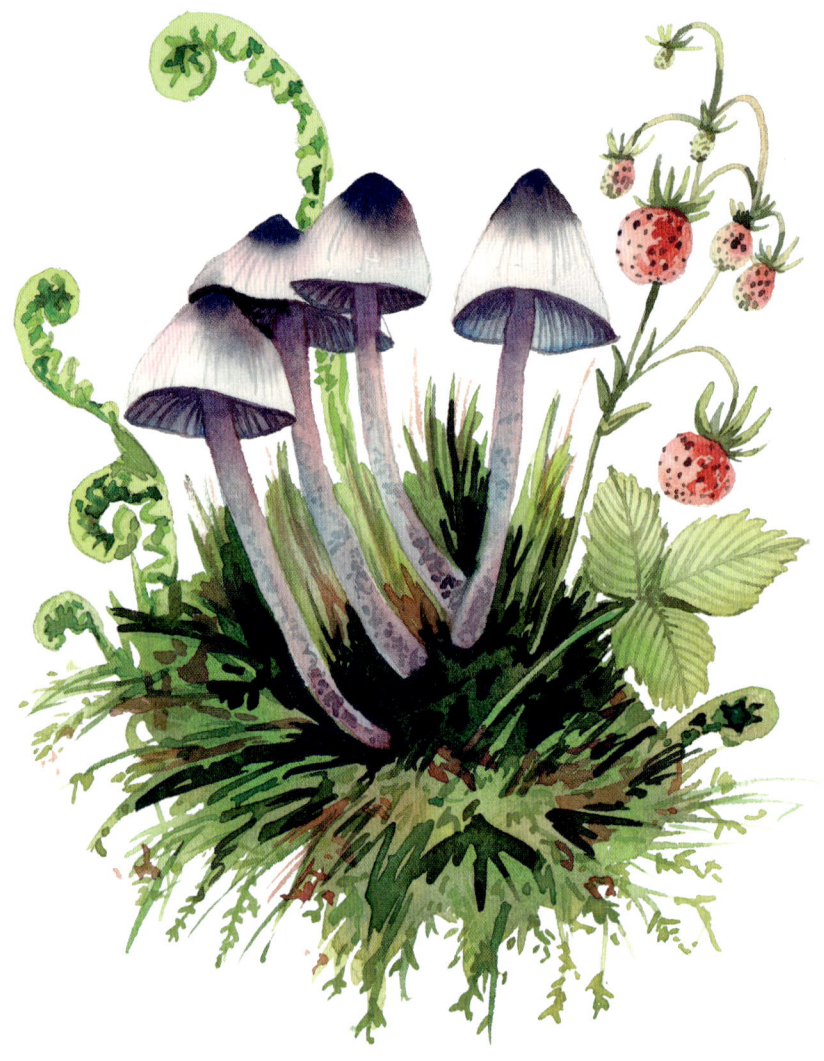

Fairy Helmet Mushrooms and Wild Strawberries

Challenge yourself with a simple yet unforgettable composition of mushrooms, woodland berries, young ferns, and thick grass. Focus on the top of the mushrooms, trying the amazing watercolor technique of "charging."

Colors

LEMON YELLOW	SAP GREEN	CADMIUM YELLOW HUE	HOOKER'S GREEN	RAW UMBER	BURNT SIENNA	LIGHT RED

ULTRAMARINE BLUE	PERMANENT ROSE	DIOXAZINE PURPLE	ALIZARIN CRIMSON	PRUSSIAN BLUE	LAMP BLACK

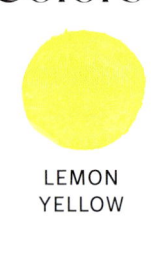
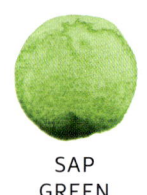

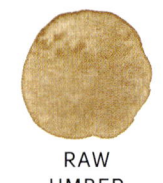
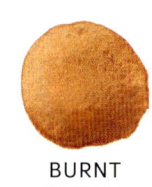
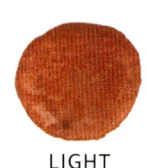

Brushes

Size 6 round brush

Size 3 round brush

Size 2/0 round brush for details

Paper

300 gsm cold-pressed

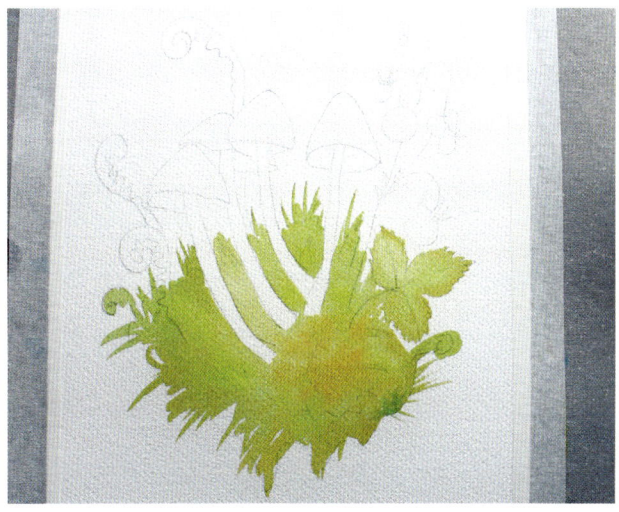

1. Mix Lemon Yellow and Sap Green (milk consistency) and paint the grass using a size 6 brush. Apply Cadmium Yellow Hue wet-on-wet in the center.

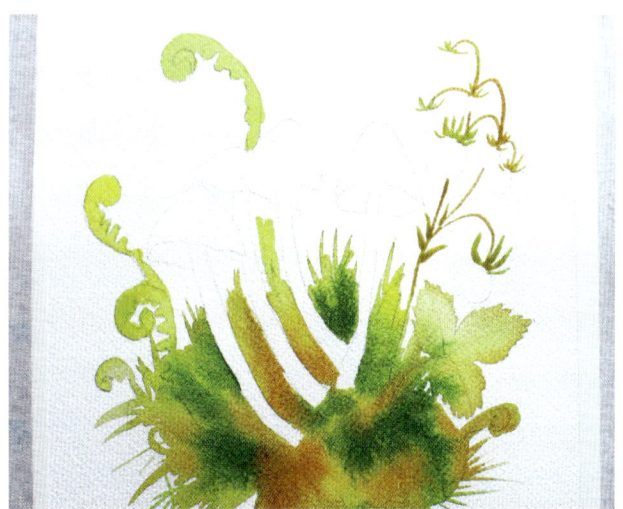

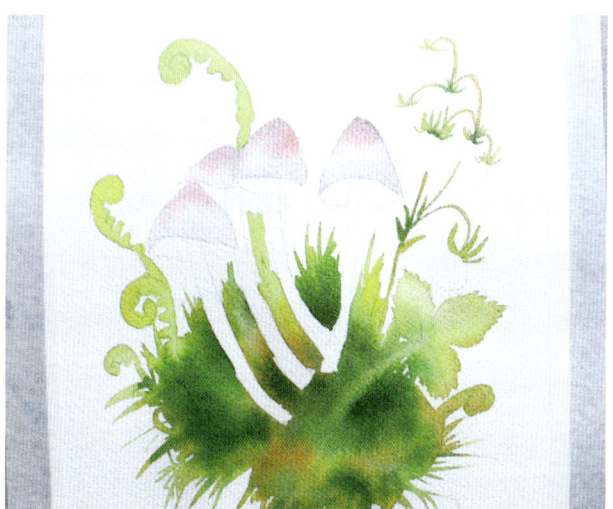

2. Apply Hooker's Green (cream consistency) wet-on-wet. Then, add Raw Umber, followed by a mix of Burnt Sienna and Raw Umber.

   Paint the strawberry's stem with a mix of Raw Umber and Sap Green using a size 2/0 brush. Add a mix of Cadmium Yellow Hue and Sap Green on top of the leaves.

   For the tops of the ferns, mix Lemon Yellow and Sap Green (milk consistency) and paint them. Let dry.

3. Apply a mix of Light Red and Ultramarine Blue (tea consistency) to all mushroom caps using a size 3 brush. Apply a mix of Burnt Sienna and Permanent Rose wet-on-wet on top of each mushroom, then add a drop of Dioxazine Purple.

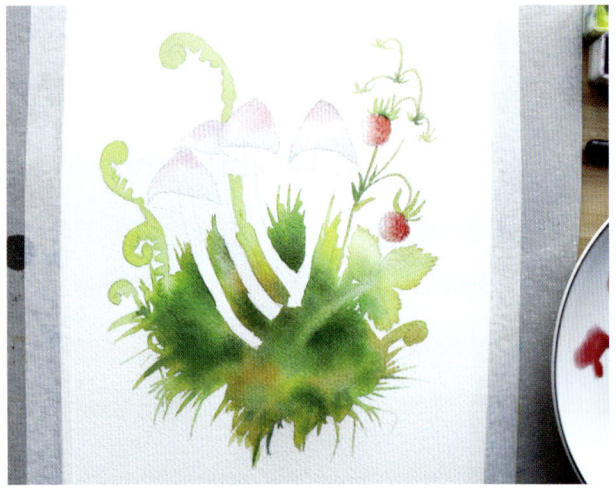

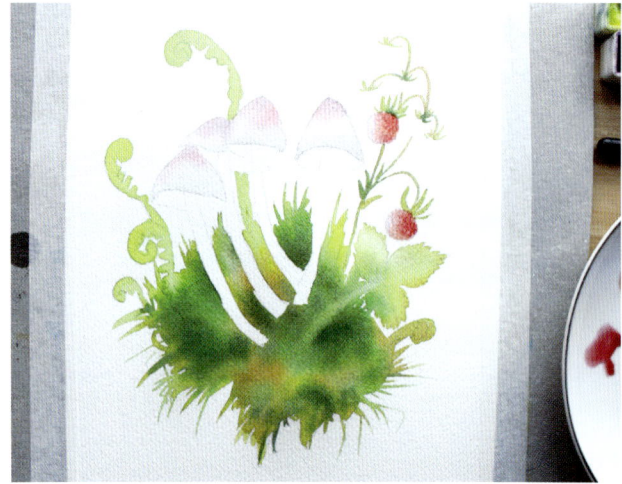

4. Paint the berries with a mix of Light Red and Ultramarine Blue (tea consistency) using a size 6 brush.

Immediately apply a mix of Alizarin Crimson and Burnt Sienna (milk consistency) wet-on-wet to the right side of the berries using a size 3 brush.

5. For the smaller berries, use a size 3 brush. Working wet-on-wet, start with a mix of Sap Green and Cadmium Yellow Hue, then add a drop of Permanent Rose to some of the berries.

Mix Light Red and Ultramarine Blue (tea consistency) and paint all stalks and inside the mushrooms using a size 3 brush.

Apply Prussian Blue wet-on-wet on the sides of the stalks and inside the caps using a size 2/0 brush. Apply a mix of Prussian Blue and Light Red wet-on-wet at the bottom of all stalks.

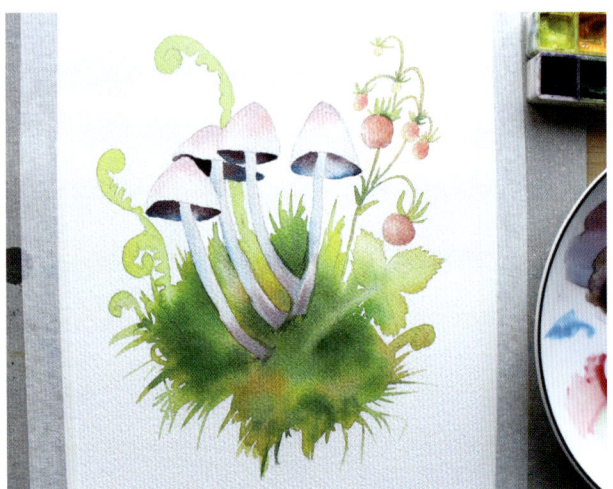

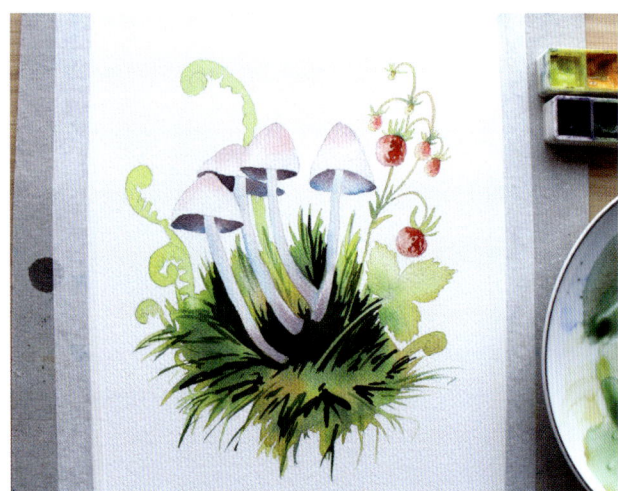

6. Apply water to all areas inside the caps, avoiding the stalks, using a size 6 brush.

Switch to a size 2/0 brush and apply the Prussian Blue and Light Red mix (cream consistency) on top for a dark purple color. Apply Prussian Blue (milk consistency) along the edges of each mushroom inside.

7. Apply Alizarin Crimson (cream consistency) wet-on-dry to paint shadows on the ripe strawberries using a size 3 brush.

Apply Hooker's Green (cream consistency) wet-on-dry to the grass areas using a size 3–6 brush.

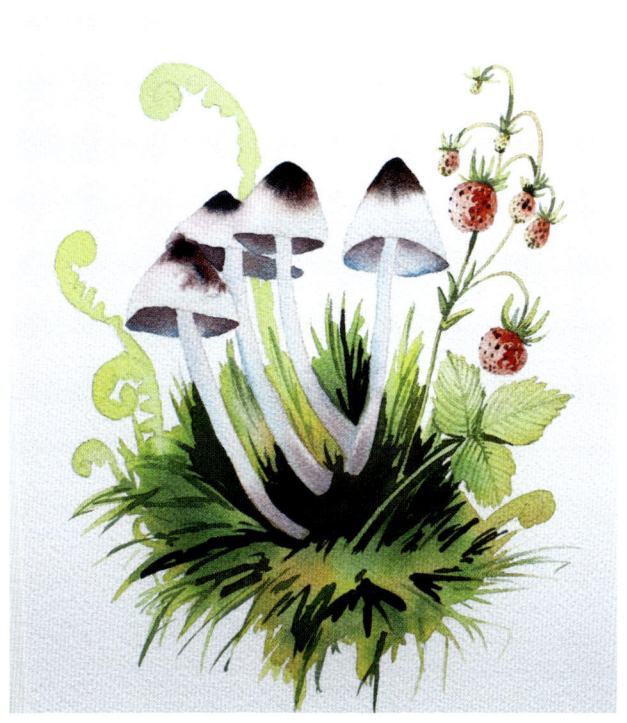

8. Apply a mix of Sap Green and Cadmium Yellow Hue to paint veins on the strawberry leaves using a size 2/0 brush. Use the same mix to define shadows on the stem and paint a few grass blades in the background.

   Mix Sap Green and Raw Umber and paint seeds on the green strawberries using a size 2/0 brush. Load your brush with a mix of Lamp Black and Alizarin Crimson and paint the remaining seeds.

   Apply Light Red and Payne's Gray (cream consistency) using a size 6 brush. Use the same brush to apply a layer of water on top of each mushroom cap. Take a size 2/0 brush, load it with the Light Red and Payne's Gray mix, and lightly touch the very top of each mushroom. This technique is called "charging" as it releases color.

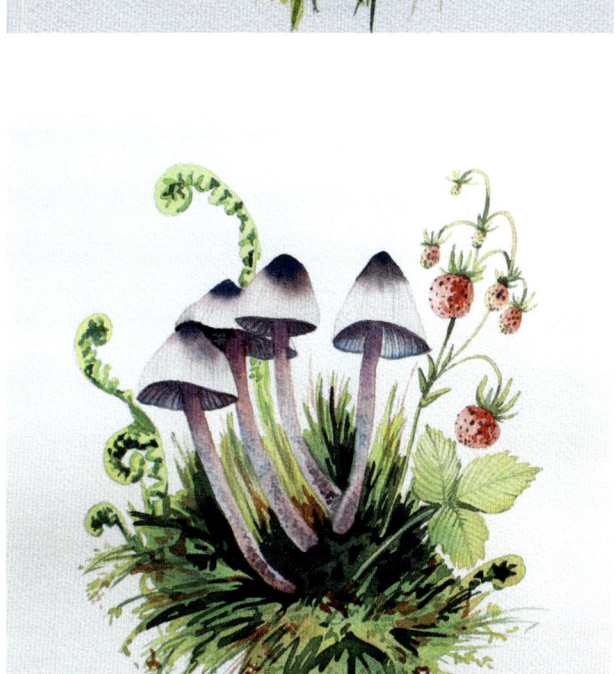

9. Mix Sap Green and Cadmium Yellow Hue using a size 3 brush to add values to the ferns, then paint the grass.

   For shadow areas, paint dots at the bottom of each stalk with a Prussian Blue and Light Red mix using a size 3 brush. Change to a lighter Prussian Blue as you move up the stalk, adding details.

   Inside the caps, paint lines with the Prussian Blue and Light Red mix using a size 2/0 brush.

   Dilute the Prussian Blue and Light Red mix to almost transparent and apply it wet-on-dry to create lines on the caps.

   Apply Cadmium Yellow Hue wet-on-dry to paint the grass using a size 3 brush.

   Apply Burnt Sienna wet-on-dry to the grass using a size 3 brush.

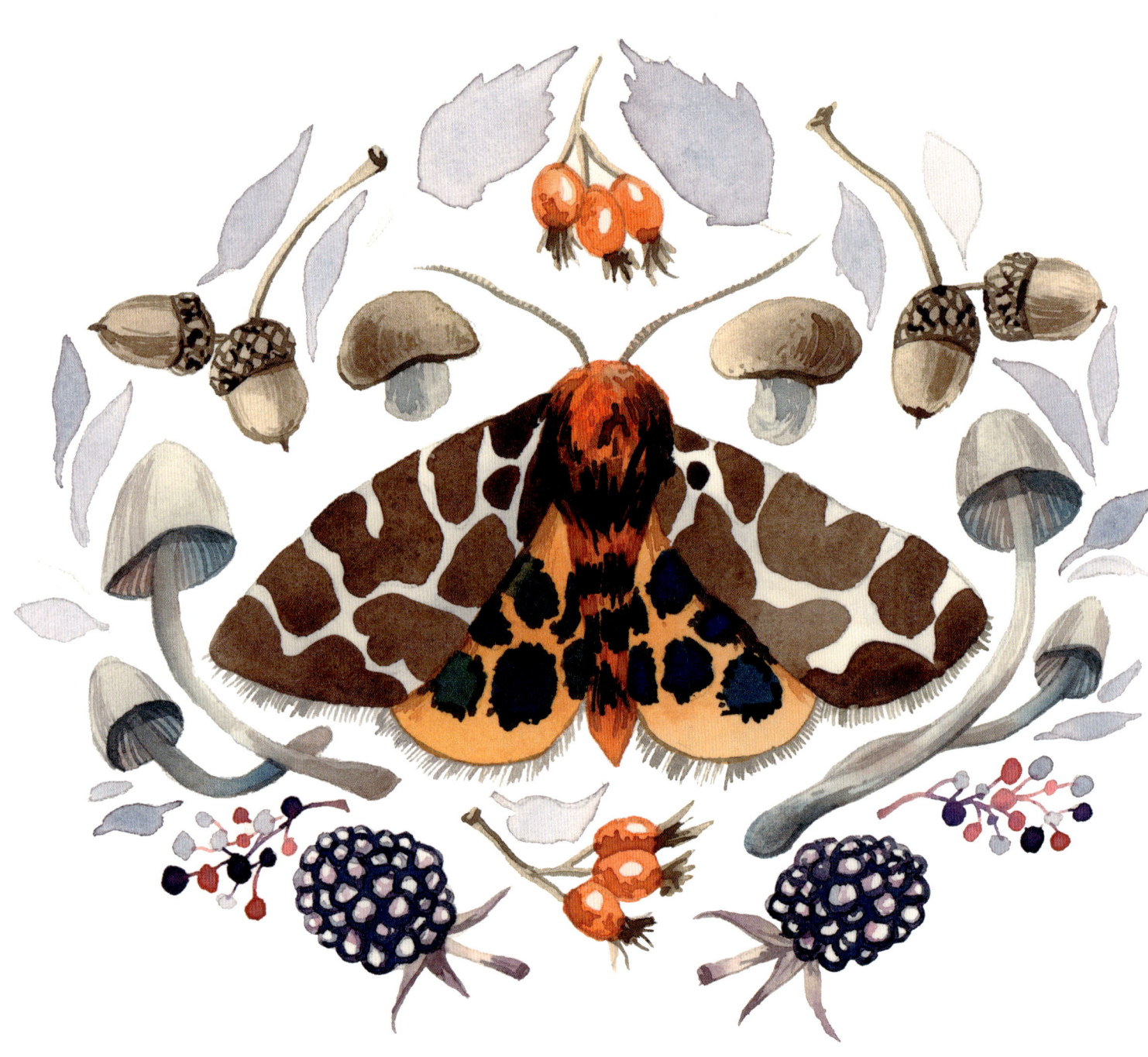

Tiger Moth with Mycena Mushrooms, Grapes, Rosehips, and Blackberries

Create a stunning composition with a beautiful moth, blackberries, and mushrooms. You'll master core watercolor techniques—wet-on-wet, wet-on-dry, and lifting pigment—for a beautifully textured painting.

Colors

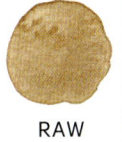		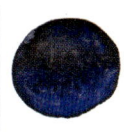	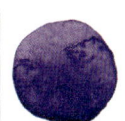	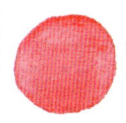	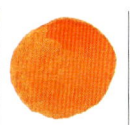	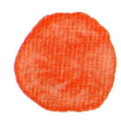	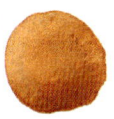	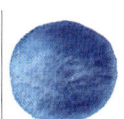	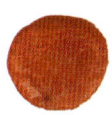
RAW UMBER	LAMP BLACK	PAYNE'S GRAY	DIOXAZINE PURPLE	PERMANENT ROSE	CADMIUM ORANGE HUE	CADMIUM RED DEEP HUE	BURNT SIENNA	PRUSSIAN BLUE	LIGHT RED

Brushes

Size 6 round brush

Size 3 round brush

Size 2/0 round brush for details

Paper

300 gsm cold-pressed

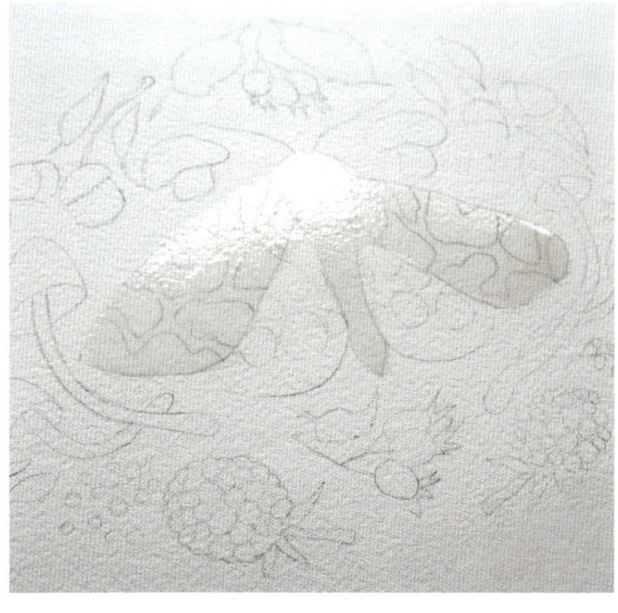

1. Start by using an eraser to remove any dark pencil marks. Apply water to the upper wings of the moth.

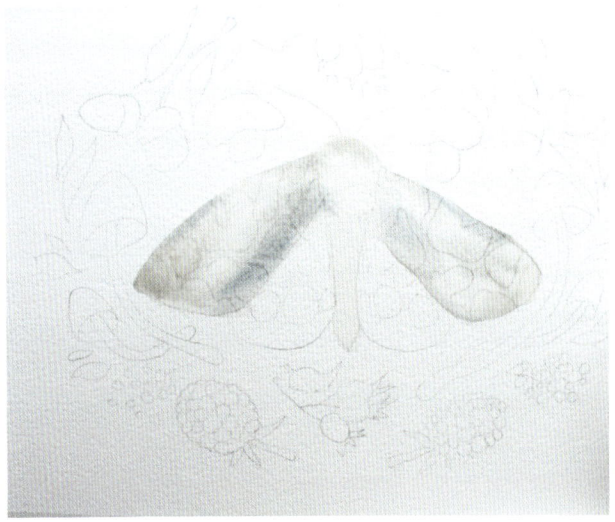

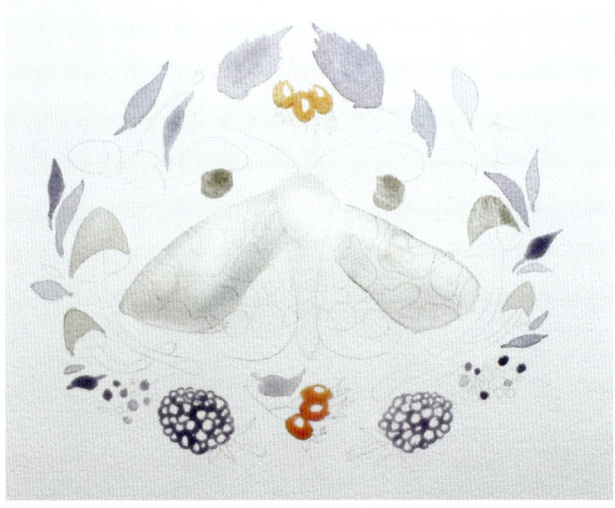

2. Apply a mix of Raw Umber and Lamp Black (tea consistency) wet-on-wet using a size 2/0 brush. Then apply Payne's Gray.

3. Mix Payne's Gray and Dioxazine Purple (tea consistency). Use this light purple mix to paint all the leaves using a size 3 brush. Use the same mix to paint the blackberries and some berries on the wild grapes. Use a mix of Payne's Gray and Raw Umber (tea consistency) to paint the mushroom caps and stalks. Mix Permanent Rose and Cadmium Orange Hue and use it to paint the rose hips.

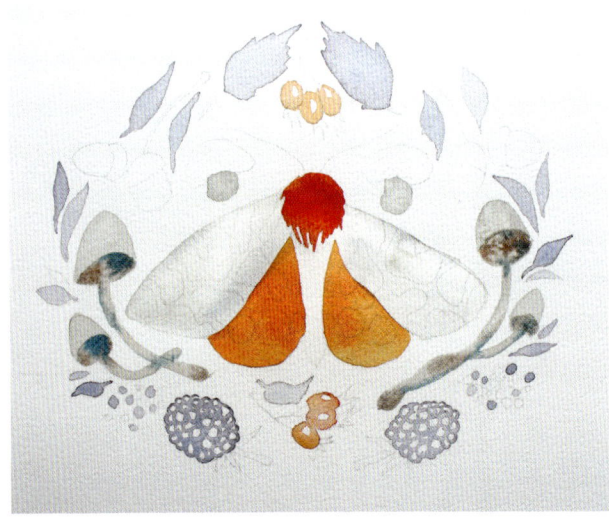

4. Combine Cadmium Orange Hue and Cadmium Red Deep Hue to paint the underside of the moth's wings using a size 3 brush. Use a mix of Cadmium Red Deep Hue and Burnt Sienna to paint the moth's red head. Use a mix of Raw Umber and Payne's Gray to apply a very weak layer on the mushroom stalks. Apply Prussian Blue wet-on-wet under the mushroom caps on one side and Light Red on the other side. Use a size 6 brush to lift pigment and create lighter areas on the stalks.

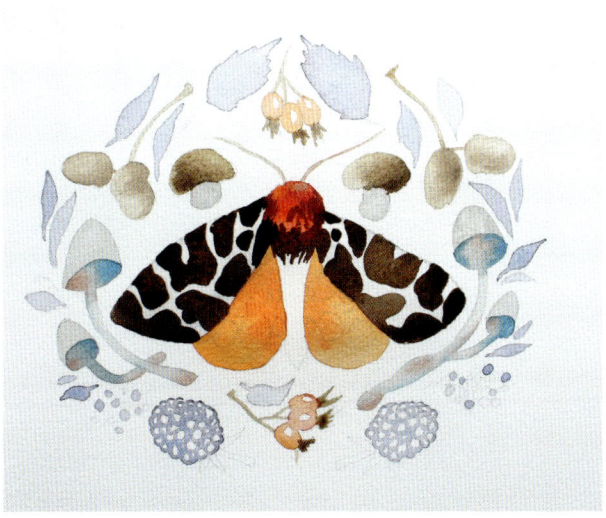

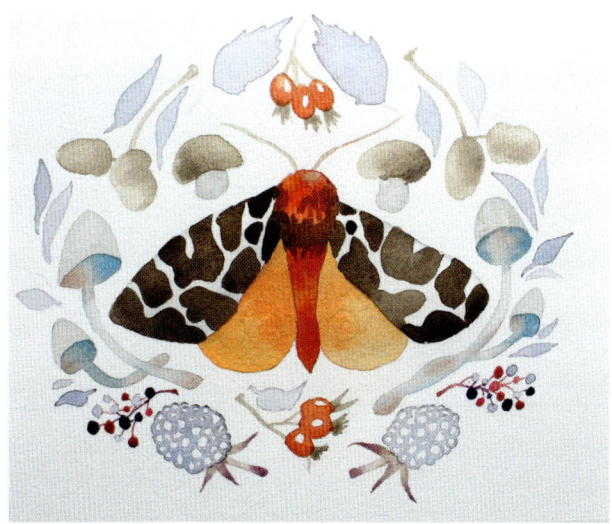

5. Mix Burnt Umber and Lamp Black and paint spots all over the upper wings of the moth. Paint the middle area between the spots with Burnt Umber. Use Raw Umber to paint the antennas on the moth, the acorns, the branches on the rose hips, and the caps on small mushrooms. Add Burnt Umber wet-on-wet on small mushrooms to create shadows using a size 3 brush.

6. Use Raw Umber to paint the leaves and sticks of blackberries wet-on-dry using a size 3 brush. Use a size 2/0 brush to add a mix of Dioxazine Purple and Permanent Rose wet-on-wet to the edges of the leaves. Use the same mix to paint the branches of wild grapes and paint a few berries.

7. Apply a mix of Burnt Sienna and Cadmium Orange Hue to paint the body of the moth using a size 3 brush.

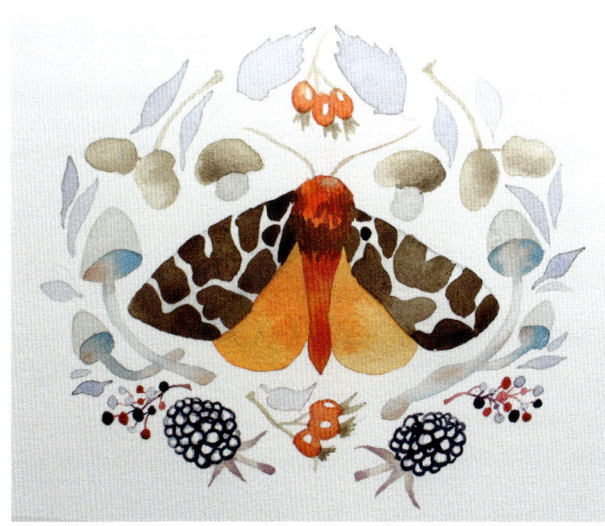

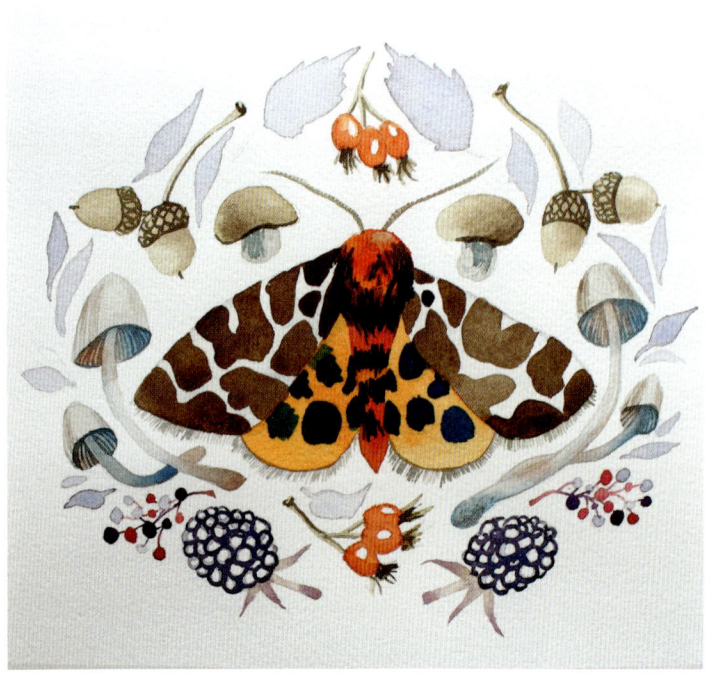

8. Apply a mix of Burnt Umber and Raw Umber to add details to the acorns, rose hips, antennas, shadows under the small mushrooms, and hairs around the moth's wings with a 2/0 brush. Apply Prussian Blue (cream consistency) wet-on-dry to paint spots on the moth wings using a size 3 brush. Use a mix of Dioxazine Purple and Payne's Gray to paint blackberries with the same brush. Use Lamp Black to make black, hairy spots on the moth's body and around the head. Use a mix of Burnt Sienna and Cadmium Red Deep Hue to darken the rose hips. Paint details inside the mushroom caps with a mix of Prussian Blue and Light Red using a size 2/0 brush. Add Prussian Blue to the ends of the mushroom stalks and apply a mix of Prussian Blue and Raw Umber to the stalks of the small mushrooms.

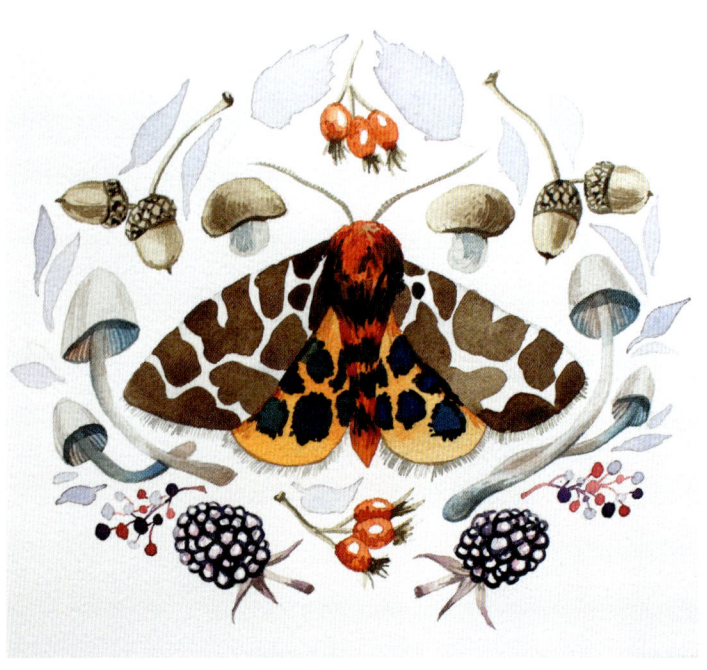

9. Paint around the dark blue spots with Lamp Black using a size 3 brush. Use a mix of Burnt Umber and Lamp Black to make darker values on the caps of acorns with a size 2/0 brush and on the rose hips. Add a darker value of the Burnt Sienna and Cadmium Red Deep Hue mix to the rose hips using a size 3 brush. Use a mix of Lamp Black and Dioxazine Purple to paint circles over the blackberries again.

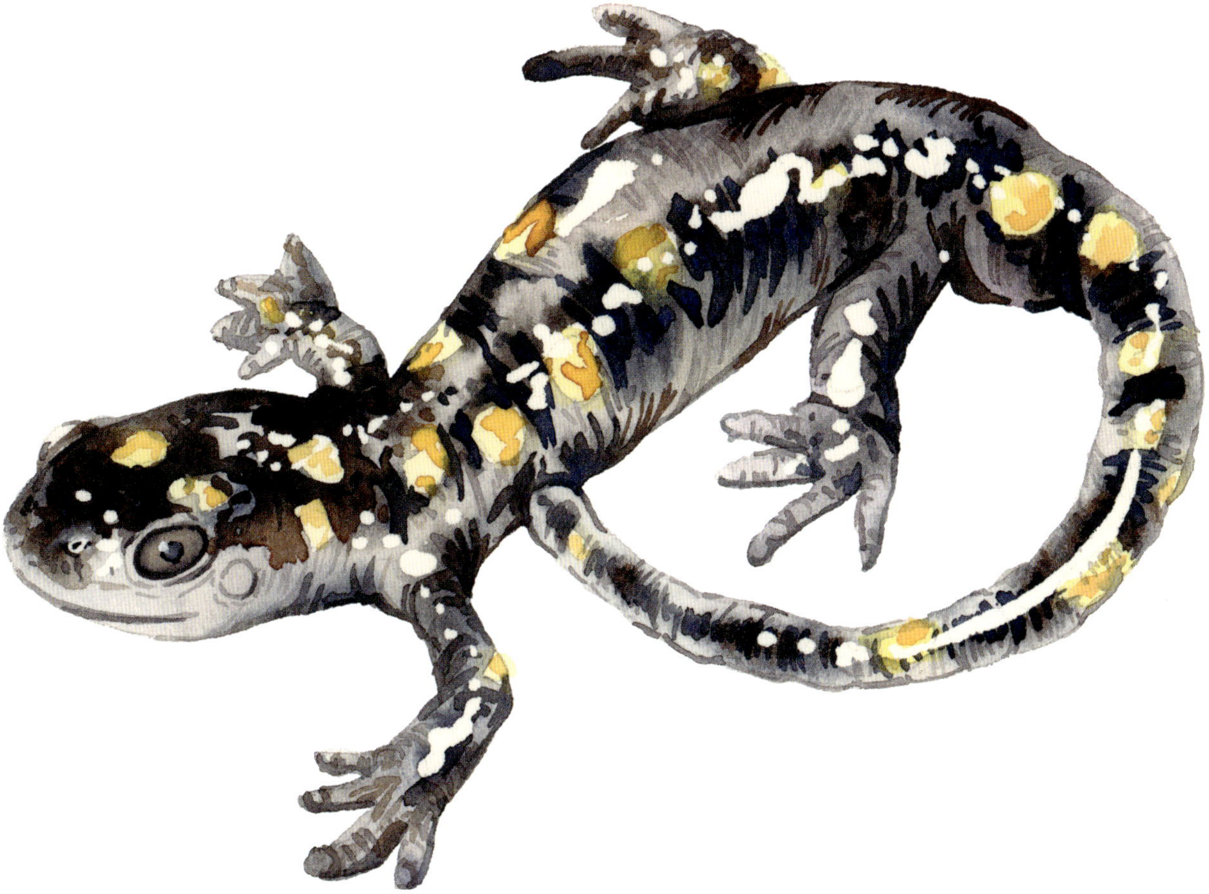

Tiger Salamander

These amphibians are so adorable, but capturing their glossy appearance can be tricky. In this lesson, you'll learn how to use contrast to create shiny effects in watercolor. Masking fluid will help you create stunning reflections and highlights on a slimy salamander.

Colors

  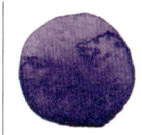  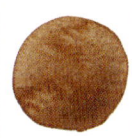 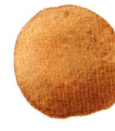 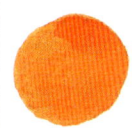  

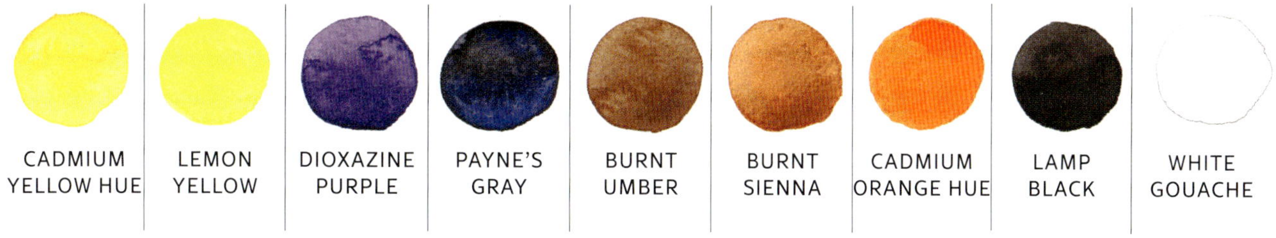

| CADMIUM YELLOW HUE | LEMON YELLOW | DIOXAZINE PURPLE | PAYNE'S GRAY | BURNT UMBER | BURNT SIENNA | CADMIUM ORANGE HUE | LAMP BLACK | WHITE GOUACHE |

Brushes

Size 6 round brush

Size 3 round brush

Size 2/0 round brush for details

Old brush for masking fluid

Paper

300 gsm cold-pressed

Other

Masking fluid

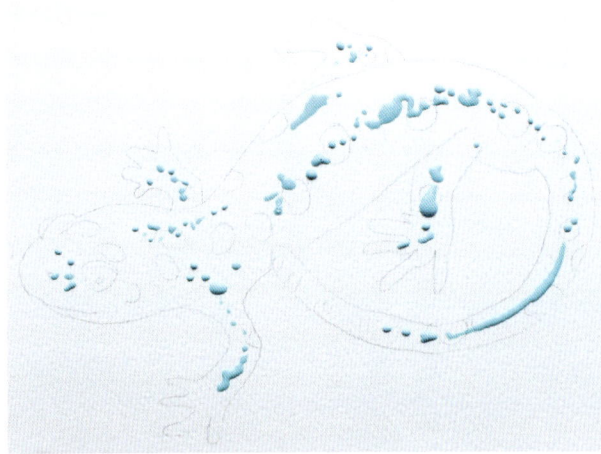

1. Apply masking fluid to the areas where you want to preserve highlights. After applying the masking fluid, leave it to dry completely. It will darken as it dries. You can check if it's ready by gently touching it with your finger—if it doesn't leave any marks, it's dry.

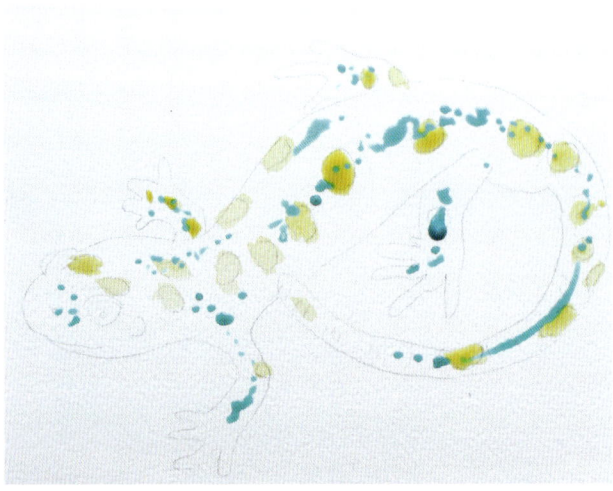

2. Apply a mix of Cadmium Yellow Hue with a bit of Lemon Yellow wet-on-dry to the yellow spots using a size 3 brush. Let it dry.

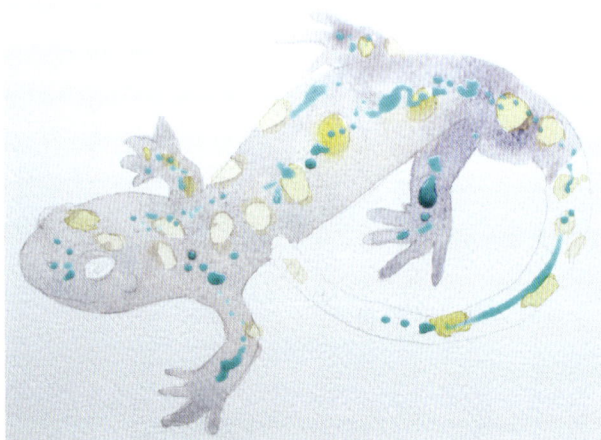

3. Apply a mix of Dioxazine Purple and Payne's Gray (tea consistency) wet-on-dry using a size 6 brush, covering the whole body of the salamander while avoiding the yellow patches. You can apply more Dioxazine Purple at the back of the salamander.

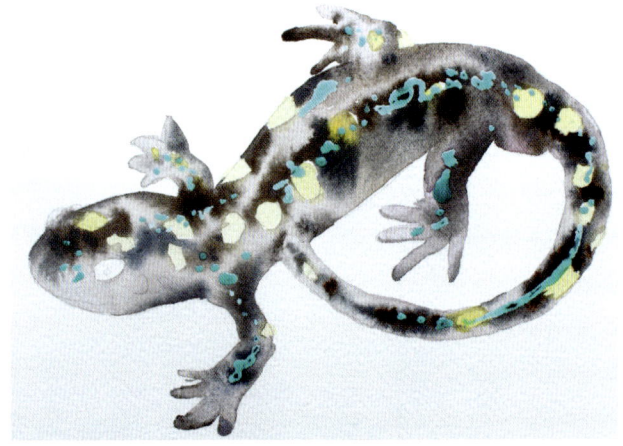

4. Once the body is fully covered with the wet mix, apply Burnt Umber and Payne's Gray (cream consistency) wet-on-wet to paint the darker areas using a size 2/0 brush. Using a thin brush but loading it with thick pigment helps control the size of your watercolor bleeds. Now, use Payne's Gray and Burnt Umber separately, touching just the tip of your brush to areas where you want more contrast.

Lift off excess pigment while it's still wet using a size 6 brush. Let it dry completely.

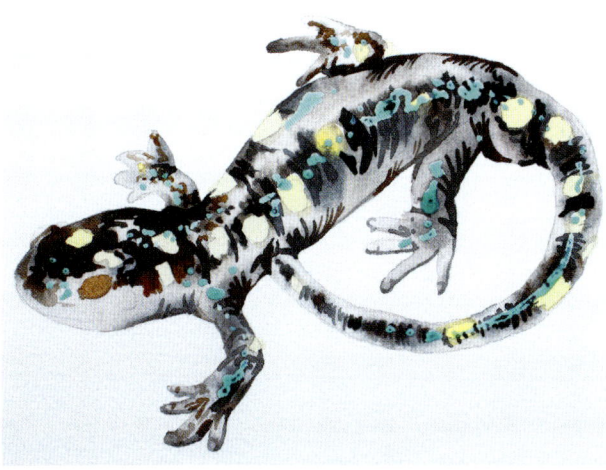

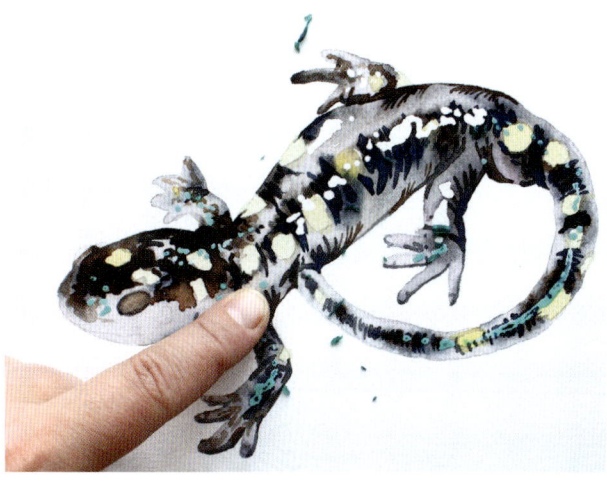

5. Apply a mix of Payne's Gray and Burnt Umber (milk consistency) wet-on-dry to paint lines and wrinkles on the body using a size 3 brush. Apply Burnt Sienna wet-on-dry to the eye and add a few drops of Burnt Sienna into the freshly painted wrinkles. Let it dry.

6. Using your fingers and applying some pressure, gently remove the masking fluid to reveal the white spots.

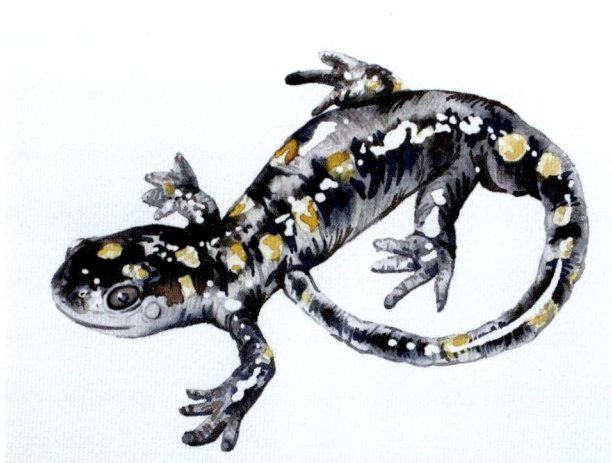

7. Mix Cadmium Orange Hue and Cadmium Yellow Hue (milk consistency) to create a darker value for the yellow spots. Apply wet-on-dry using a size 3 brush. Use Payne's Gray and Dioxazine Purple to add more details using their lightest and middle values (tea consistency first, then milk consistency) using a size 2/0 brush. Add curved wrinkles around the tail, middle body, face, and toes. Apply Lamp Black in the center of the eye wet-on-dry to paint the pupil using a size 3 brush. Let it dry, and then finish by adding white gouache for reflections in the eye.

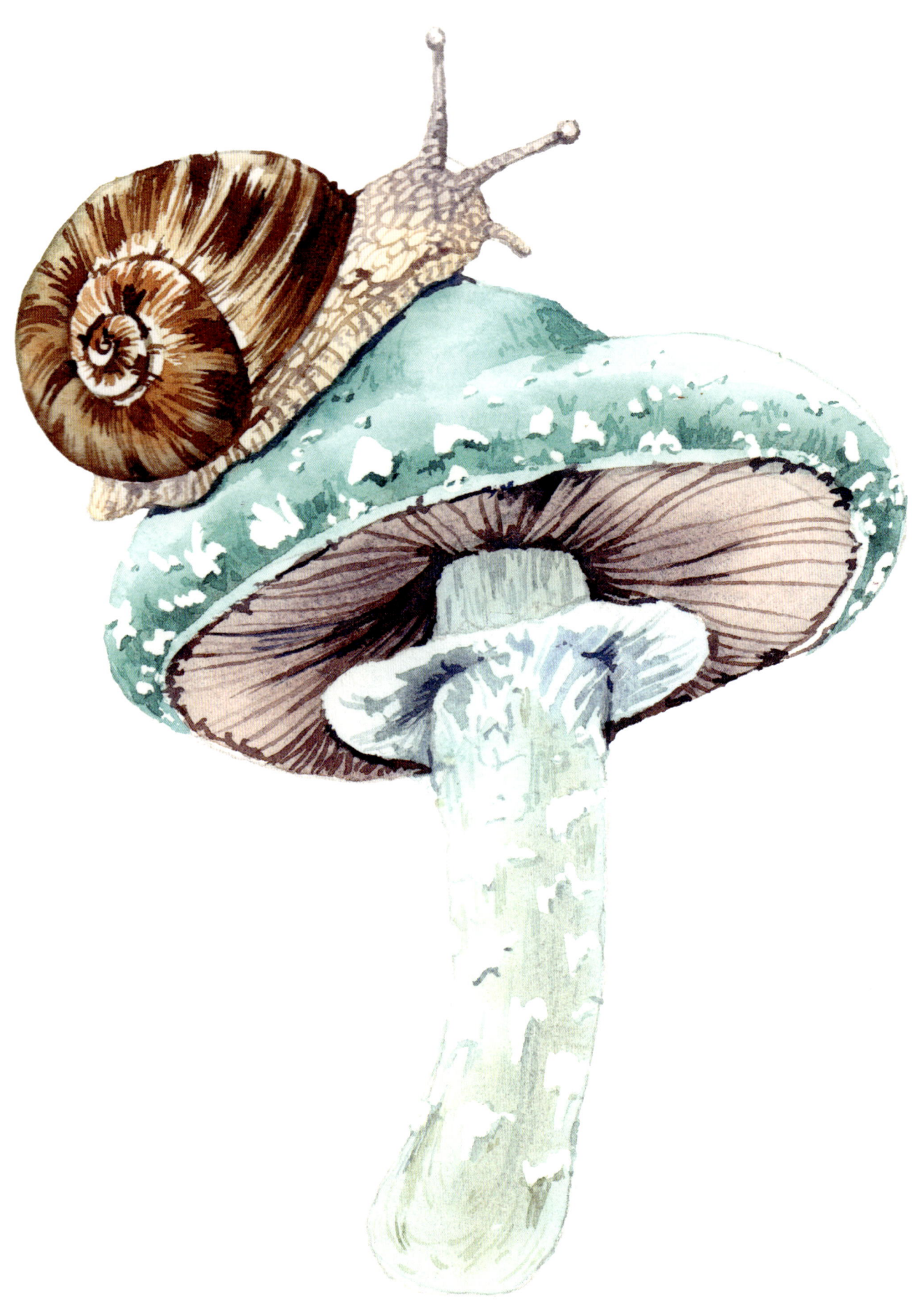

Blue Roundhead Mushrooms with Garden Snail

Painting a little snail perched atop a mushroom (in this case, *Stropharia caerulea*) is a whimsical delight and a great exercise in painting dimension. By adding darker layers gradually and strategically, you can create the look of roundness in the snail's shell and sturdiness in the mushroom. You'll also get practice in using masking fluid.

Colors

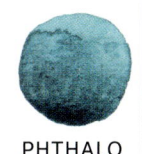   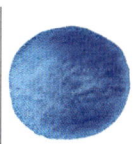 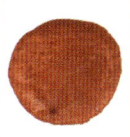 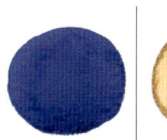  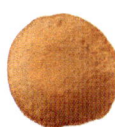 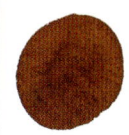

| PHTHALO TURQUOISE | EMERALD GREEN | RAW UMBER | PRUSSIAN BLUE | LIGHT RED | ULTRAMARINE BLUE | YELLOW OCHRE | BURNT SIENNA | VAN DYKE BROWN |

Brushes

Size 6 round

Size 3 round

Size 2/0 round for details

Old brush for applying masking fluid

Paper

300 gsm cold-pressed

Other

Masking fluid

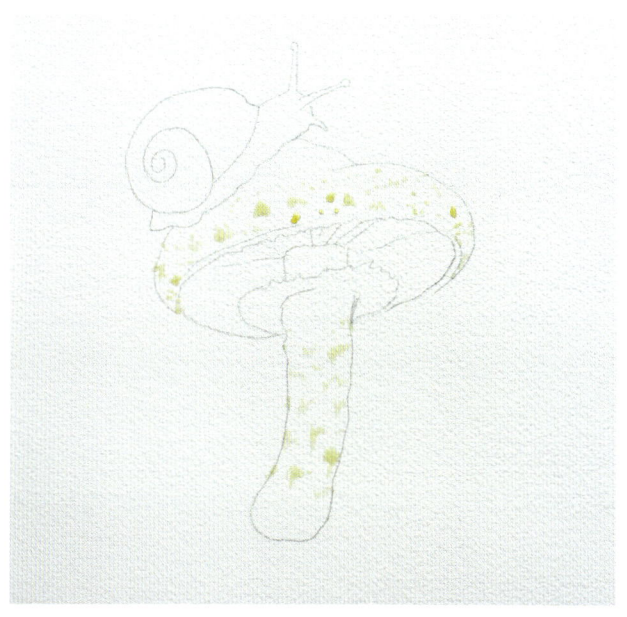

1. Draw or transfer the sketch onto the paper. Attach the watercolor paper to a board or your table using masking tape. Apply masking fluid to the white areas on the mushroom using an old brush. Allow it to dry completely; the fluid usually changes to a darker color when it's dry. It's very important to let it dry 100 percent before you start painting.

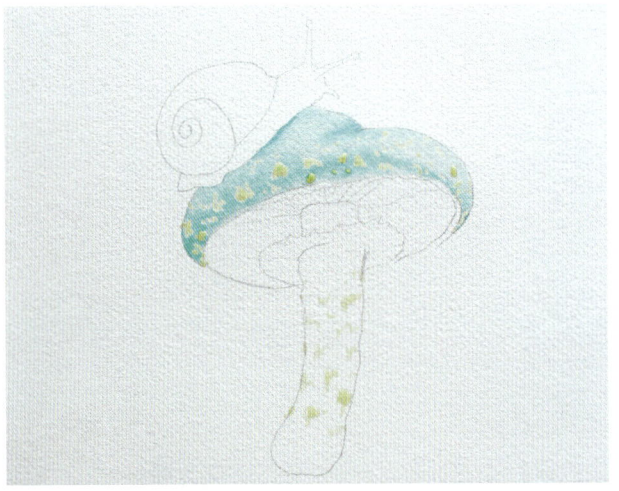
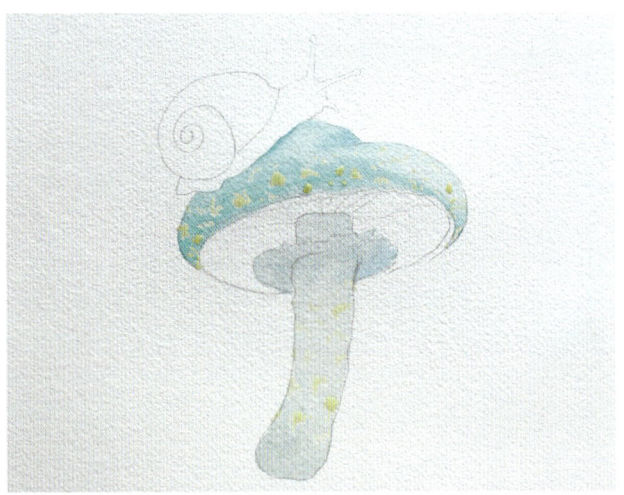

2. Apply a mix of Phthalo Turquoise and Emerald Green (tea consistency) wet-on-dry to the cap of the mushroom, using a size 6 brush and avoiding the masking fluid.

    Adjust the water-to-paint ratio to have slightly more paint and less water. Use the same brush to apply this mix to create shadow areas under the snail and on the cap of the mushroom. Leave it to dry.

3. Apply a mix of Raw Umber and Prussian Blue (tea consistency) to the mushroom stalk. Leave it to dry.

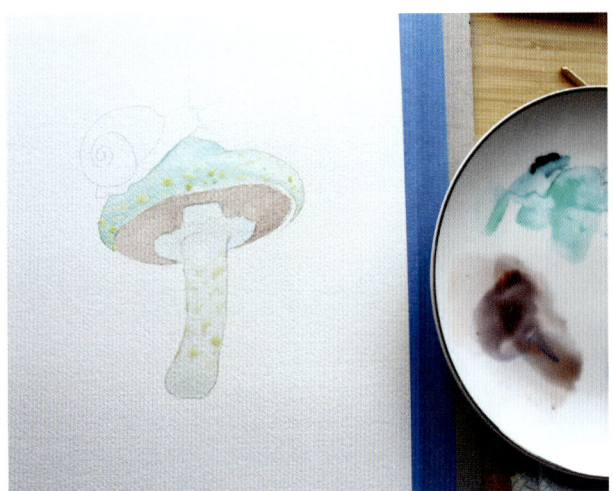
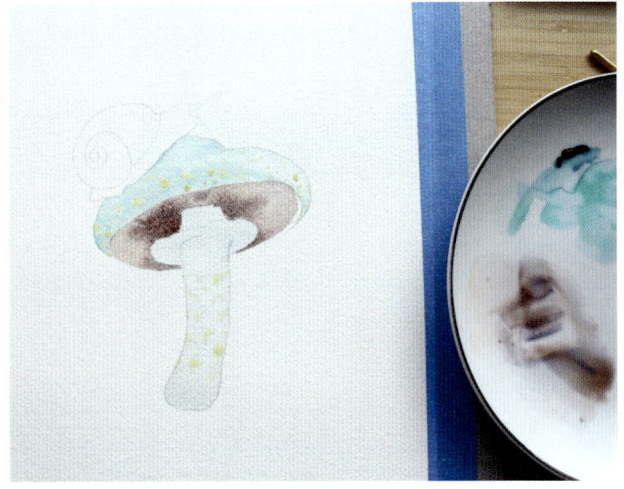

4. Apply a mix of Light Red and Ultramarine Blue (coffee consistency) wet-on-dry to paint the area under the cap to achieve a muted shade of purple.

5. Apply a darker mixture of Light Red and Ultramarine Blue with less water wet-on-wet to create shadow areas. Leave it to dry.

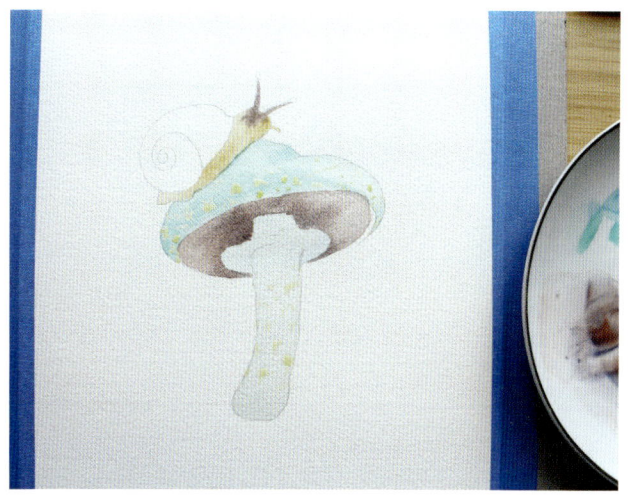

6. Let's paint the snail! Using a size 6 brush, apply a layer of Yellow Ochre (tea consistency) wet-on-dry to the entire snail, except for the shell. Use a mix of Light Red and Ultramarine Blue (tea consistency) to paint the snail's antennas and to create a shadow area under the shell. Let it dry.

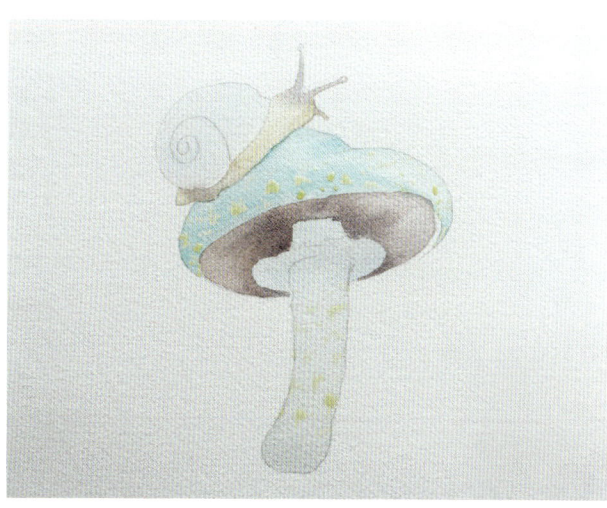

7. Apply Ultramarine Blue (tea consistency) to the entire shell area wet-on-dry so it's almost as white as the paper.

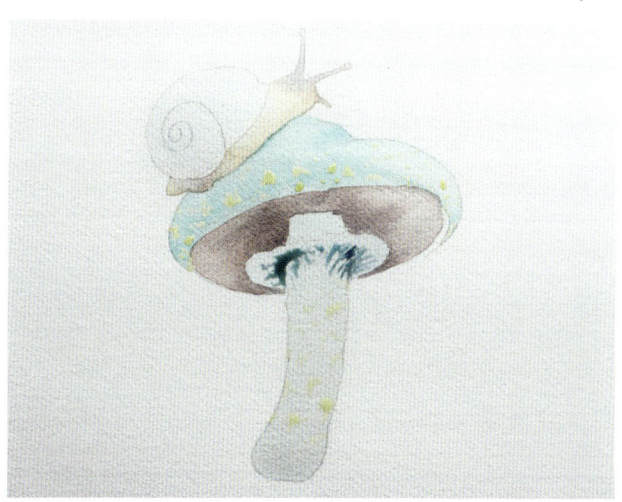

8. Returning to the stalk, use a mix of Raw Umber and Prussian Blue to paint shadow areas on the stalk using a size 3 brush.

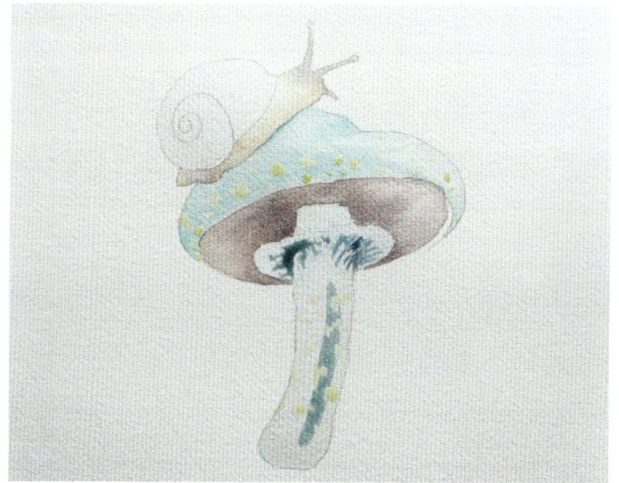

9. With a size 6 brush, use the same mixture to paint a shadow in the center of the stalk. Then, soften the edges on both sides with water. Apply Raw Umber wet-on-wet to the shadowed area of the stalk. Next, apply a mix of Phthalo Turquoise and Emerald Green (milk) wet-on-dry to create a shadow line across the cap. Soften it with a slightly damp brush. Work on the shadows under the snail the same way. Use a size 2/0 brush to apply a mix of Phthalo Turquoise and Emerald Green (butter) wet-on-wet to the darkest areas of the mushroom.

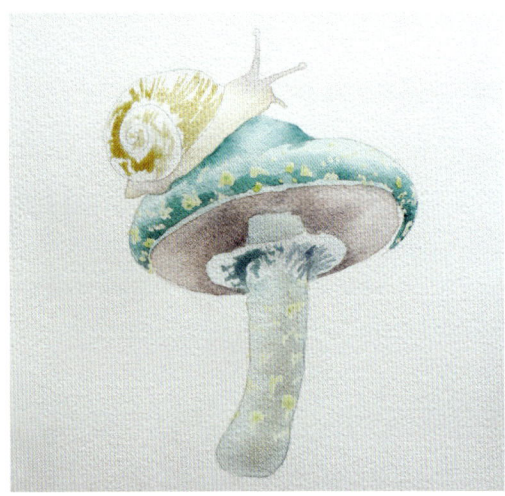

10. For the snail's shell, use a size 6 brush with Yellow Ochre (coffee consistency). Try to follow the spiral pattern with your brushstrokes while leaving some white areas.

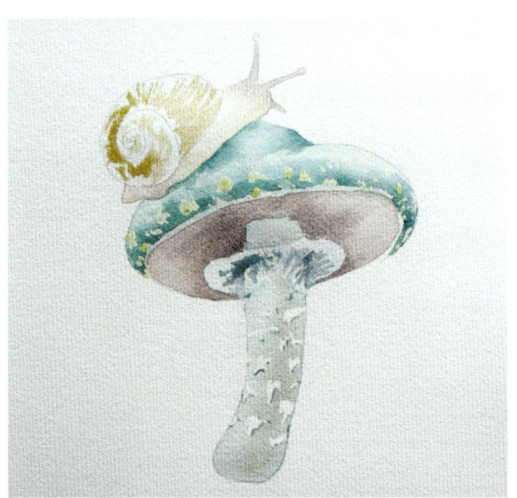

11. Before removing the masking fluid from the stalk, lightly touch the paper in the areas with the masking fluid. If it feels dry, gently rub off the masking fluid with light pressure. Using a size 2/0 brush, mix Raw Umber and Prussian Blue and paint shadows under the white areas of the stalk. You can also add more details to the stalk by painting vertical brushstrokes with the same Raw Umber and Prussian Blue mixture.

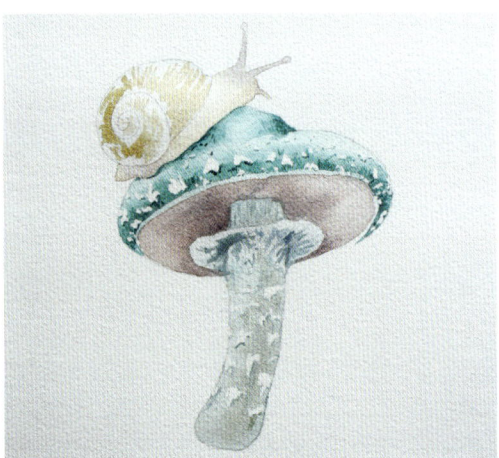

12. Peel off the masking fluid from the cap. Use the 2/0 brush to apply shadows under the white spots with the Phthalo Turquoise and Emerald Green mix.

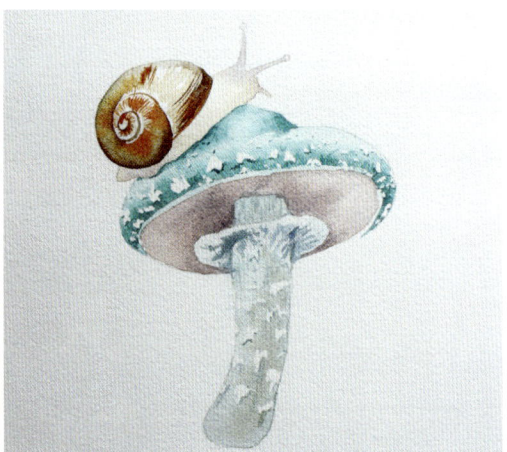

13. Apply Raw Umber using a size 6 brush to paint half of the shell. Then, use Van Dyke Brown to paint the bottom of the shell. Using a size 3 brush, apply a few brushstrokes of Van Dyke Brown wet-on-dry to the shell, following the curve of the shell. Add more to the left side of the shell wet-on-dry, then apply a mix of Burnt Sienna and Yellow Ochre wet-on-wet to the shell with the same brush.

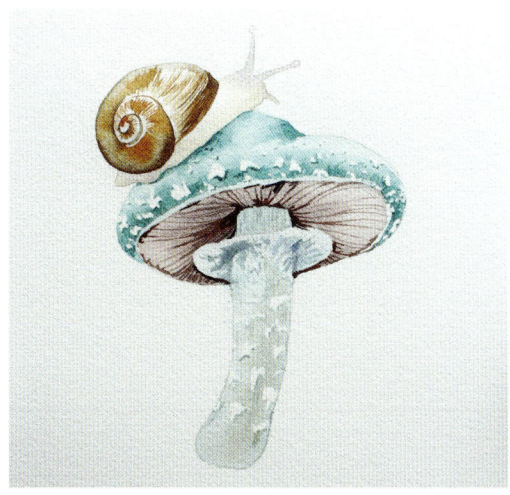

14. Apply the Burnt Sienna and Yellow Ochre mix to the shell with fine brushstrokes using a size 2/0 brush.

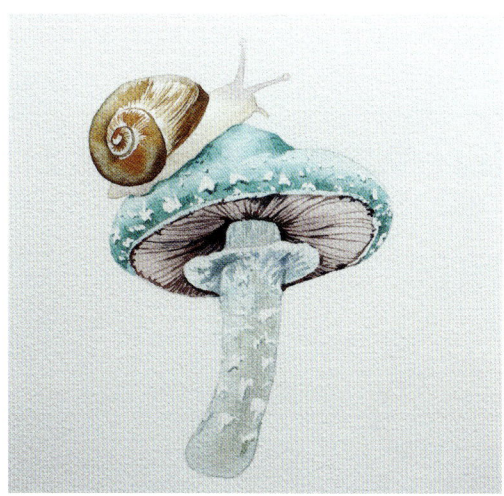

15. To add depth under the cap, mix Light Red and Ultramarine Blue with more pigment and less water to create a dark, muddy purple. Make sure the area is dry before applying slightly curved brushstrokes using a size 2/0 brush to follow the natural pattern of the mushroom.

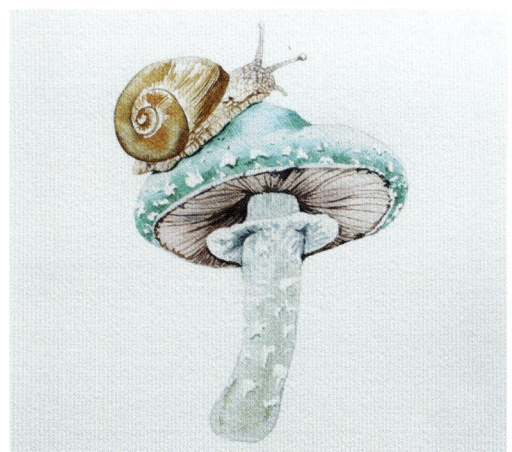

16. Mix Light Red and Prussian Blue to create a very dark shade. Use it to add the darkest tonal values and details. You can also apply a few brushstrokes to the stalk.

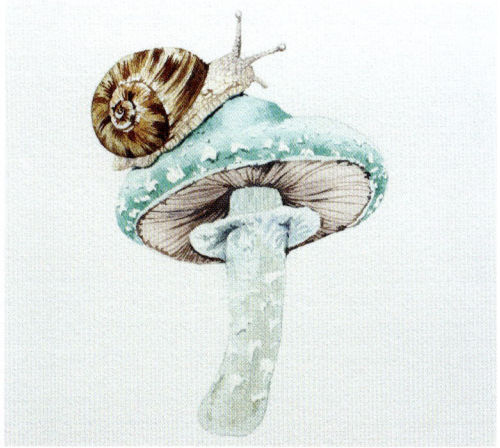

17. Apply Yellow Ochre (tea consistency) wet-on-dry using a size 2/0 brush to work on the snail's body. Use more of the Light Red and Ultramarine Blue mix to paint the area next to the snail's head and its antennae.

Complete the painting by applying Van Dyke Brown using a size 2/0 brush to add fine brushstrokes to the shell.

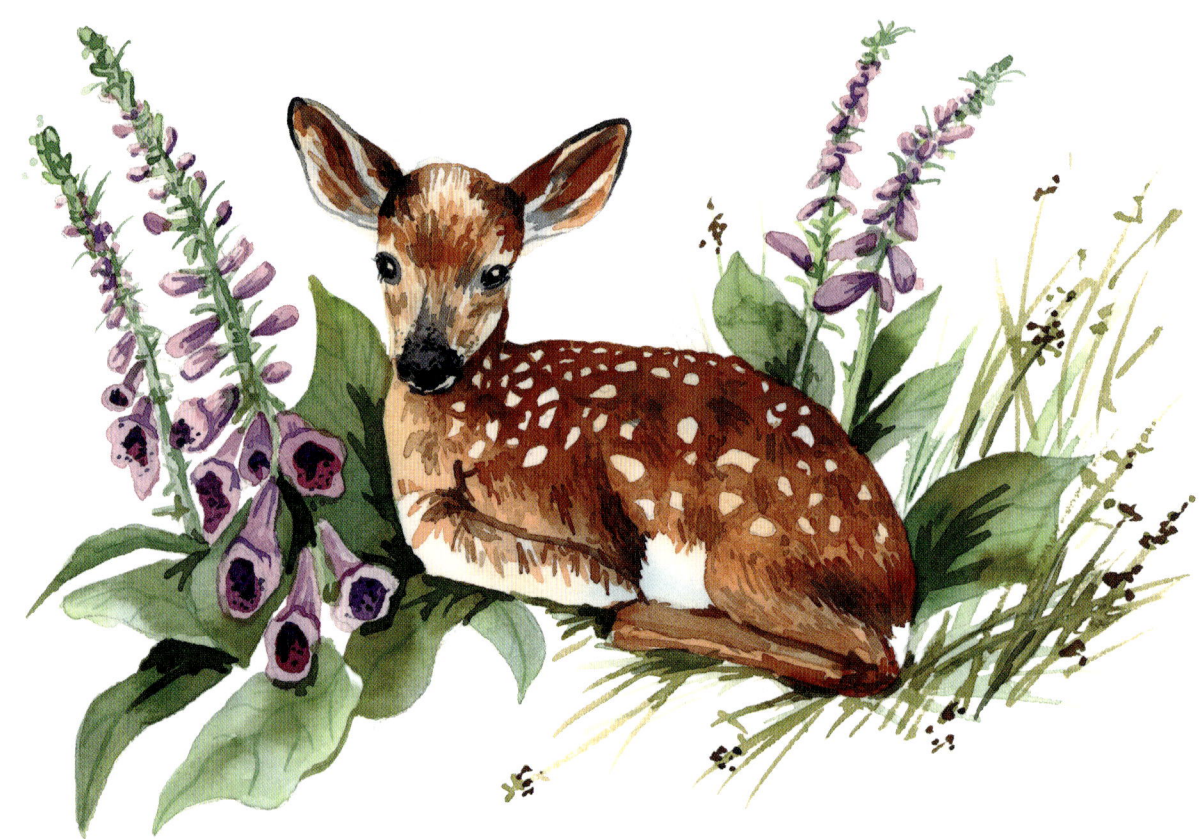

Fallow Deer and Foxgloves

Let's paint this adorable little deer nestled among the foxgloves, enjoying the warmth of summer.

Colors

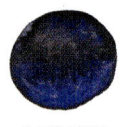       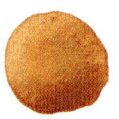 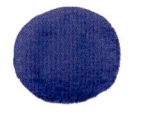

PAYNE'S GRAY	PRUSSIAN BLUE	YELLOW OCHRE	COBALT BLUE	PERMANENT ROSE	RAW UMBER	BURNT SIENNA	ULTRAMARINE BLUE

      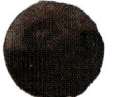

SAP GREEN	LEMON YELLOW	BURNT UMBER	DIOXAZINE PURPLE	HOOKER'S GREEN	CADMIUM YELLOW HUE	LAMP BLACK

Brushes

Size 6 round brush

Size 3 round brush

Size 2/0 round brush for details

Paper

300 gsm cold-pressed

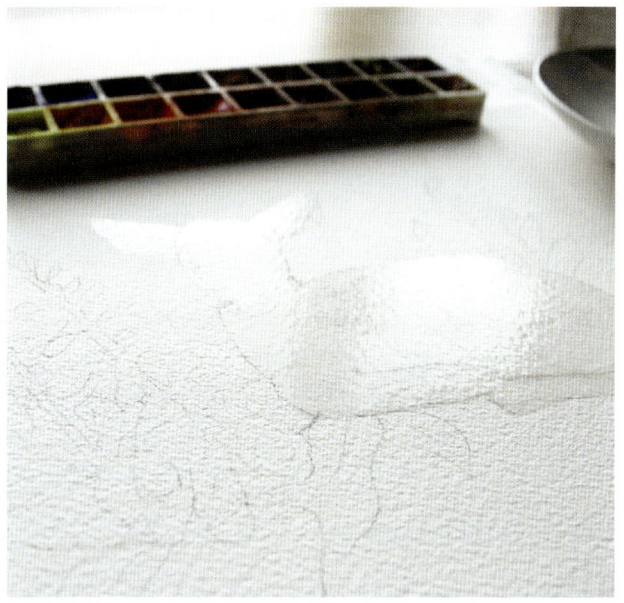

1. Apply a thick layer of water to the whole area of the deer using a size 6 brush.

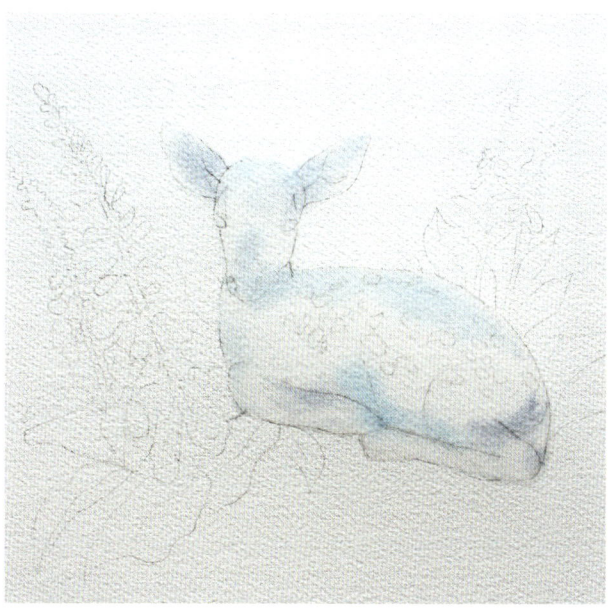

2. Apply Payne's Gray (tea consistency) wet-on-wet using a size 3 brush. Add Prussian Blue (tea consistency) after.

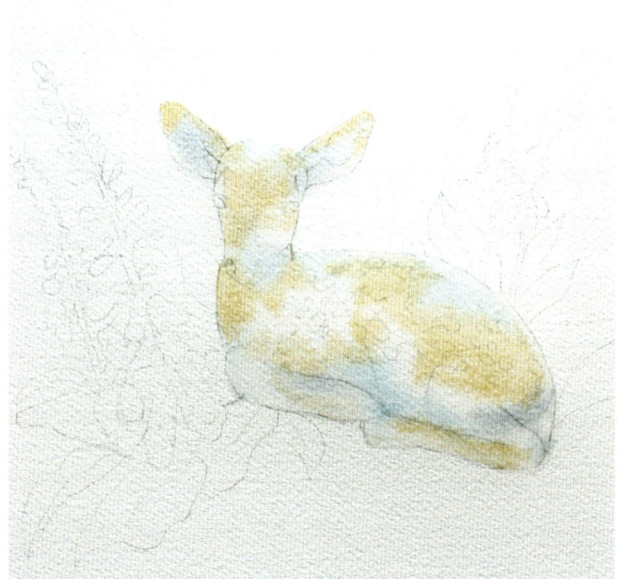

3. While it's still wet, add Yellow Ochre (tea consistency).

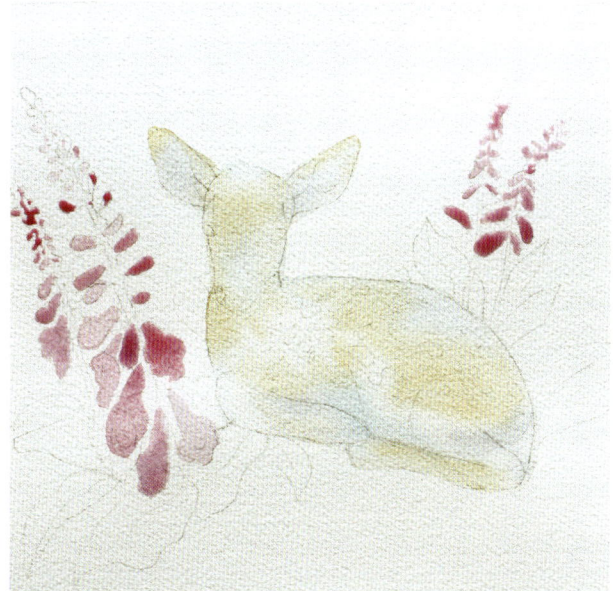

4. Apply a mix of Cobalt Blue and Permanent Rose (tea consistency) wet-on-dry on all flowers using a size 3 brush.

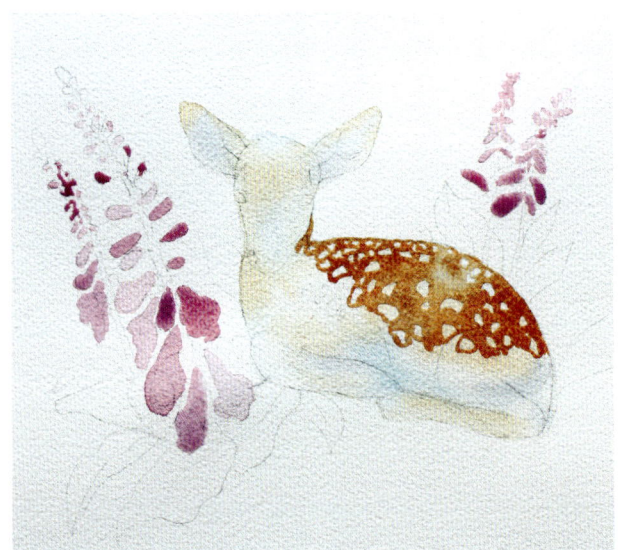

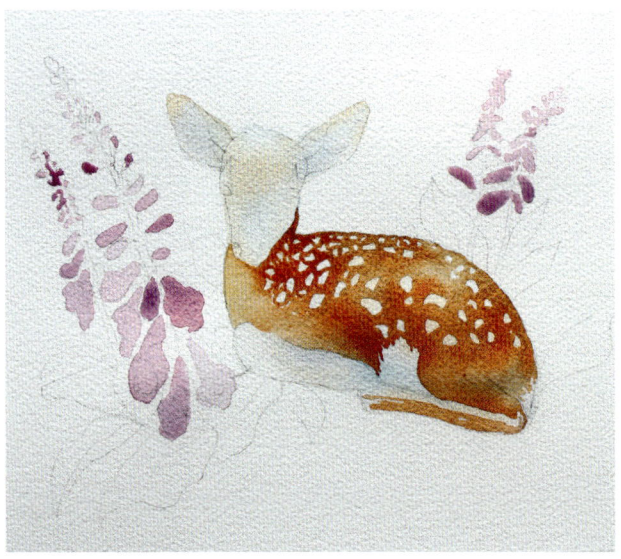

5. Apply a mix of Raw Umber and Burnt Sienna (milk consistency) wet-on-dry using a size 3 brush, avoiding the white dots. Add Burnt Sienna wet-on-wet on shaded areas next to the neck and on the back.

6. Using the Raw Umber and Burnt Sienna mix (tea consistency), paint light brushstrokes on the head and legs.

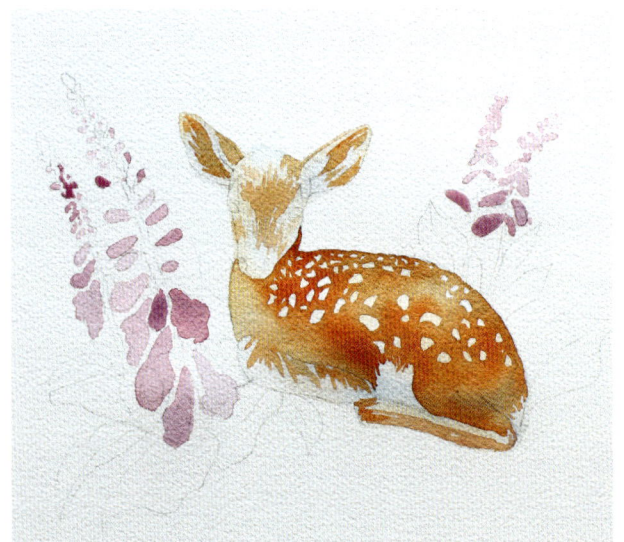

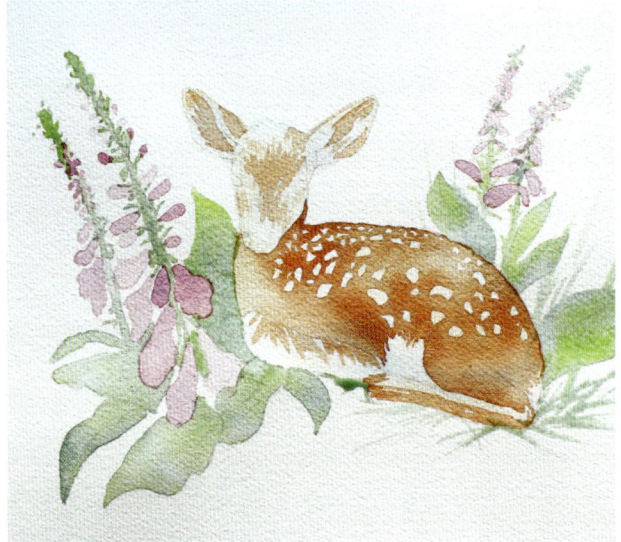

7. Apply a mix of Ultramarine Blue and Sap Green (tea consistency) wet-on-wet to the leaves and stems using a size 3–6 brush. Add a mix of Lemon Yellow and Sap Green wet-on-wet to some areas on the leaves.

8. Apply Burnt Sienna to the deer's back wet-on-dry, gradually activating most of its back with wetness. Use Burnt Umber to add shadow areas using a size 3 brush.

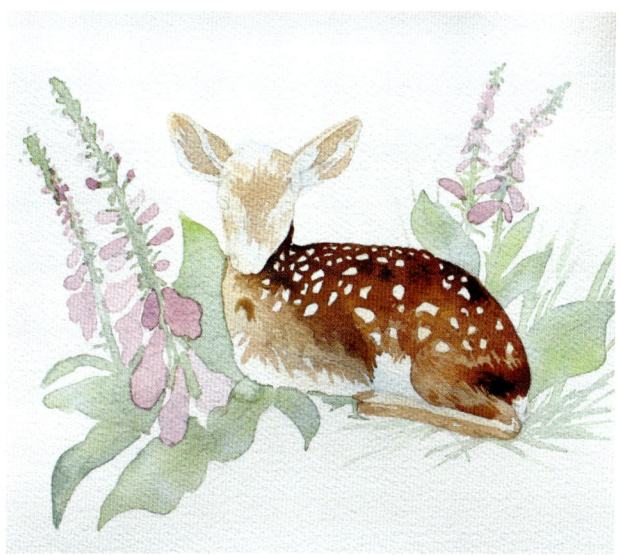

9. Use Payne's Gray with a size 2/0 brush to add gray and black tones, painting the nose, eyes, tops of the ears, and areas on the body. Use Burnt Sienna to paint details inside the ears and on the forehead, changing to Burnt Umber to paint darker hair on the deer's legs.

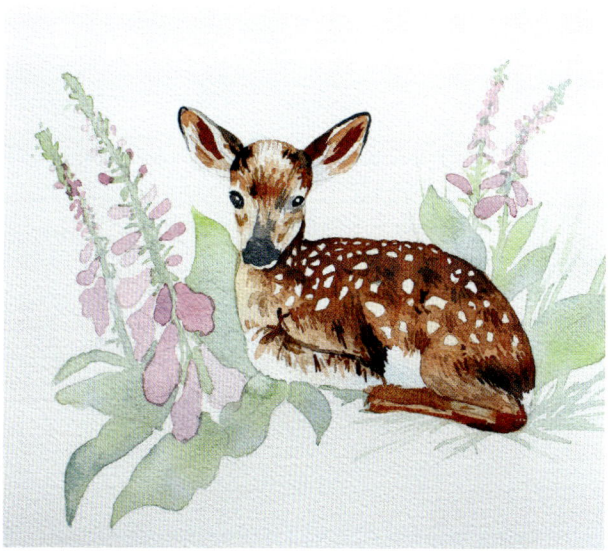

10. Paint veins with a mix of Sap Green and Ultramarine Blue (tea consistency) using a size 2/0 brush. Add shadow areas on stems.

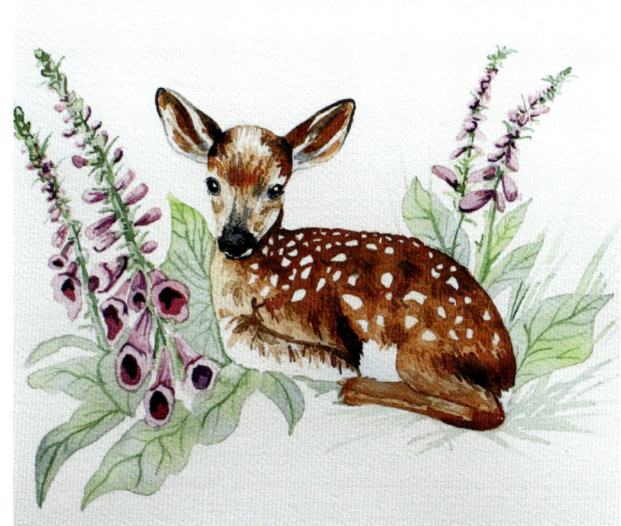

11. Apply a mix of Sap Green and Ultramarine Blue (tea consistency) to paint grass on the right using a size 3 brush. Mix Permanent Rose and Cobalt Blue (milk consistency) and paint darker values on flowers using a size 3 brush. Apply an intense mix of Permanent Rose and Dioxazine Purple to paint inside some flowers.

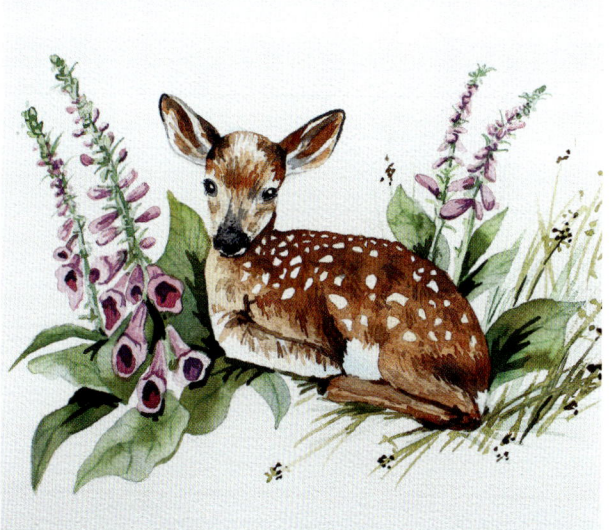

12. Use a mix of Hooker's Green and Burnt Umber to paint shadows under the leaves using a size 3 brush. Apply a mix of Cadmium Yellow Hue and Sap Green wet-on-dry to paint grass on the right-hand side with a size 3 brush. Paint darker details with Burnt Umber using a size 2/0 brush. Use Lamp Black to paint dots around the face, define the eyes, and paint dots on the foxgloves.

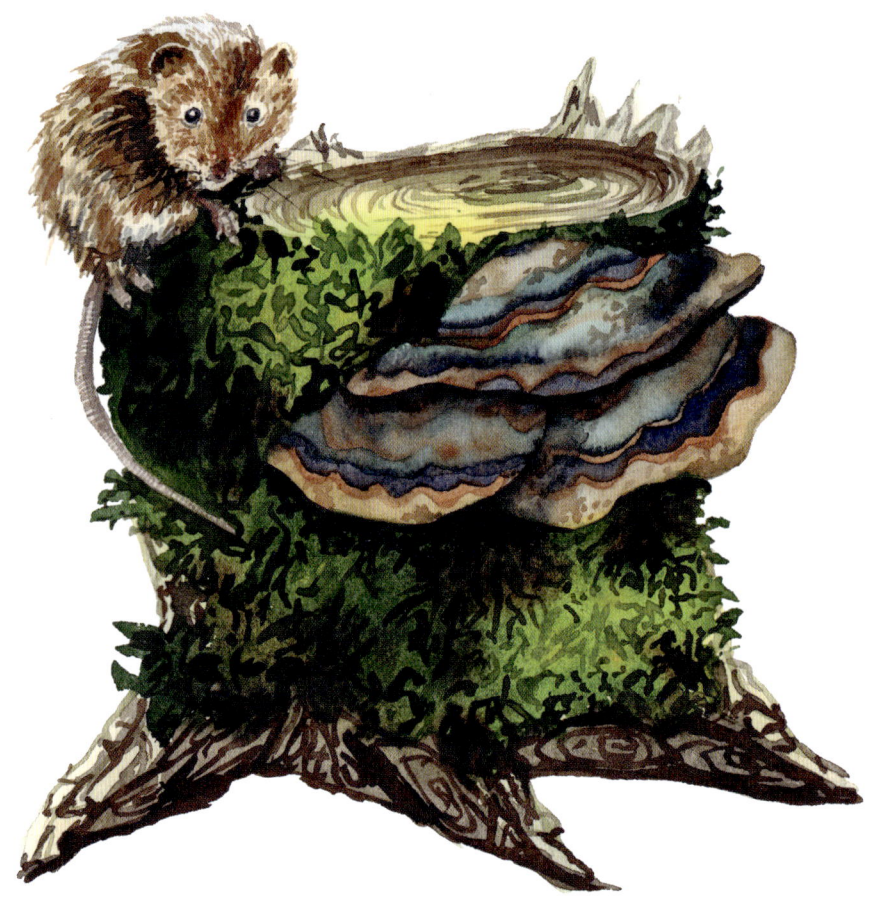

Harvest Mouse and Turkey Tail Mushrooms

Here's a gorgeous forest scene to paint: A harvest mouse has stopped on a stump overtaken by moss and turkey tail mushrooms.

Colors

CADMIUM
YELLOW HUE

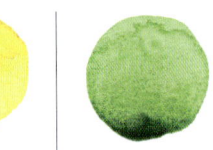
SAP
GREEN

RAW
UMBER

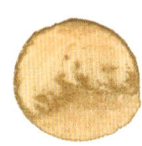
YELLOW
OCHRE

ULTRAMARINE
BLUE

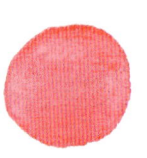
PERMANENT
ROSE

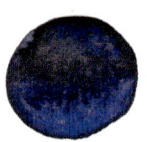
PAYNE'S
GRAY

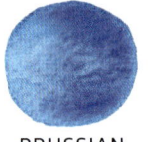
PRUSSIAN
BLUE

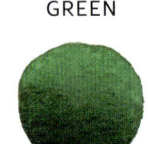
HOOKER'S
GREEN

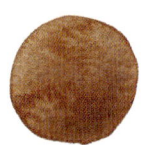
BURNT
UMBER

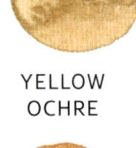
BURNT
SIENNA

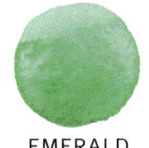
EMERALD
GREEN

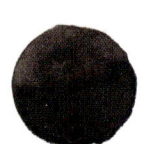
LAMP
BLACK

Brushes

Size 8 round brush

Size 6 round brush

Size 3 round brush

Size 2/0 round brush for details

Paper

300 gsm cold-pressed

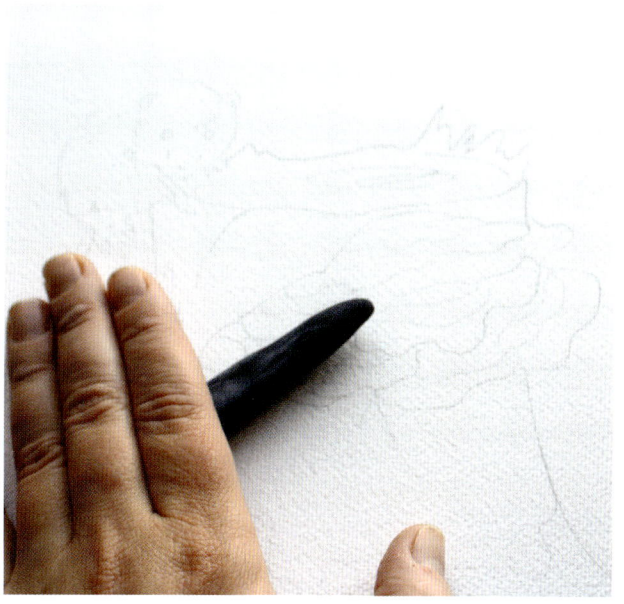

1. Rub off some dark graphite marks using an eraser.

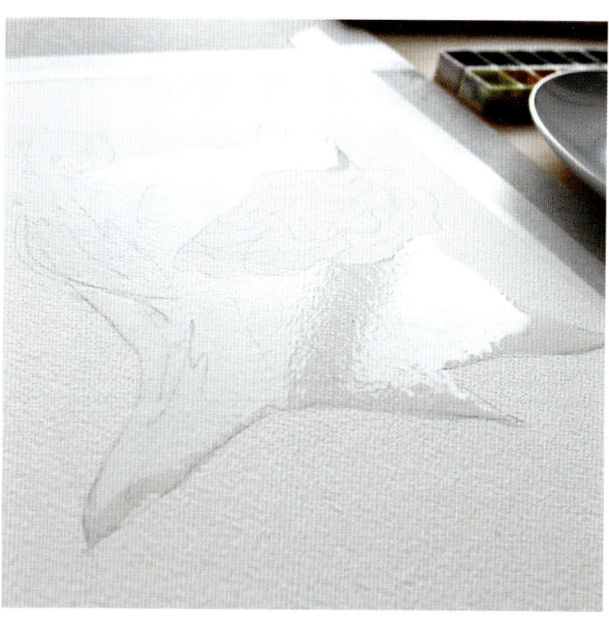

2. Wet the entire area of the stump using a size 8 brush with an even layer of water.

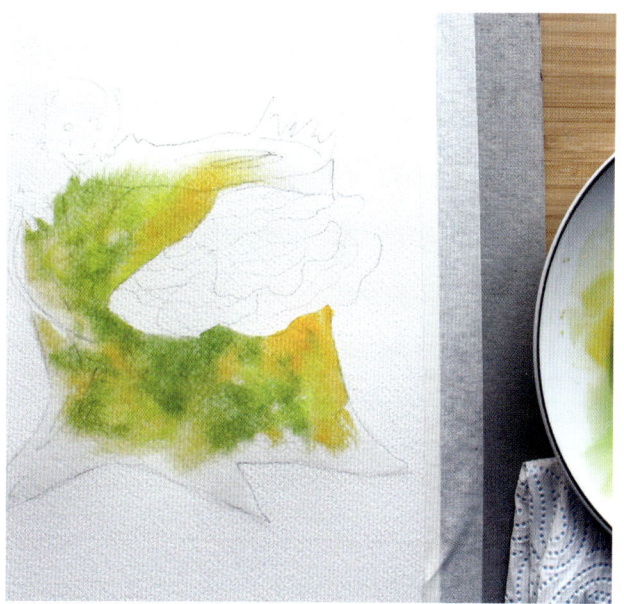

3. Add colors wet-on-wet using a size 6 brush, starting with Cadmium Yellow Hue, then Sap Green.

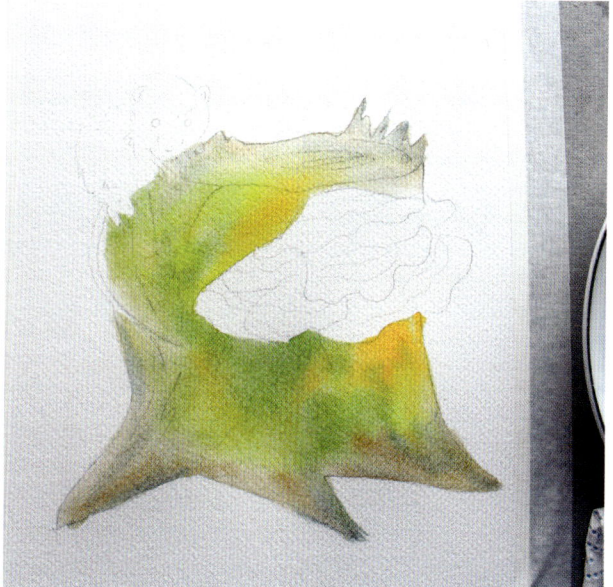

4. Mix Raw Umber and Yellow Ochre (tea consistency), then add this mix to the bottom and top of the stump. Use a size 3 brush to apply Ultramarine Blue (tea consistency) on top. Let it dry.

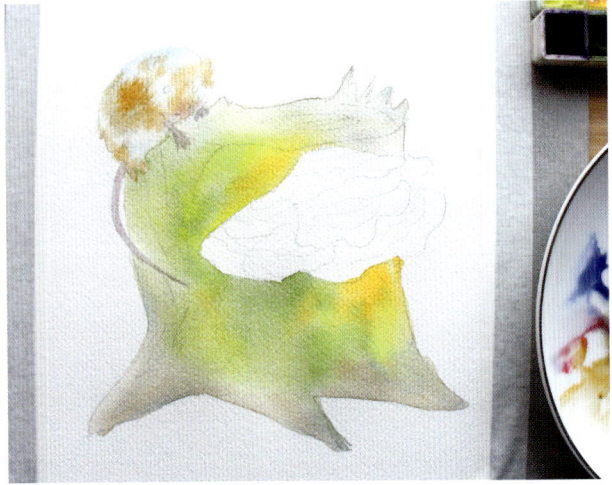

5. Apply water to the mouse using a size 3 brush. Add Ultramarine Blue (tea consistency) on top of the mouse. Wash your brush, then immediately add Yellow Ochre (tea consistency). Mix Permanent Rose and Payne's Gray (tea consistency) and apply it to the paws and tail using a size 3 brush. Let it dry.

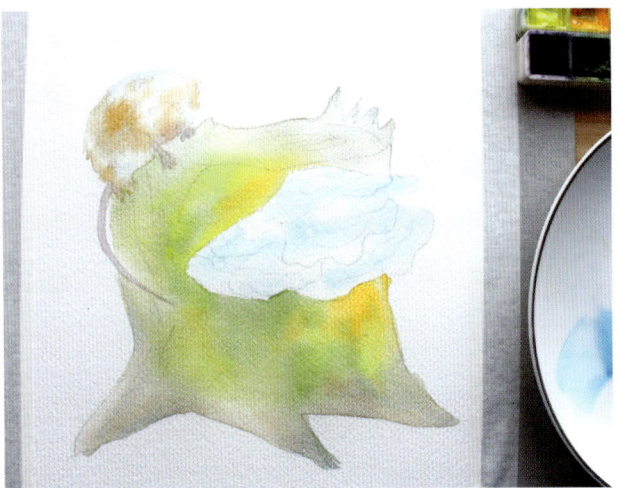

6. Add water to the turkey tail mushroom using a size 6 brush. Add some Prussian Blue (tea consistency) to the mushroom wet-on-wet using a size 6 brush.

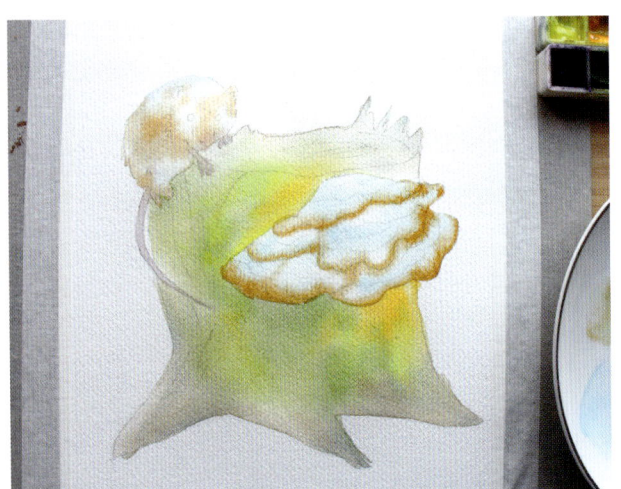

7. Apply Yellow Ochre when the mushroom is damp, focusing on the edges. Let it dry.

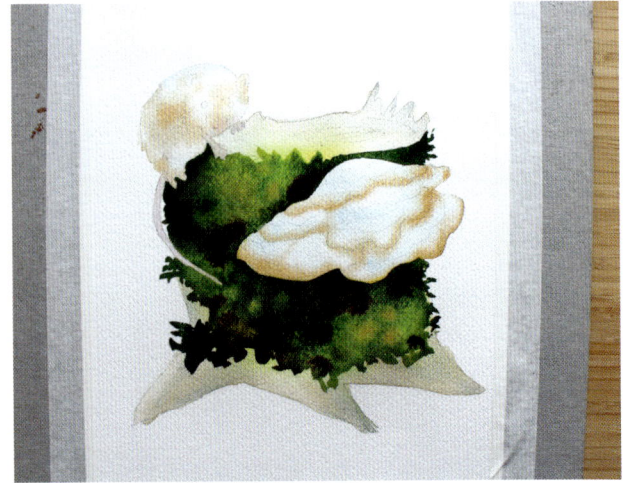

8. Prepare the following mixes to paint the moss, in this order:
   - Cadmium Yellow Hue + Sap Green
   - Hooker's Green + Burnt Umber
   - Hooker's Green + Ultramarine Blue
   - Burnt Umber

   All mixes should be at a milk consistency, full of color. Begin adding the lightest colors using a size 6 brush. Let it dry.

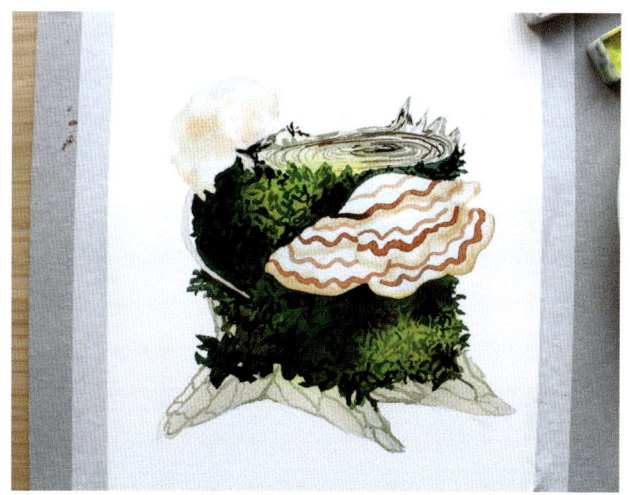
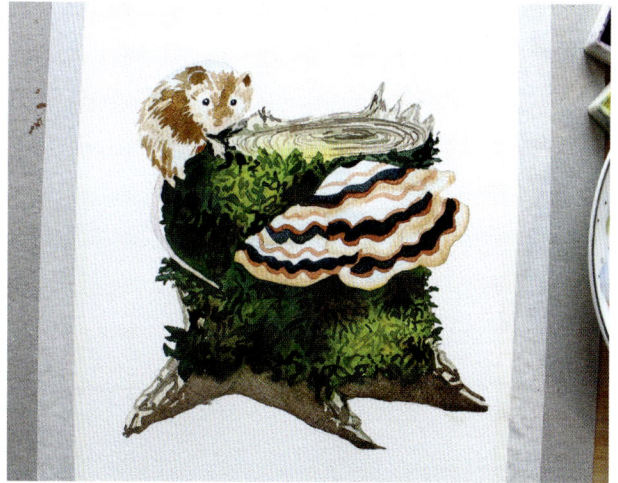

9. Use Burnt Sienna to paint lines on the mushrooms wet-on-dry using a size 6 brush. Apply Burnt Umber and Raw Umber (tea consistency) separately using a size 2/0 brush to make lines inside the stump.

Use the same mixes we used for the background color to work wet-on-dry, defining the moss. Start with the lighter colors and move to darker areas. Switch to a size 2/0 brush for smaller details.

Use Raw Umber and a size 6 brush to break the bark into fragments.

10. Paint lines on the mushrooms with Payne's Gray wet-on-dry using a size 6 brush. Use a mix of Burnt Umber and Raw Umber to paint shadow areas on the bottom of the stump.

Switch to a size 3 brush and apply Raw Umber wet-on-dry to the mouse. Add Payne's Gray to paint the eyes, leaving a white space in the middle of each eye, using a size 2/0 brush.

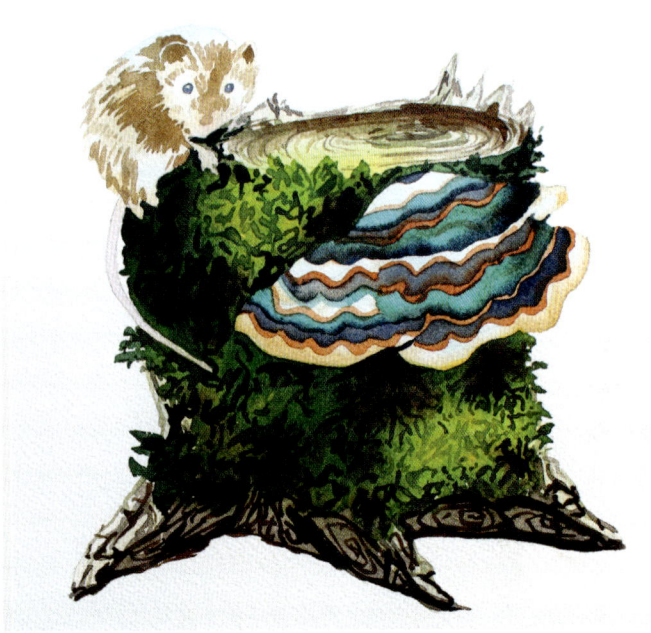

11. Use Burnt Umber (cream consistency) to define shadows at the bottom and top of the stump using a size 3 brush. Apply a mix of Emerald Green with a bit of Payne's Gray wet-on-dry to the mushrooms. Add a few drops of Burnt Sienna on top of the Emerald Green lines. Lift some paint to allow highlights.

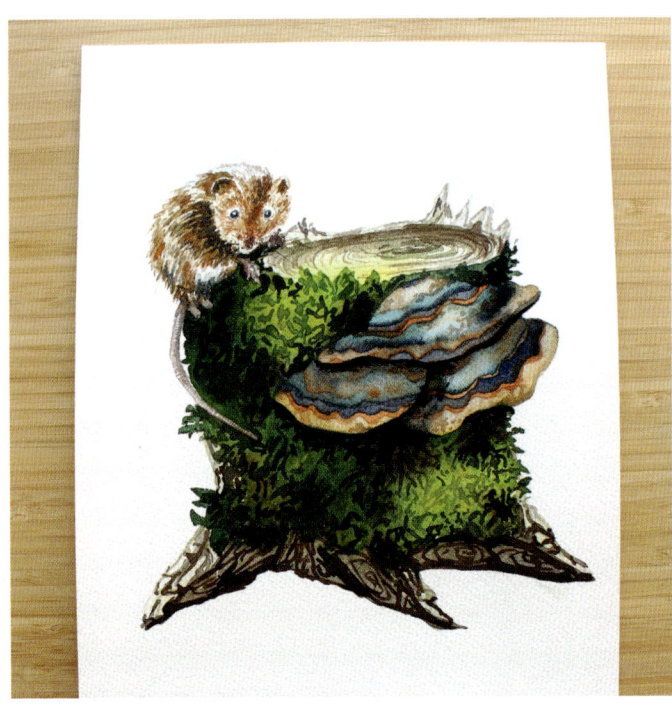

12. Let's paint the mouse: Apply a mix of Permanent Rose and Raw Umber wet-on-dry to create a pink nose using a size 2/0 brush. With the same brush, add Burnt Sienna for fur around the mouse, followed by Raw Umber, then Burnt Umber, and finally a mix of Payne's Gray and Burnt Umber. Apply all colors wet-on-dry to allow layering from light to dark values.

Mix Payne's Gray and Permanent Rose and use a size 2/0 brush to paint lines over the tail, then add a shadow on the right side of the tail. Add the same details to the paws. Paint the eyes with Lamp Black, add dots around the face, and paint the whiskers.

Color the remaining lines on the mushroom with Burnt Sienna. Let it dry. Use Lamp Black and a size 3 brush to paint shadows separating the turkey tail mushrooms and darken the shadows under the mushroom.

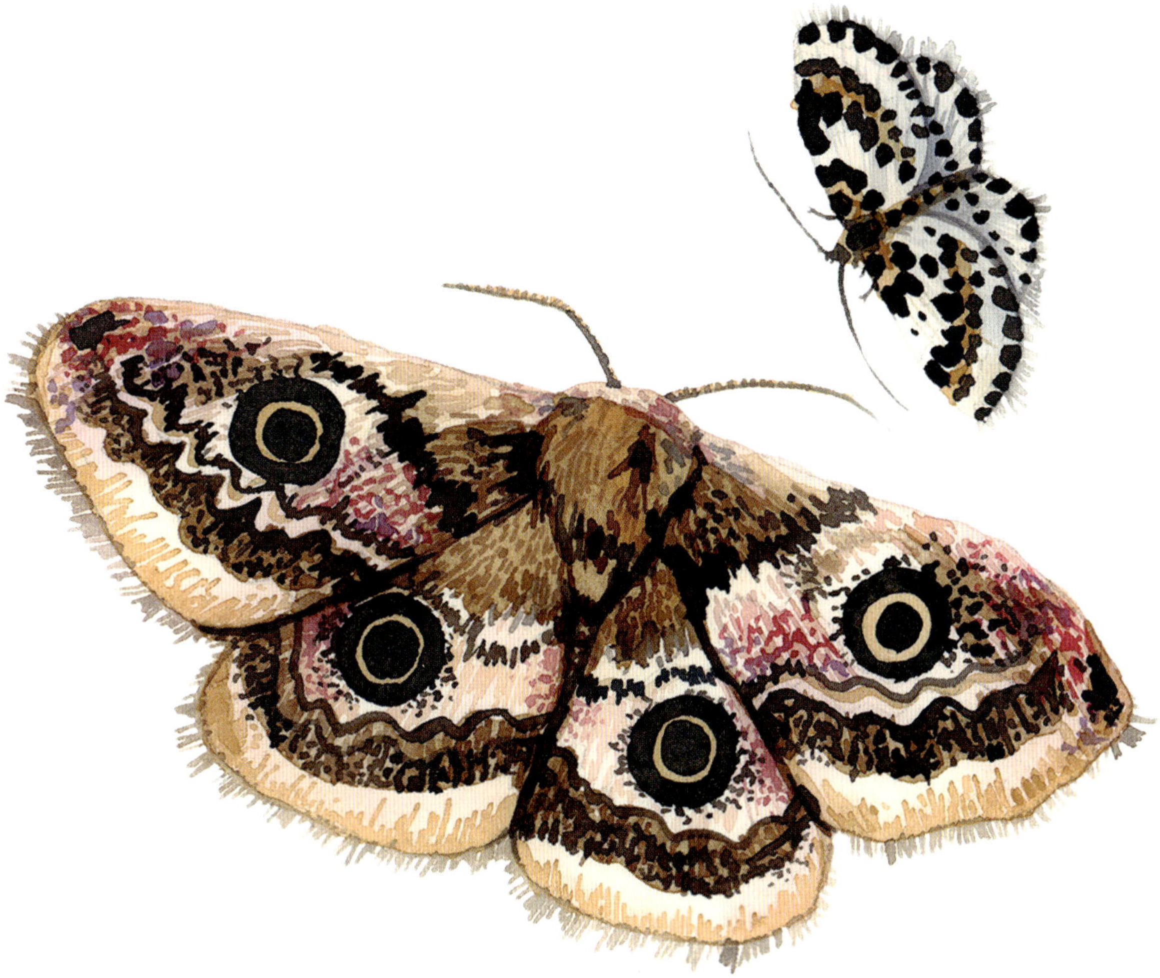

Emperor and Magpie Moths

Moths will circle around night-blooming flowers, attracted to the white light of the blossoms. These fluffy, delicate moths are a joy to paint.

Colors

 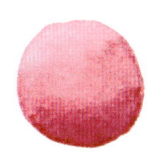 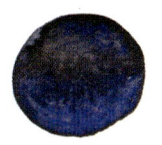 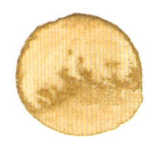 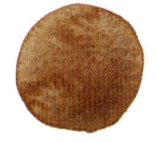 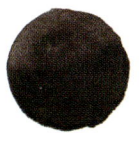

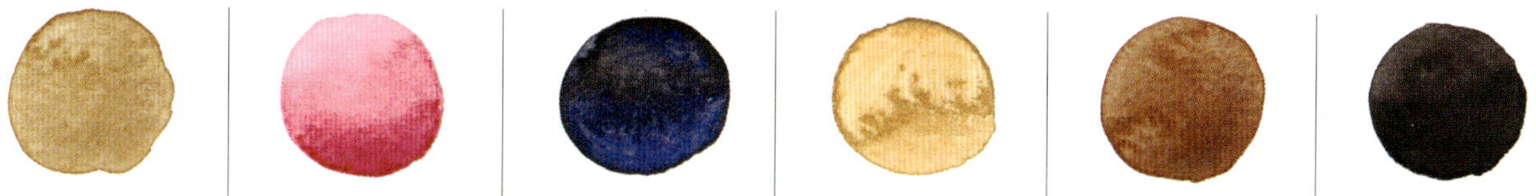

| RAW UMBER | PERMANENT ROSE | PAYNE'S GRAY | YELLOW OCHRE | BURNT UMBER | LAMP BLACK |

Brushes

Size 6 round brush

Size 3 round brush

Size 2/0 round brush for details

Paper

300 gsm cold-pressed

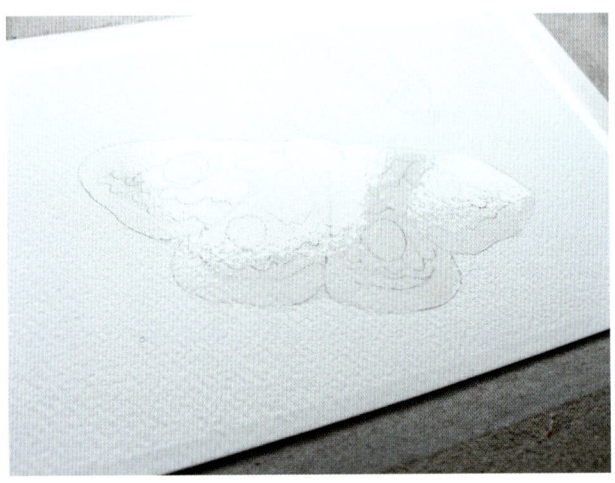

1. Apply an even, thick layer of water to the whole area of the larger moth using a size 6 brush. For the smaller moth, cover it with water using a size 3 brush. Avoid puddles, and ensure your brush covers all the edges with water.

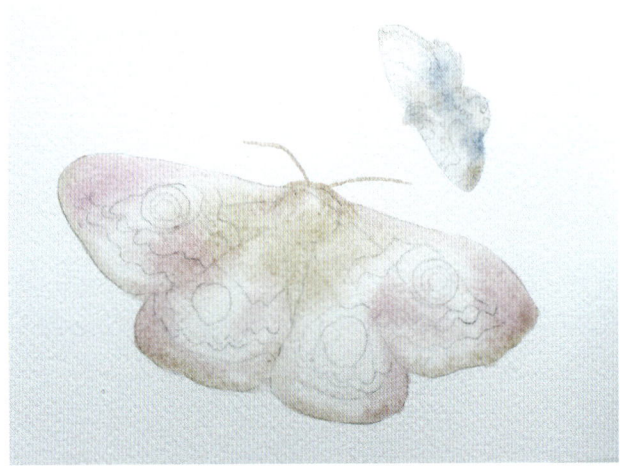

2. Prepare three mixes (tea consistency) on your ceramic palette: Raw Umber, Permanent Rose, and Payne's Gray. Apply Raw Umber wet-on-wet first, then follow with Permanent Rose on the larger moth.

Use a size 3 brush to apply Raw Umber in the middle of the smaller moth, then apply Payne's Gray over the same area. Let it dry.

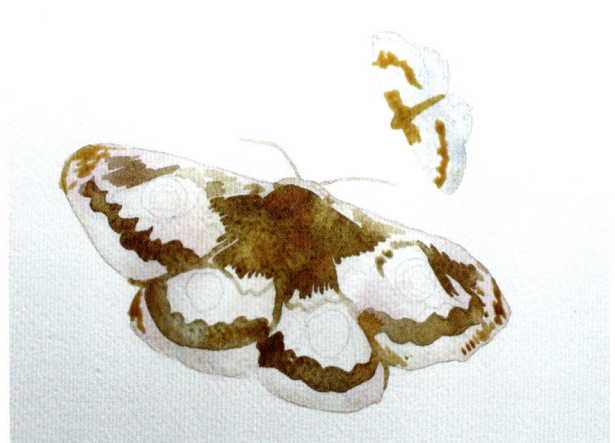

3. Apply Raw Umber (milk consistency) wet-on-dry using a size 3 brush.

Next, apply Yellow Ochre to the edges of the upper wings and on top of the Raw Umber.

Use Yellow Ochre to paint warm areas on the smaller moth, applying it to the middle and upper wings. Let it dry.

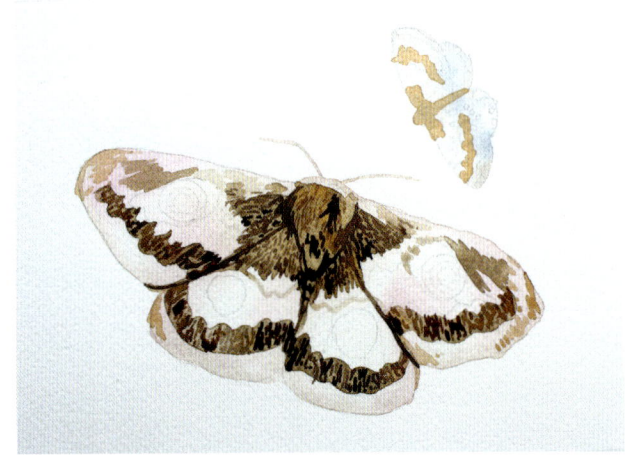

4. Apply Burnt Umber (milk consistency) with short brushstrokes covering areas in light brown, imitating scales, using a size 2/0 brush.

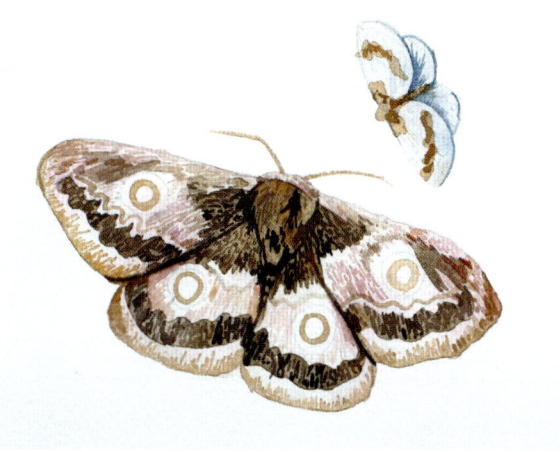

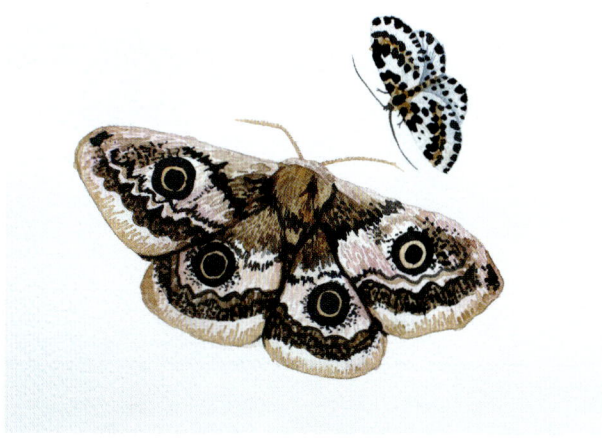

5. Apply Permanent Rose (tea consistency) to areas that should have a slightly pinkish color.

Then, apply Yellow Ochre with short brushstrokes along the edges of the wings of the larger moth and on the antennas.

Apply Payne's Gray (tea consistency) to paint darker values on the smaller moth using a size 2/0 brush. Add a few long brushstrokes to create texture.

6. Use Lamp Black wet-on-dry to paint the darkest values using a size 2/0 brush. Combine dots and short brushstrokes to paint all the black circles and dots around them. Add black dots to the smaller moth using a size 3 brush. Then, switch to a size 2/0 brush to paint the pointy antennas.

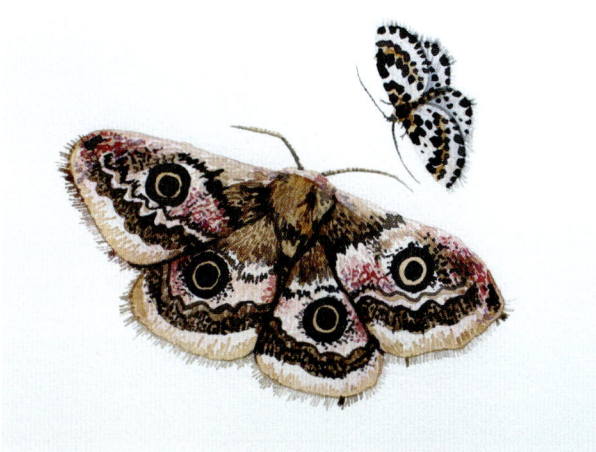

7. Use Permanent Rose to finish the larger moth, adding more details wet-on-dry.

Then load your size 2/0 brush with a mix of Raw Umber and Permanent Rose and paint a fluffy ribbon on all the wings of the larger moth. Then, switch to Payne's Gray to add fluffiness to the smaller moth.

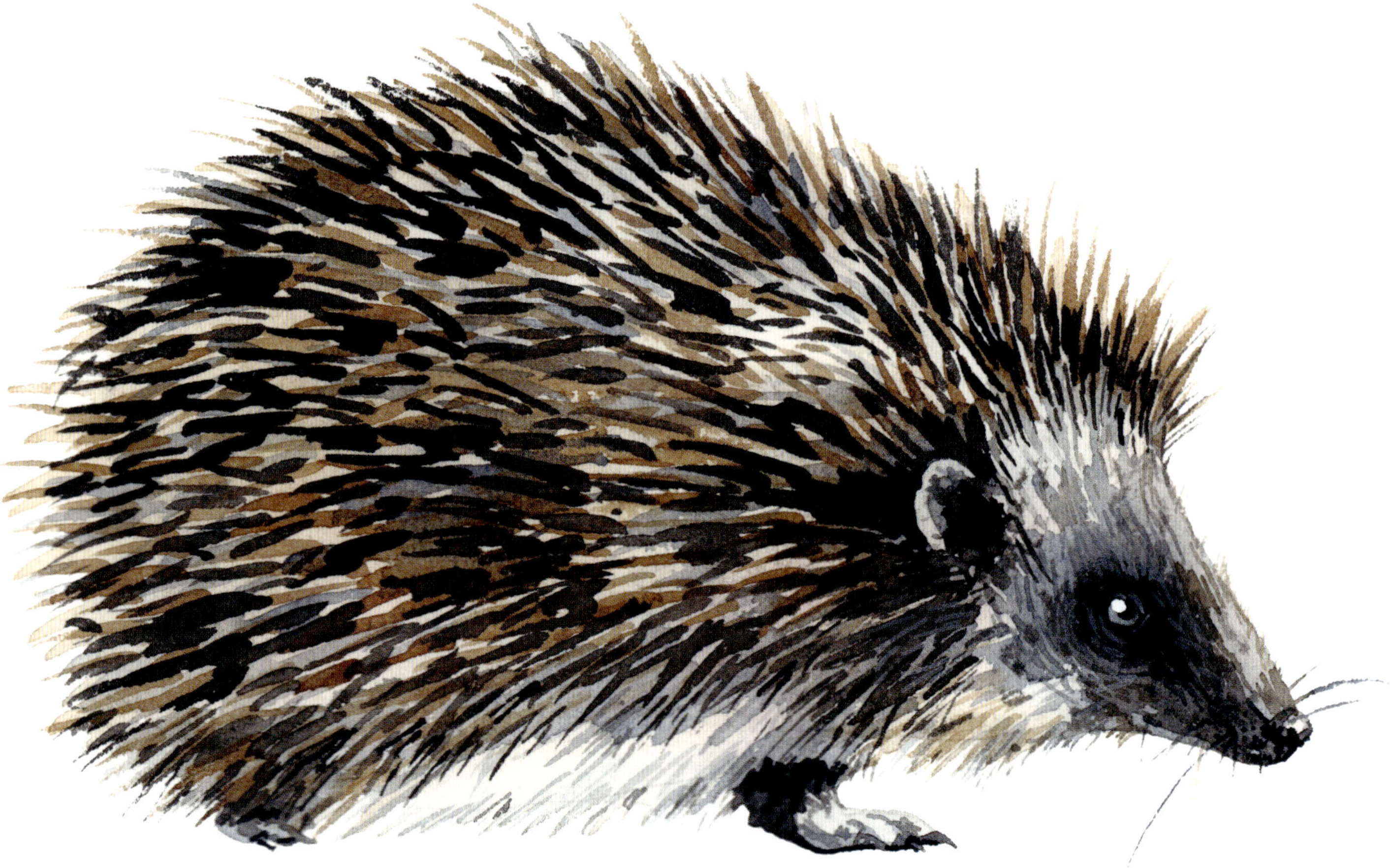

Hedgehog

A cute little hedgehog is a must in any collection of woodland paintings. These nocturnal creatures are a joy to paint, and there's nothing quite like them in the natural world.

Colors

  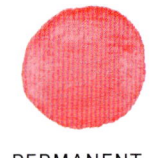 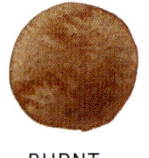  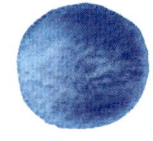 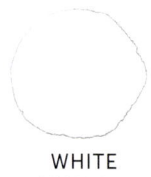

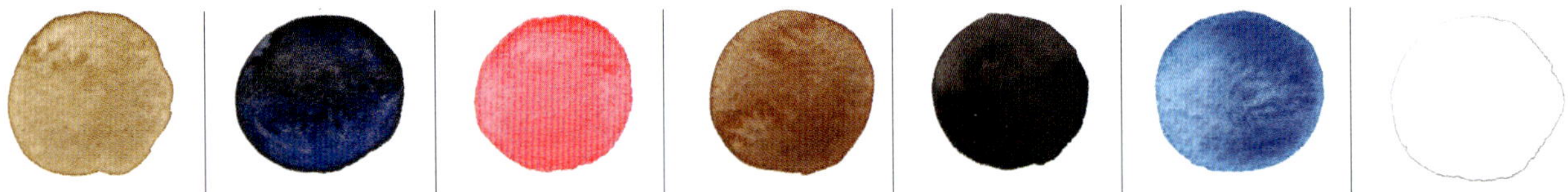

RAW UMBER	PAYNE'S GRAY	PERMANENT ROSE	BURNT UMBER	LAMP BLACK	PRUSSIAN BLUE	WHITE GOUACHE

Brushes

Size 6 round brush

Size 3 round brush

Size 2/0 round brush for details

Paper

300 gsm cold-pressed

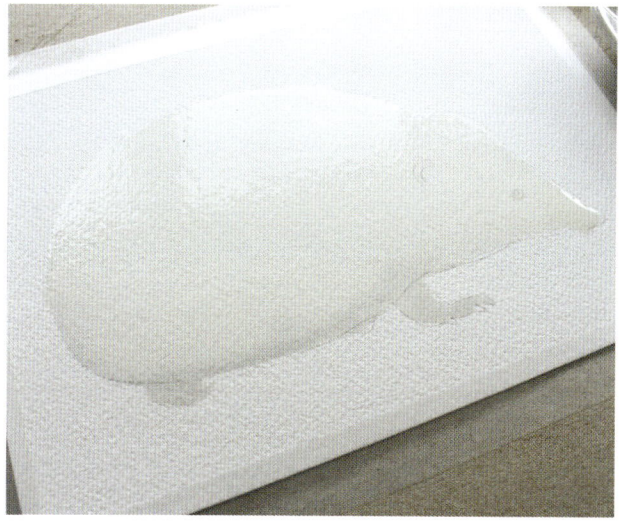

1. Apply a thick layer of water to the entire area of the hedgehog using a size 6 brush. Evenly spread the water, making sure to cover all corners up to the pencil marks. The surface should glisten evenly, without any puddles of water.

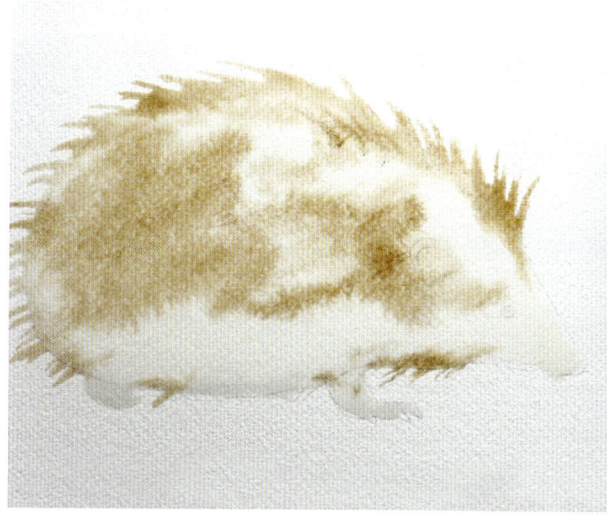

2. Prepare the following colors (tea consistency) on your ceramic palette: Raw Umber, Payne's Gray, and Permanent Rose. Using a size 3 brush, apply the Raw Umber wet-on-wet. Using only the tip of your brush, pull the Raw Umber from the edges of the pencil marks, creating the needles on the hedgehog's body.

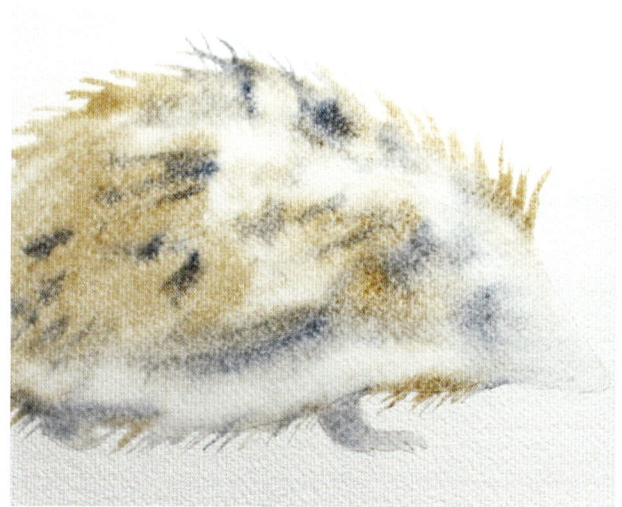

3. Next, apply Payne's Gray and wet-on-wet with the same brush.

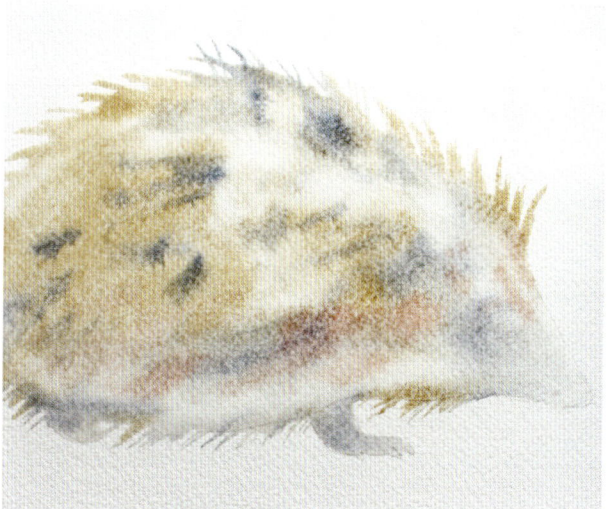

4. Apply Permanent Rose with the size 3 brush wet-on-wet. Let it dry completely.

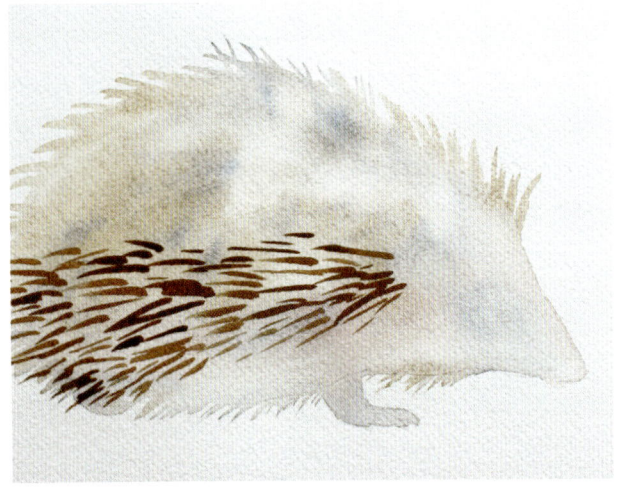

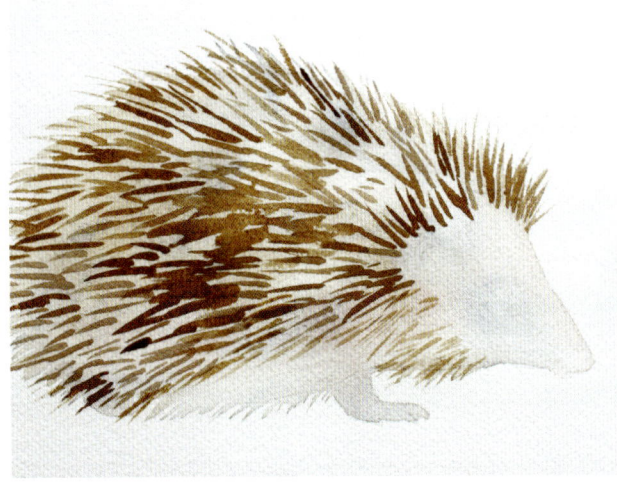

5. Apply Burnt Umber (milk consistency) wet-on-dry to create darker needles using a size 3 brush. Follow the natural curves of the needles, flicking your brush lightly from right to left to create sharp, spiky ends.

6. You can also merge some of the larger needles in the middle of the body to add shadows and depth.

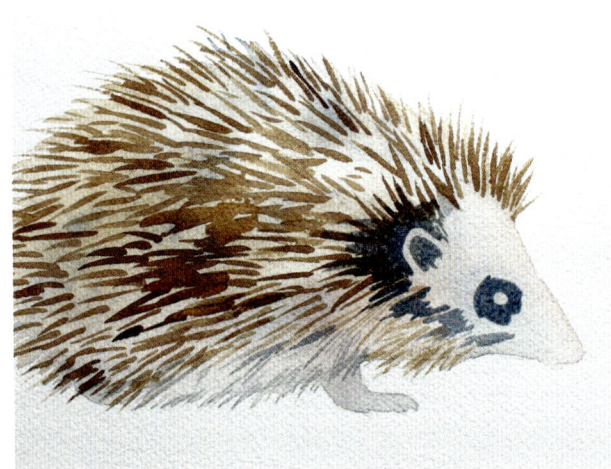

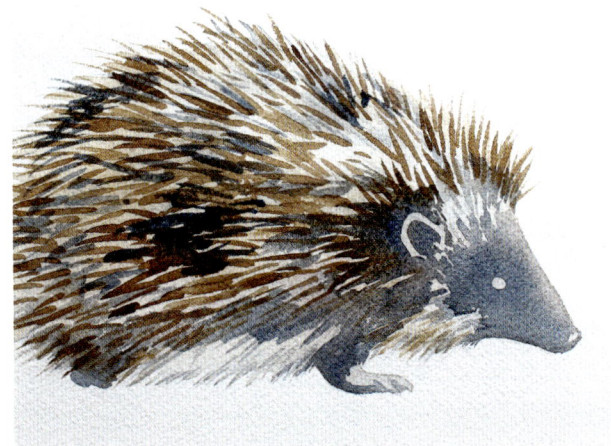

7. Load your size 3 brush with Payne's Gray and paint a few lighter needles on the belly wet-on-dry. Reload your brush with slightly more color and less water and create a shadow next to the ear and around the eye.

8. Continue with the same brush and color, painting more with Payne's Gray. Leave the belly light and darken the middle part of the body and face. Let it dry.

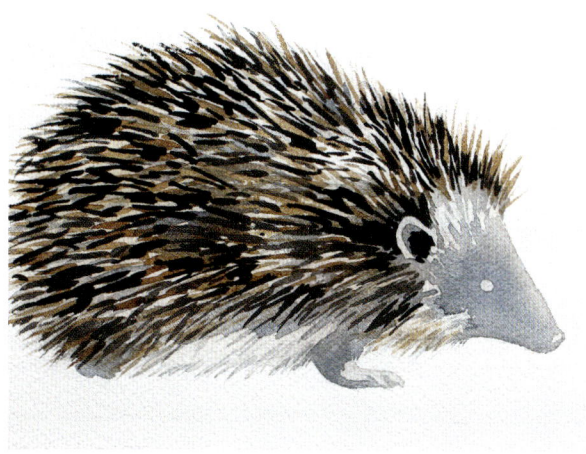

9. Apply Lamp Black (tea consistency) wet-on-dry to the body of the hedgehog using a size 3 brush, working mainly on the darker values of the needles.

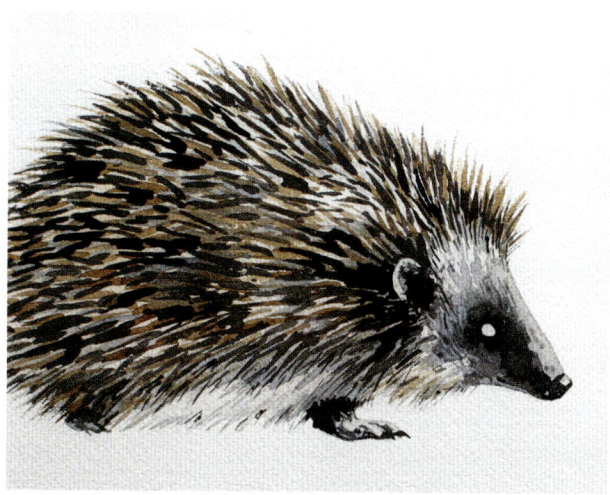

10. Switch to a size 2/0 brush to paint a few thin needles. Then, swap back to size 3 and use Raw Umber (milk consistency) to paint a few brushstrokes around the face. Apply a few more brushstrokes with Payne's Gray.

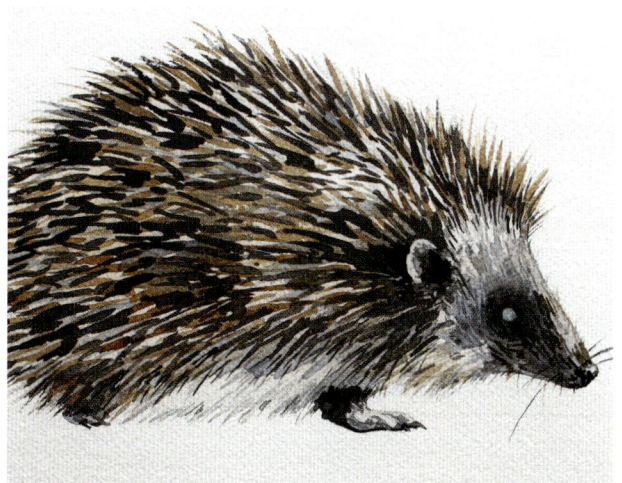

11. Mix Prussian Blue and Payne's Gray (tea consistency) and apply to the eye area to create a light gray effect using a size 3 brush. Let it dry.

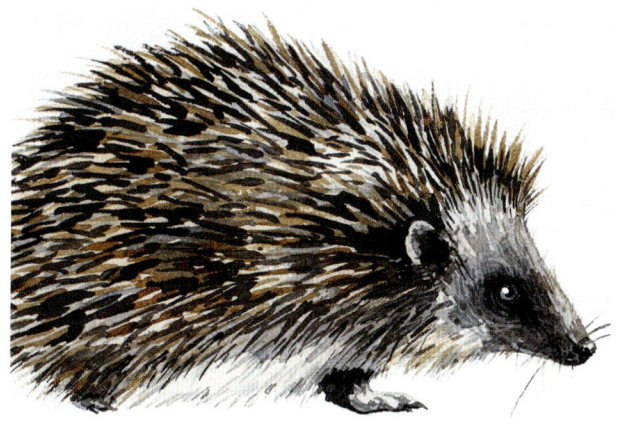

12. Once dry, use Lamp Black (cream consistency) to paint the pupil using a size 3 brush or smaller. Switch to a size 2/0 brush and use Lamp Black to paint the whiskers, starting the strokes from the body for neat, sharp ends. Apply white gouache using a size 3 brush to the dry eye, using just the tip of your brush.

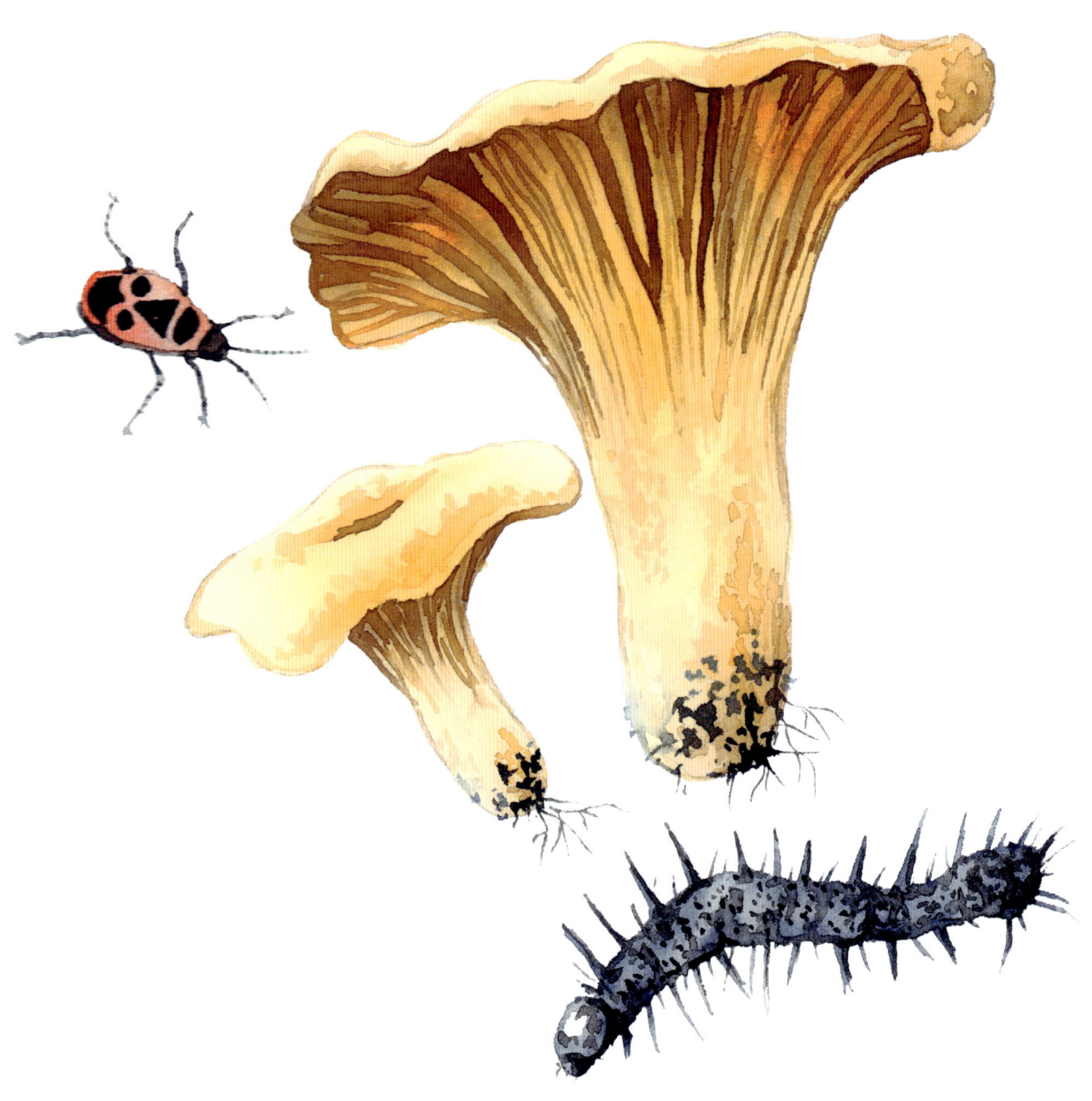

Chanterelle Mushrooms with Peacock Caterpillar and Firebug

Take a trip into a pine tree forest, where you'll find summer treasures: chanterelle mushrooms, firebugs basking in the sun, and peacock caterpillars getting ready to pupate. These orange mushrooms offer a perfect opportunity to practice complementary colors and create natural shades.

Colors

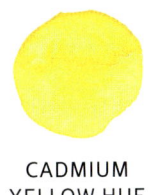 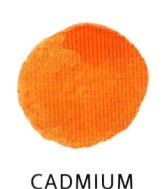  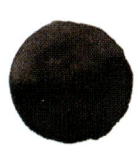  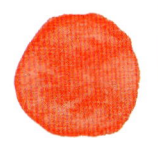 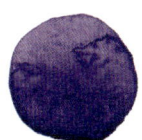

| CADMIUM YELLOW HUE | CADMIUM ORANGE HUE | PAYNE'S GRAY | LAMP BLACK | ULTRAMARINE BLUE | CADMIUM RED DEEP HUE | DIOXAZINE PURPLE |

Brushes

Size 6 round brush

Size 3 round brush

Size 2/0 round brush for details

Paper

300 gsm cold-pressed

1. Apply an even, thick layer of water using a size 6 brush to the entire area of the two mushrooms, making sure to cover all edges.

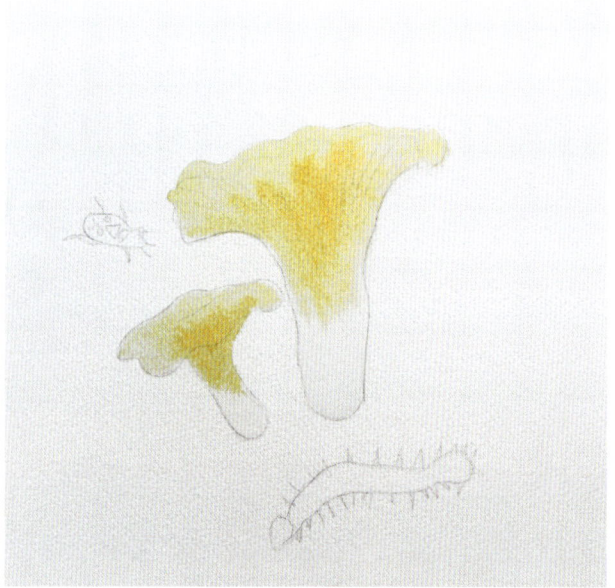

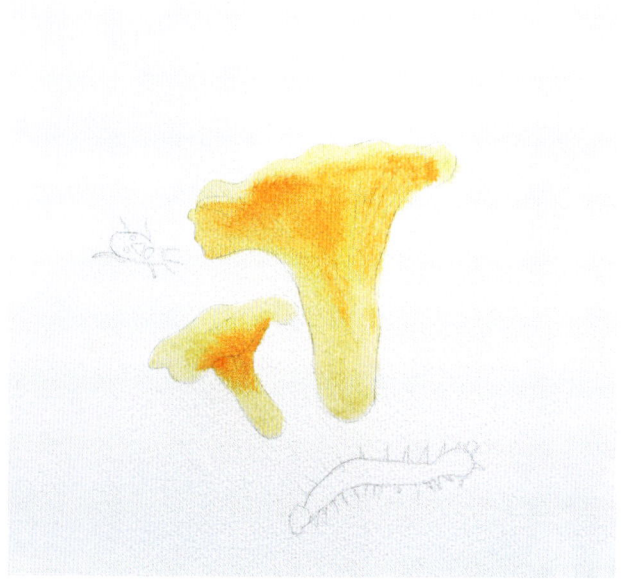

2. Start with the tops of both mushrooms. Apply Cadmium Yellow Hue (tea consistency) wet-on-wet using a size 6 brush. Immediately mix Cadmium Yellow Hue with Cadmium Orange Hue and apply this slightly darker, more orange color wet-on-wet under the caps.

3. Keep the tops of the mushrooms lighter. Mix more Cadmium Orange and apply a thicker consistency of this color wet-on-wet using a size 3 brush.

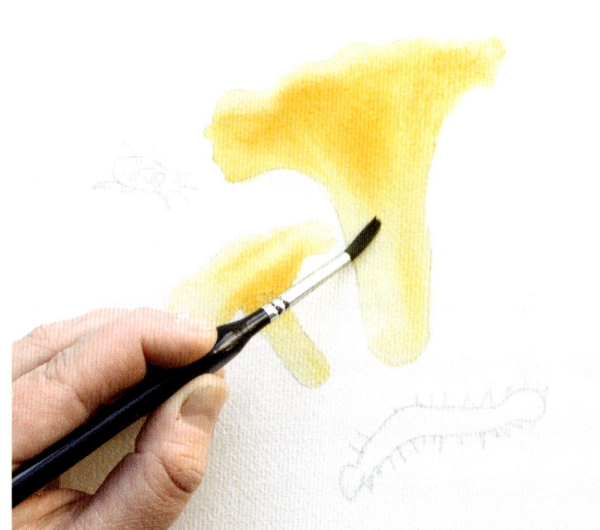

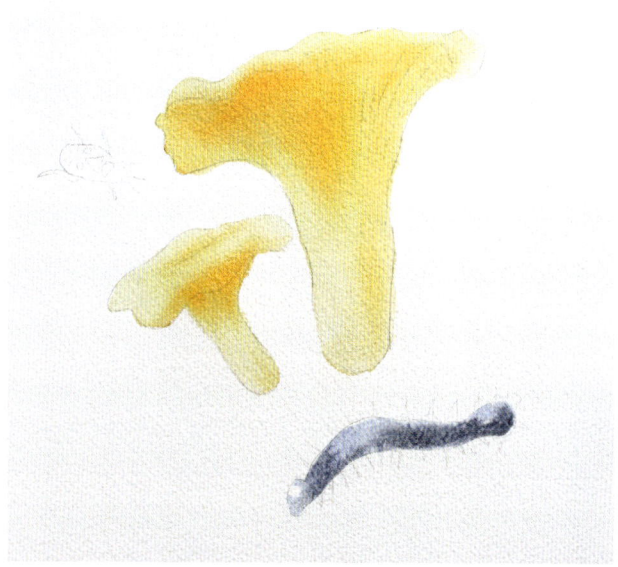

4. Remove excess color by lifting pigment while it's still wet or damp using a size 6 brush.

5. Apply Payne's Gray (tea consistency) using a size 3 brush. Then, use a thicker consistency of Payne's Gray (cream consistency) and apply it wet-on-wet in some areas of the caterpillar.

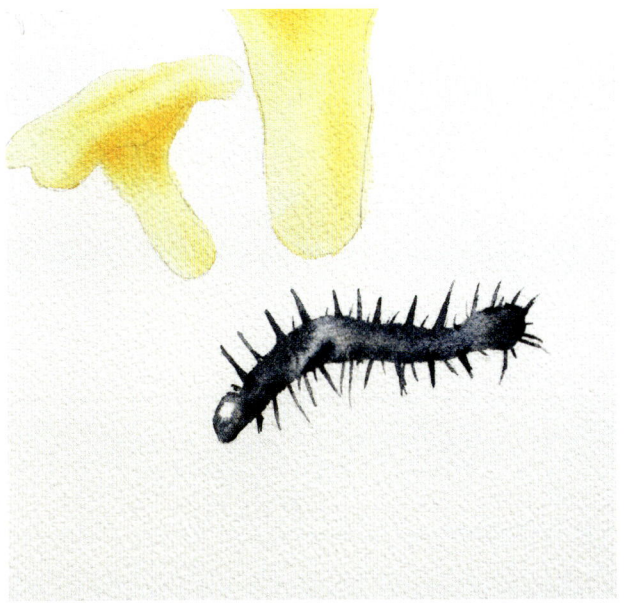

6. Apply a mix of Payne's Gray and Lamp Black wet-on-wet to the caterpillar and paint the spikes, dragging color out from the body to create neat, pointy ends, using a size 2/0 brush. Leave it to dry.

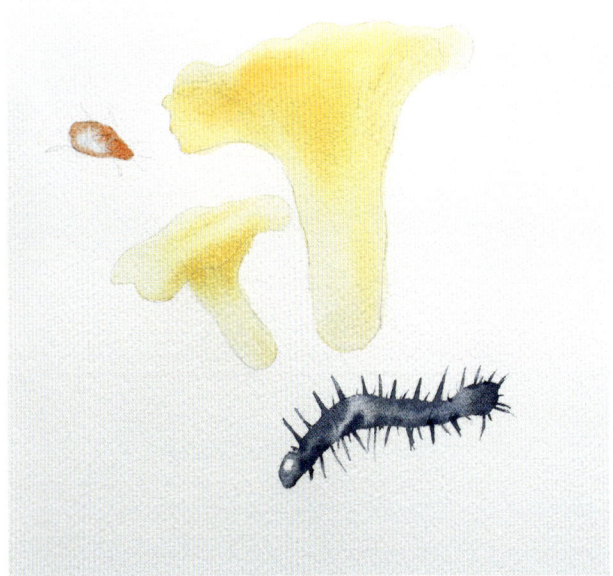

7. Paint the firebug with Ultramarine Blue (tea consistency) using a size 3 brush. Then, apply a mix of Cadmium Red Deep Hue and Cadmium Orange Hue wet-on-wet around the edge of the bug, leaving the center lighter, using a size 2/0 brush.

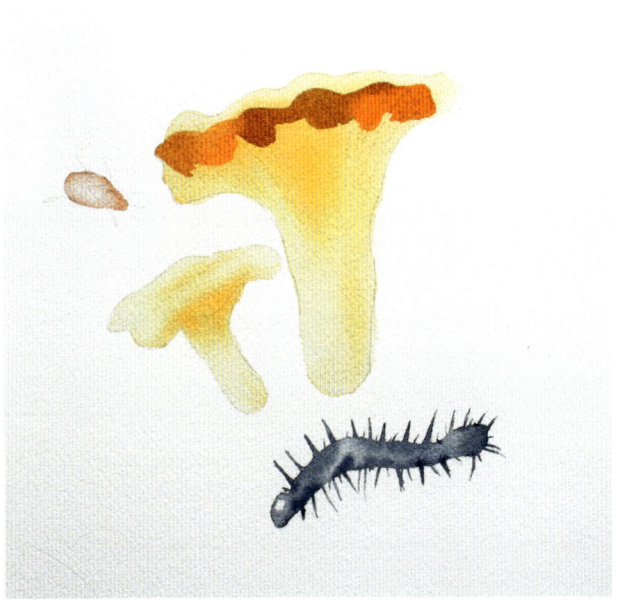

8. Prepare two mixes on the palette: one with Cadmium Orange Hue and Dioxazine Purple, and the other with just Cadmium Orange Hue. These complementary colors (orange and purple) will help create natural-looking shadows.

Paint the line under the cap of the mushroom with Cadmium Orange Hue (milk consistency) wet-on-dry using a size 6 brush. Then, wash your brush and apply the complementary mix of Cadmium Orange Hue and Dioxazine Purple wet-on-wet.

Wash your brush again and use it to soften the edges, reapplying some wetness to the rest of the mushroom.

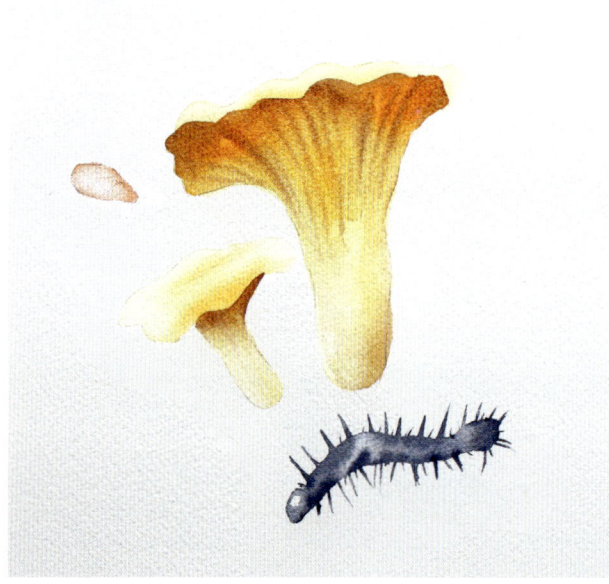

9. For the smaller mushroom, apply the Cadmium Orange Hue and Dioxazine Purple mix to paint lines on the larger mushroom, making them blurry, using a size 2/0 brush.

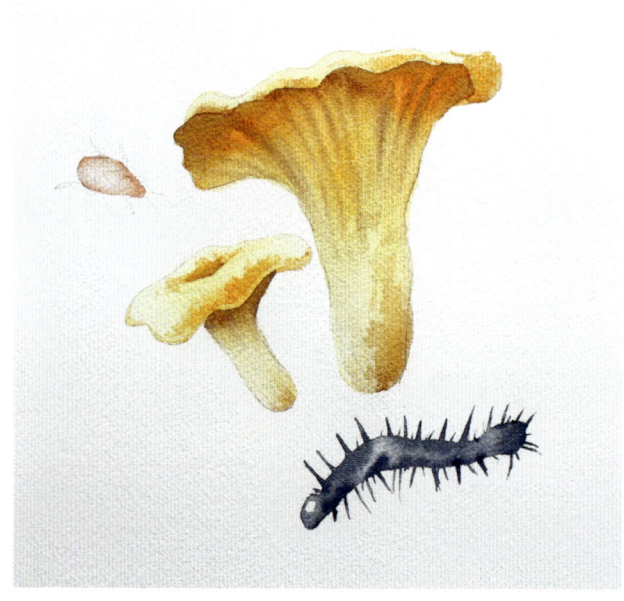

10. Apply Cadmium Orange wet-on-dry to add darker values to the caps of the mushrooms using a size 3 brush.

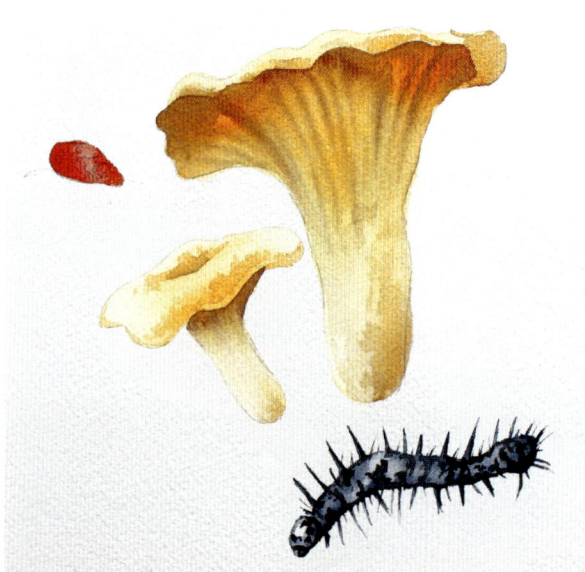

11. Dilute the Cadmium Orange Hue and Dioxazine Purple mix and apply it to create texture and volume on the stalks.

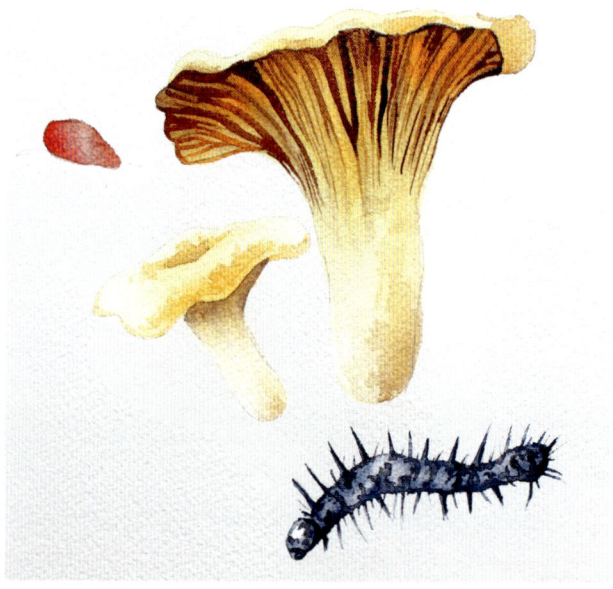

12. Apply Lamp Black wet-on-dry to the caterpillar to add details using a size 2/0 brush. Reapply Cadmium Red Deep Hue to make the bug appear brighter.

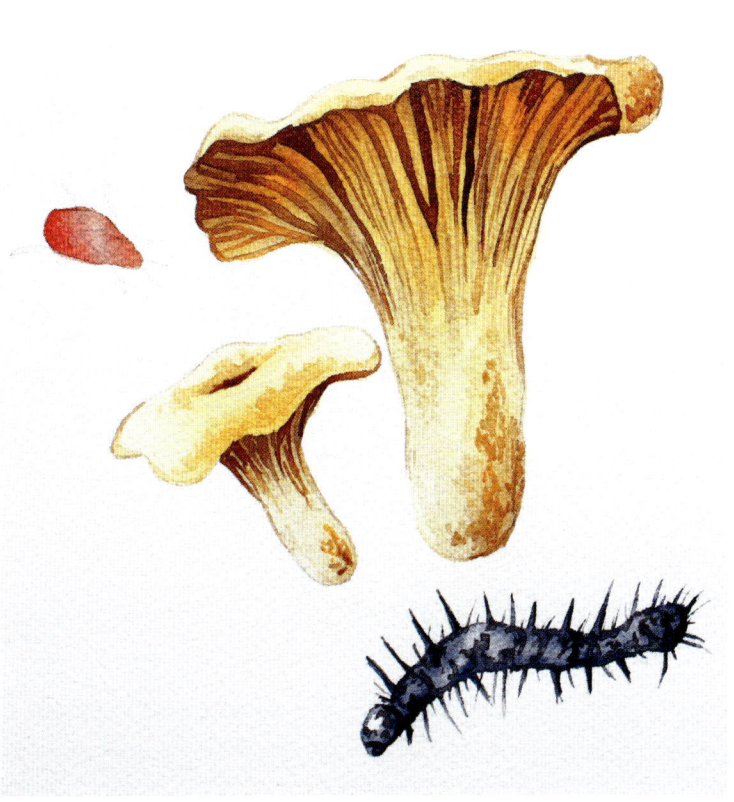

13. Mix Cadmium Orange Hue and Dioxazine Purple (cream consistency) and paint lines using size 3 and 2/0 brushes. Combine different intensities—some lines will be much darker, while others can be lightened on the palette by adding water.

For the smaller mushroom, apply Cadmium Orange wet-on-dry in the form of dots to the shadow areas using a size 3 brush. Mix Cadmium Orange Hue with a little Dioxazine Purple and paint a few different colored dots.

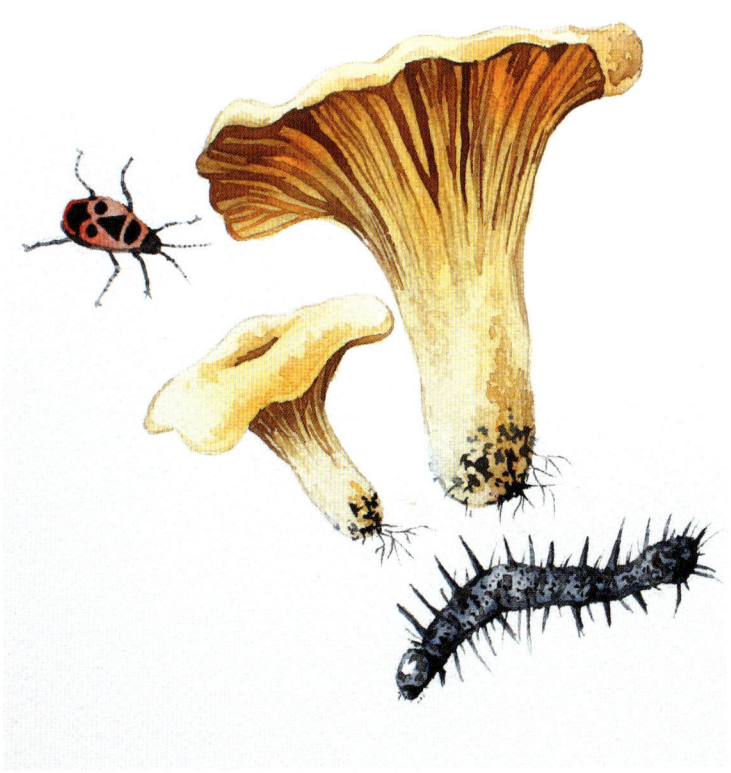

14. Apply Lamp Black wet-on-dry to add black details to the bug, paint black dots on the caterpillar, and paint bits of soil and roots on both mushrooms using a size 2/0 brush.

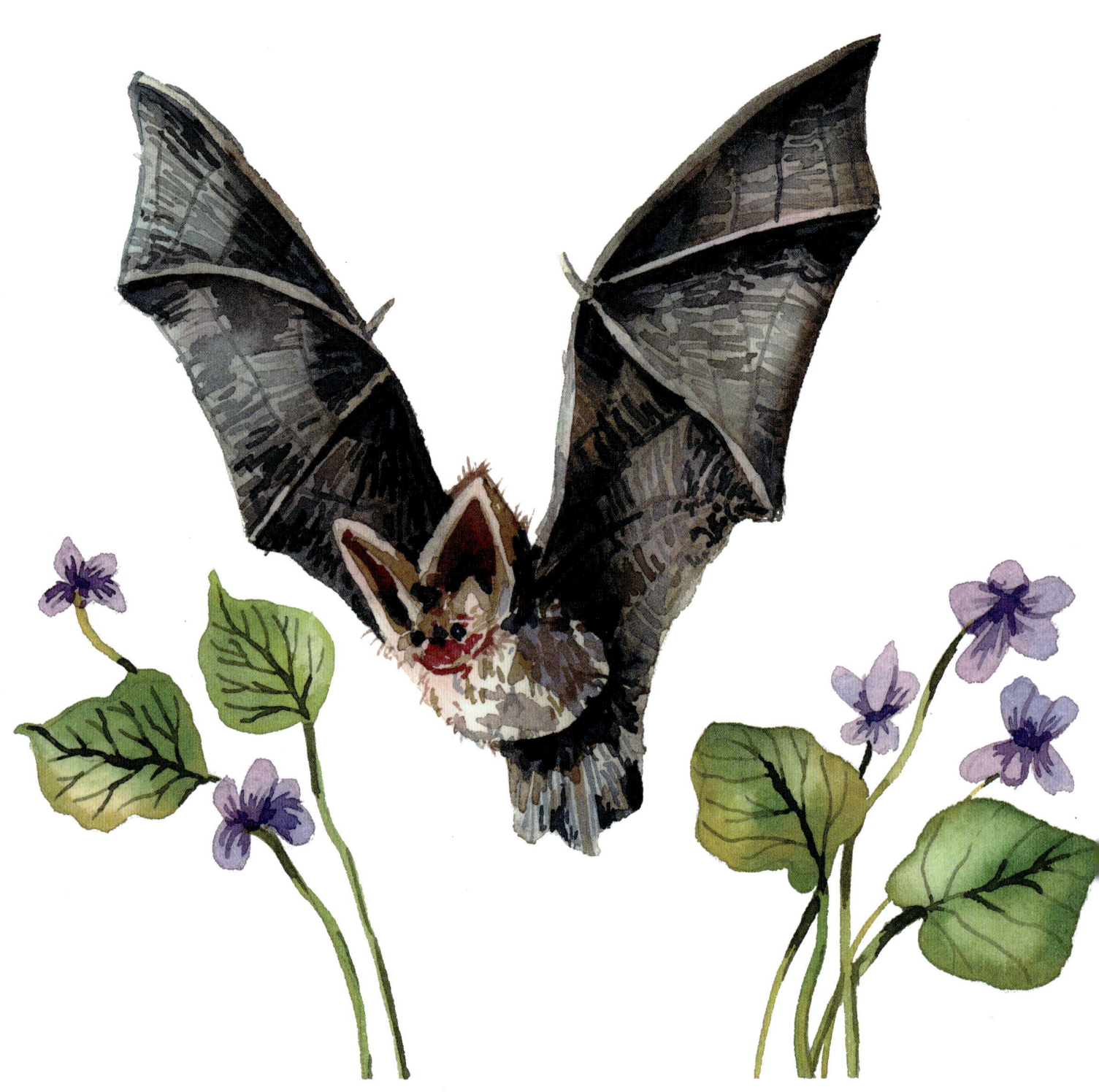

Horseshoe Bat with Sweet Violets

Spring is one of my favorite seasons, especially when bats emerge from hibernation and take to the warm evenings filled with the scent of the first flowers.

Colors

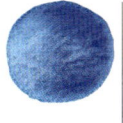 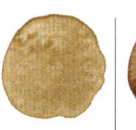 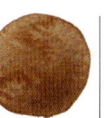 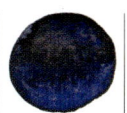 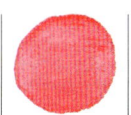  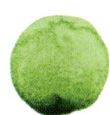 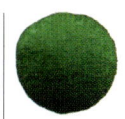  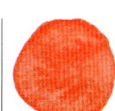

PRUSSIAN BLUE	RAW UMBER	BURNT UMBER	PAYNE'S GRAY	PERMANENT ROSE	CADMIUM YELLOW HUE	SAP GREEN	HOOKER'S GREEN	COBALT BLUE	CADMIUM RED DEEP HUE

Brushes

Size 6 round brush

Size 3 round brush

Size 2/0 round brush for details

Paper

300 gsm cold-pressed

1. Apply an even thick layer of water to the whole area of the bat using a size 6 brush. Avoid making puddles and make sure your brush will cover all the edges of the animal with water. This is essential to a successful wet-on-wet technique.

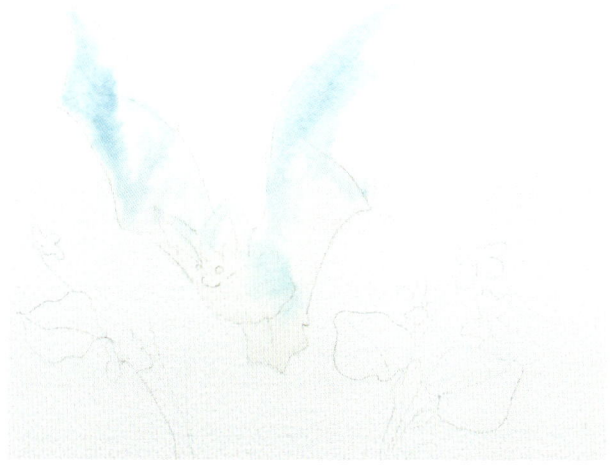

2. Apply Prussian Blue (tea consistency) wet-on-wet using a size 3–6 brush.

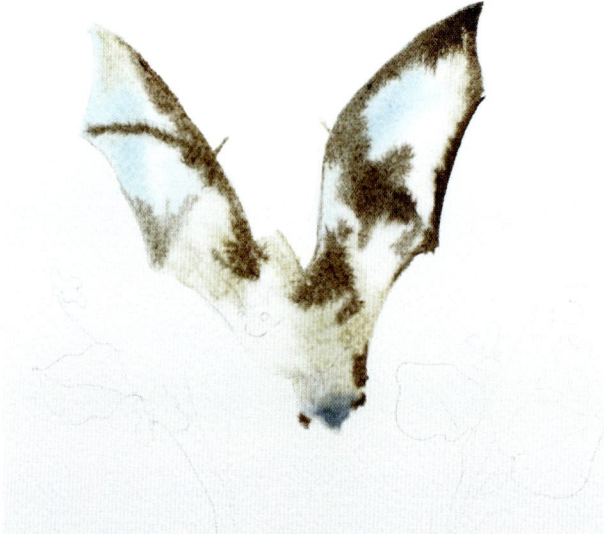

3. Apply Raw Umber (tea consistency), then Burnt Umber, then Payne's Gray (on the tail) wet-on-wet.

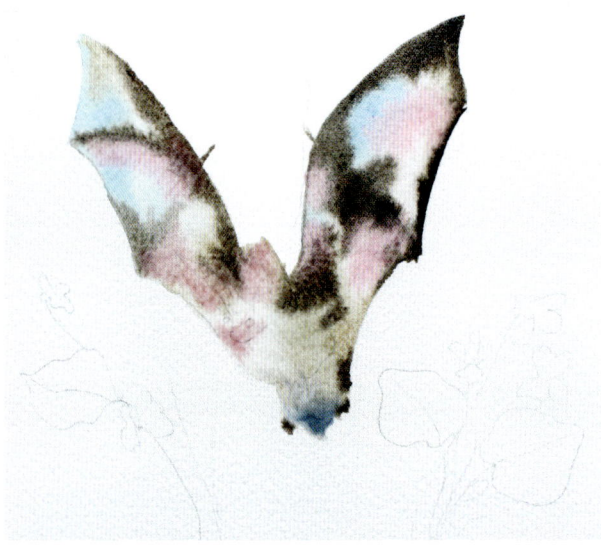

4. Apply Permanent Rose. If your mixes traveled too far, use a size 6 brush to lift some colors and create very light areas on the wings. Leave it to dry.

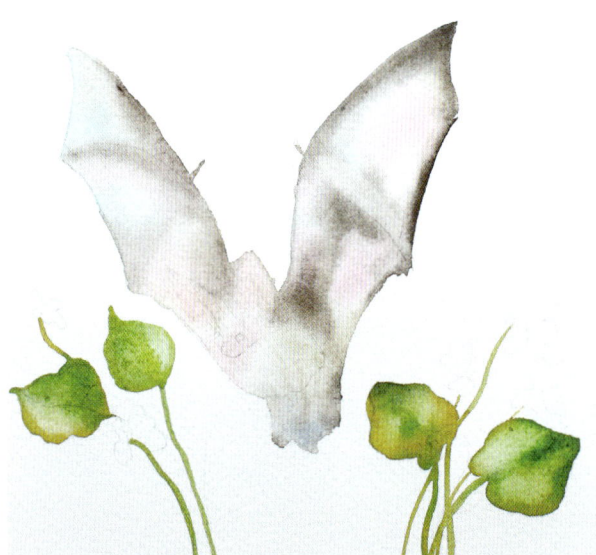

5. Apply a mix of Cadmium Yellow Hue and Sap Green wet-on-dry to the leaves using a size 3 brush, giving some leaves more of the Cadmium Yellow Hue. Apply Hooker's Green wet-on-wet on some areas of the leaves. Paint the stems using Cadmium Yellow Hue with a little bit of Sap Green. Lift some areas with a brush, collecting paint from highlight areas. Leave it to dry.

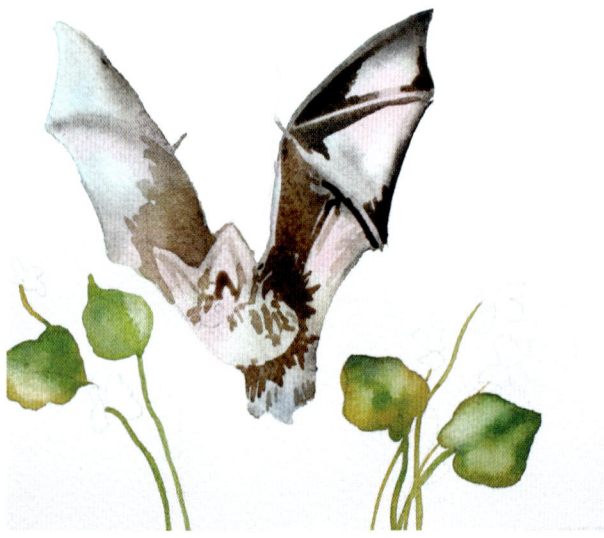

6. Apply Raw Umber wet-on-dry to paint the fur using a size 3 brush.

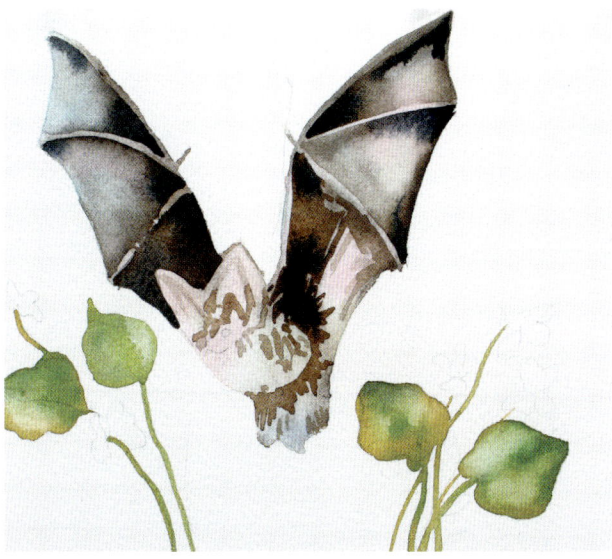

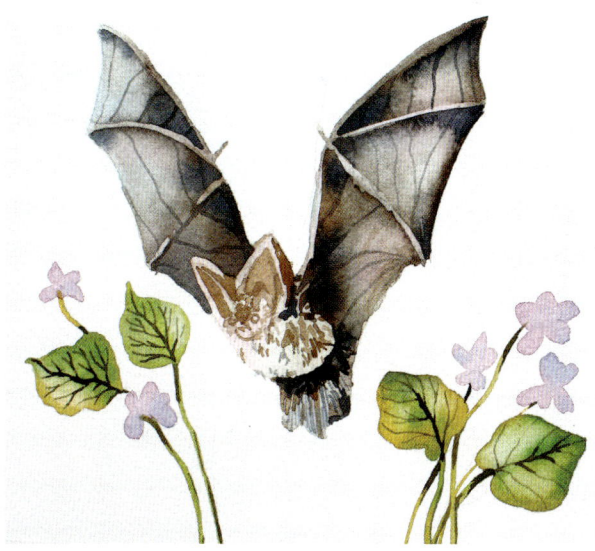

7. Use your brush to wet segments on the wing with water. Then add a mix of Payne's Gray and Burnt Umber (cream consistency) to the corners wet-on-wet using a size 2/0 brush.

8. Use Payne's Gray on its own for the corners.

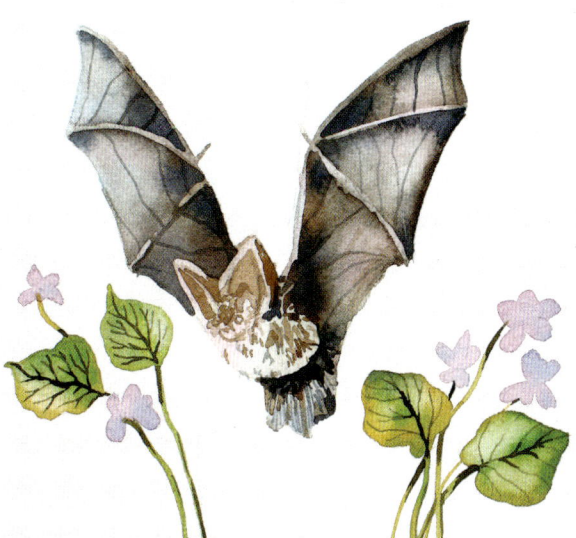

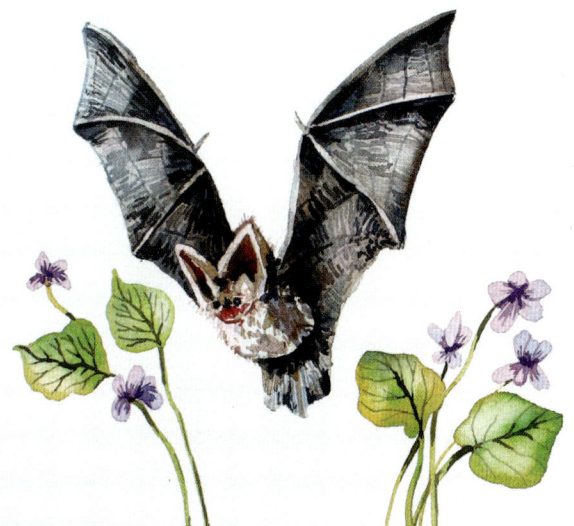

9. Paint the flowers using a mix of Cobalt Blue and Permanent Rose (tea consistency) wet-on-dry using a size 3 brush. Add more Cobalt Blue wet-on-wet. Mix Hooker's Green and Burnt Umber and paint veins on the leaves and shadows on the stems wet-on-dry using a size 3 brush. Add almost transparent lines on the wings with Payne's Gray. Use Raw Umber to paint inside the ears and on the face and body of the bat wet-on-dry using a size 3 brush.

10. Apply more of the Cobalt Blue and Permanent Rose mix to paint darker values on the flower using a size 2/0 brush. Combine Payne's Gray and Burnt Umber to paint more details on the wings. Use a mix of Burnt Umber and Cadmium Red Deep Hue to darken inside the ears and to add more details to the face. Using Payne's Gray on its own, paint the darkest values: the eyes, shadows, and inside the ears.

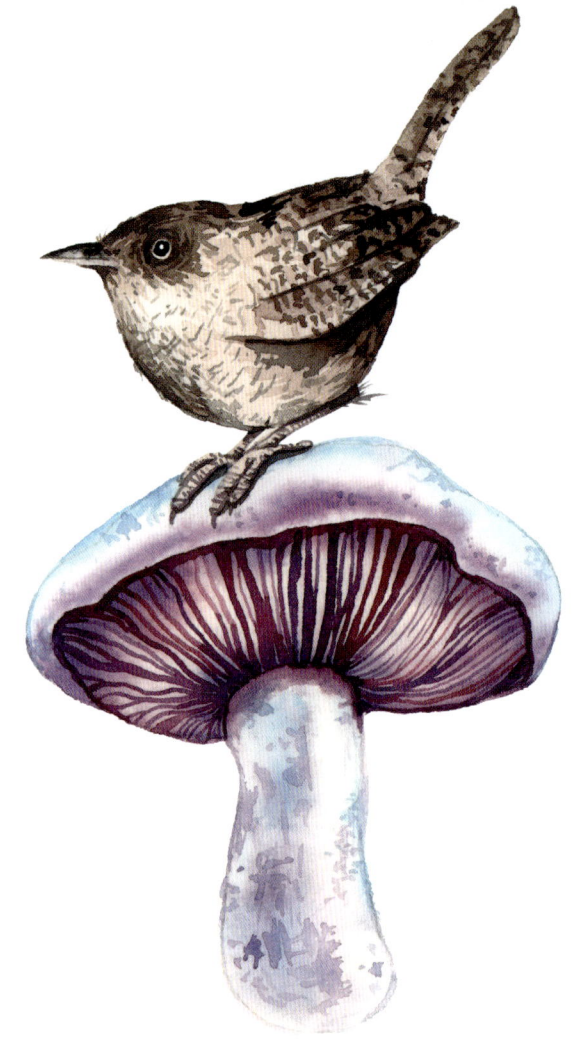

Wren on a Purple Laccaria Mushroom

Paint a lovely purple mushroom with a sweet songbird perched on top, combining techniques and building values with each step to create a detailed, colorful painting.

Colors

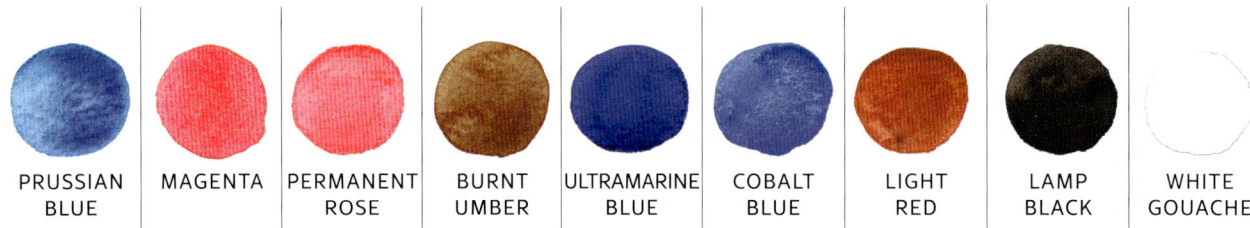

| PRUSSIAN BLUE | MAGENTA | PERMANENT ROSE | BURNT UMBER | ULTRAMARINE BLUE | COBALT BLUE | LIGHT RED | LAMP BLACK | WHITE GOUACHE |

Brushes

Size 6 round brush

Size 3 round brush

Size 2/0 round brush for details

Paper

300 gsm cold-pressed

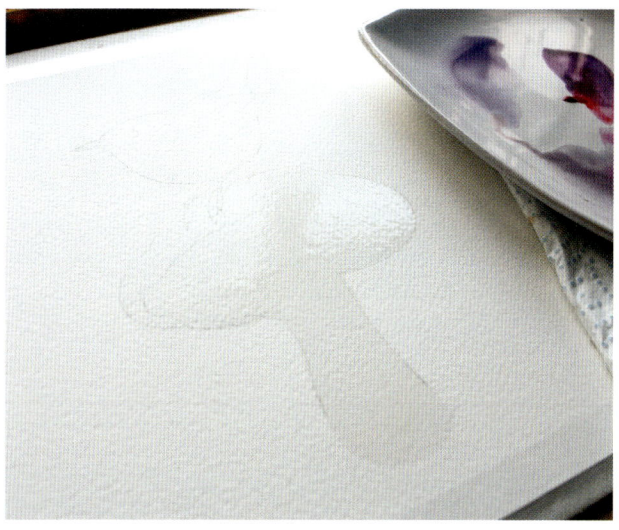

1. Apply a thin layer of water to the entire mushroom with a size 6 brush.

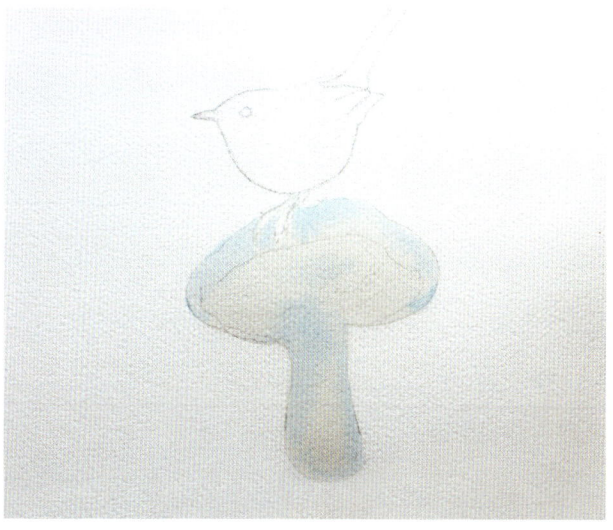

2. Apply Prussian Blue (tea consistency) wet-on-wet using a size 3 brush.

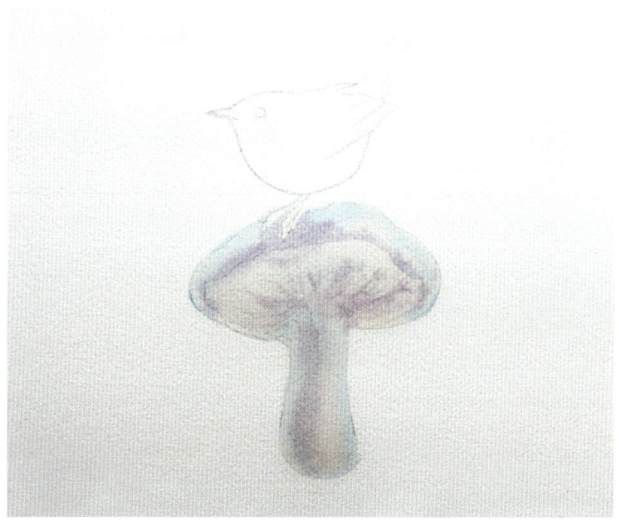

3. Apply a mix of Prussian Blue and Magenta (or Permanent Rose) (tea consistency) wet-on-wet using a size 2/0 brush.

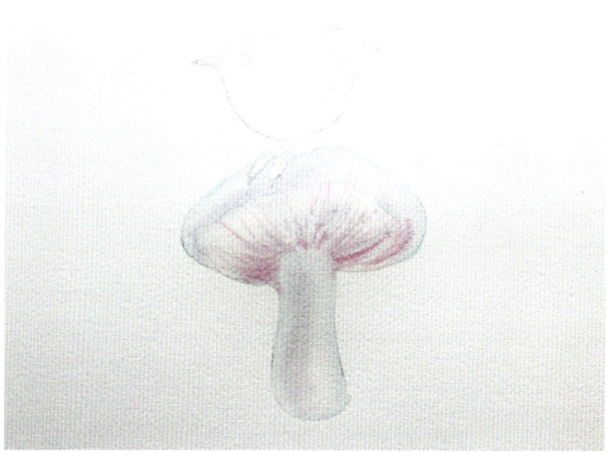

4. Apply Permanent Rose to damp paper using a size 2/0 brush.

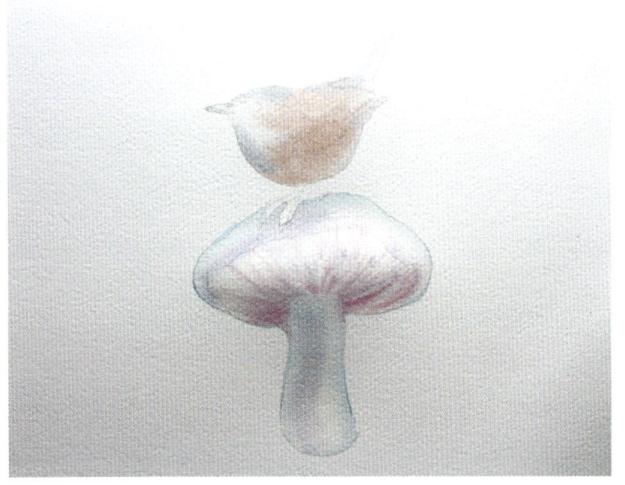

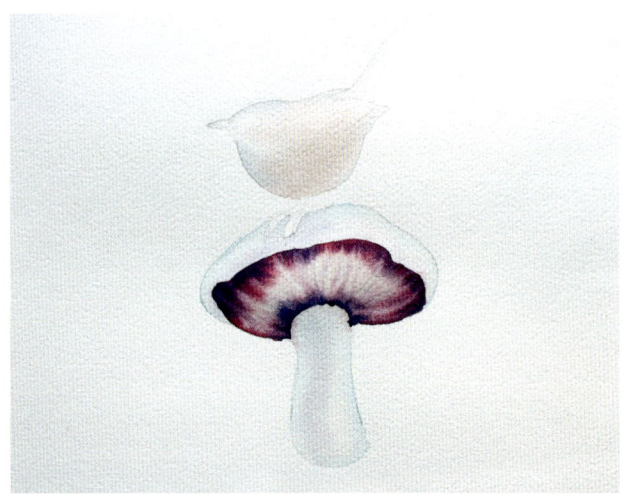

5. Wet the entire bird area with a size 6 brush. Mix Permanent Rose and Burnt Umber (tea consistency) and apply to the bird. Also, apply Ultramarine Blue (tea consistency) wet-on-wet on the bird. Let it dry.

6. Wet the area under the mushroom's cap. Apply a mix of Permanent Rose and Magenta (milk consistency) wet-on-wet under the cap and where the cap meets the stalk using a size 2/0 brush.

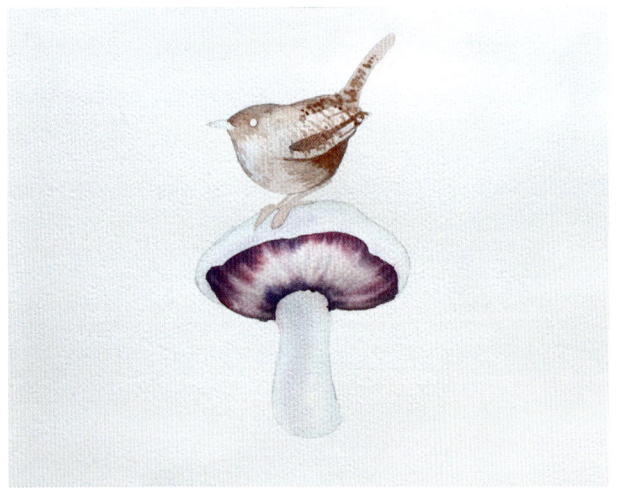

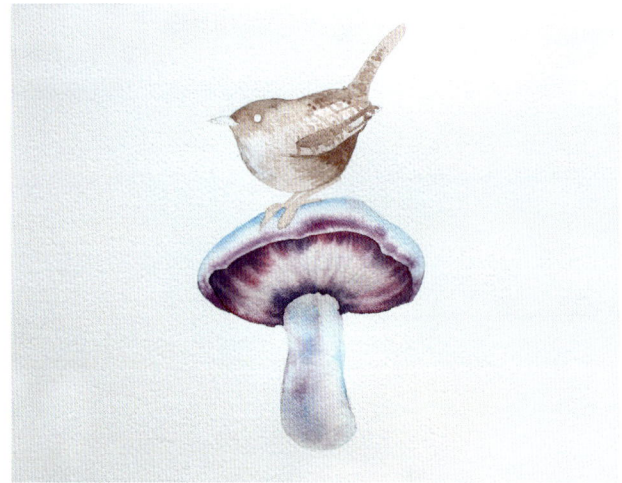

7. Apply a mix of Magenta and Cobalt Blue (cream consistency) to the bottom of the cap, leaving a clean, light area in the center. Use a size 3 brush to lift pigment and create lines on the mushroom. The ideal time for lifting is when it's damp, as this gives you more control.

Apply a mix of Burnt Umber and Light Red (tea consistency) wet-on-dry to define shadows and values on the bird.

8. Activate the mushroom stalk with water. Apply a mix of Permanent Rose and Prussian Blue (tea consistency) wet-on-wet in the middle of the stalk, adding a few lines. Wash your brush and add Prussian Blue (tea consistency) in small patches using a size 3 brush.

Next, apply water to the top of the mushroom using a size 6 brush. Apply a mix of Permanent Rose and Cobalt Blue (cream consistency) to paint shadows using a size 2/0 brush, leaving a small gap at the edge. You can drop a few saturated drops of Permanent Rose to brighten areas. Wash your brush and use Prussian Blue to add color to the mushroom top while it's still wet.

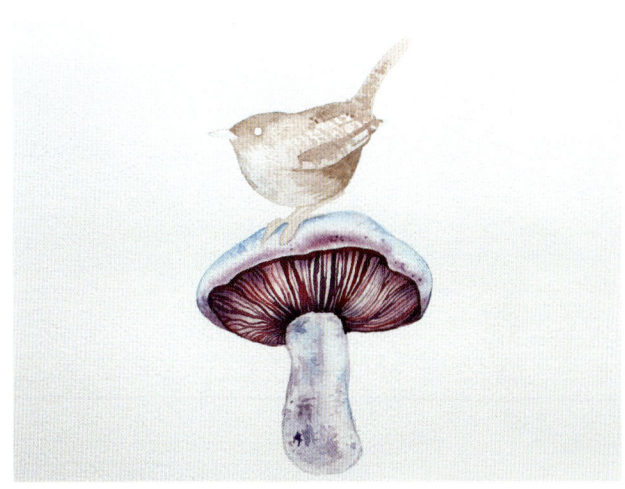

9. Apply a mix of Magenta and Prussian Blue (cream consistency) wet-on-dry to paint lines under the mushroom cap using a size 2/0 brush.

   Apply a mix of Cobalt Blue and Permanent Rose (tea consistency) to the stalk for texture and detail. Then, use a mix of Prussian Blue and Cobalt Blue (tea consistency)—almost transparent—to add more details. Use the same colors to add dots and details to the cap, making them darker where the Prussian Blue is and more purple over the shadow areas on the cap.

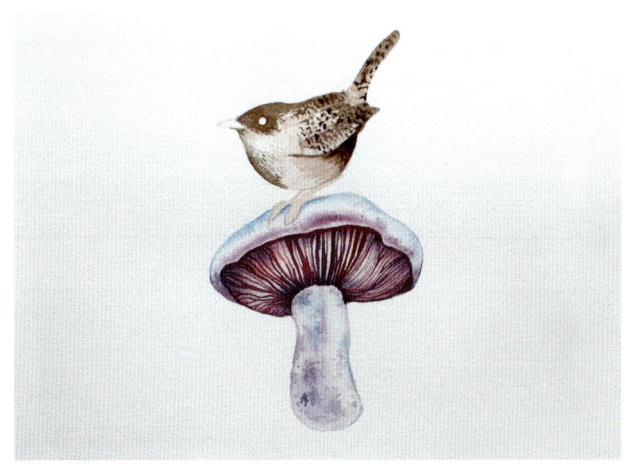

10. Mix three puddles (milk consistency) separately on your palette: Burnt Umber, Permanent Rose, and Lamp Black. Start by applying the Burnt Umber on top of the bird, following the pattern on the wren's back. Use a size 2/0 brush to make small brown dots.

    Apply color around the face and under the belly. Use a mix of Burnt Umber and Permanent Rose to create a darker shadow on the right side.

    Apply the same mix (tea consistency) to paint the bird's feet with a very watery layer using a size 3 brush. Let it dry.

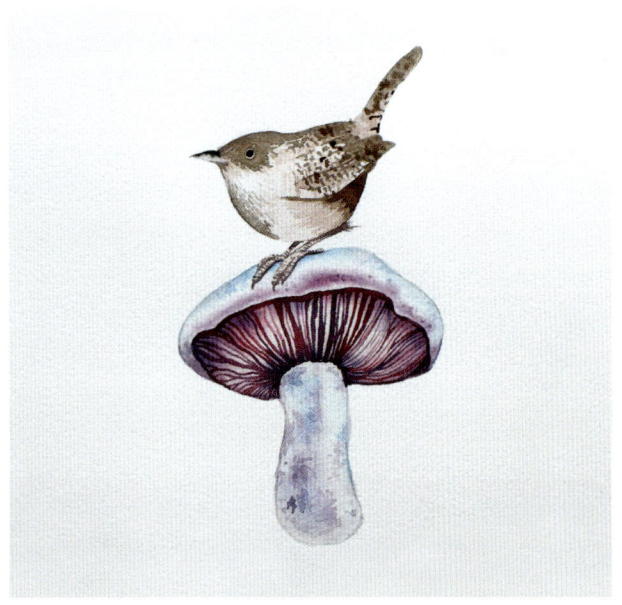

11. Use Lamp Black to color the eye.

Apply a mix of Permanent Rose and Burnt Umber (tea consistency) using a size 2/0 brush. Wash your brush, then use Lamp Black to lightly touch the top of the beak.

Apply the Permanent Rose and Burnt Umber mix wet-on-dry to paint the details on the bird's feet using a size 2/0 brush.

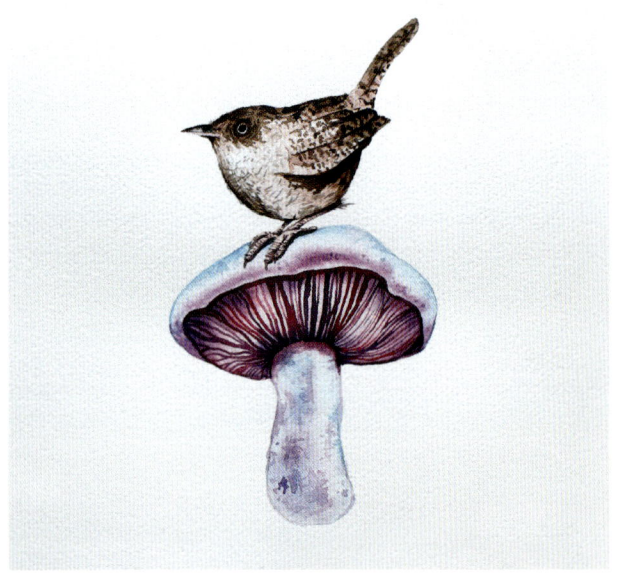

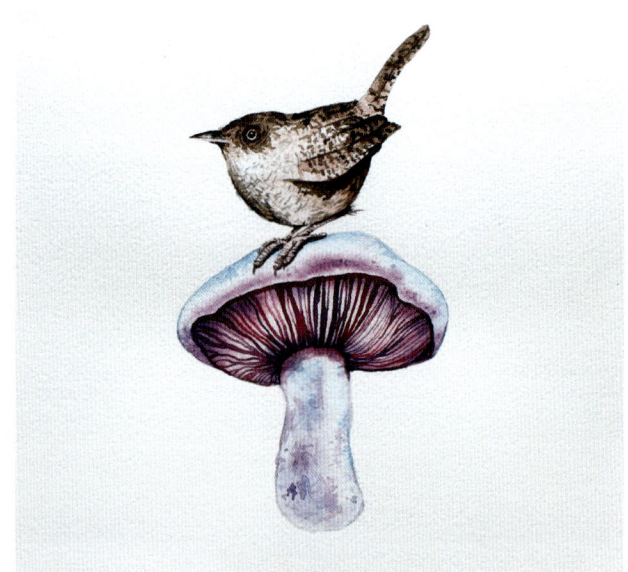

12. Apply a mix of Burnt Umber and Lamp Black (milk-to-cream consistency) for the darkest values on the bird using a size 2/0 brush.

13. Finally, use white gouache and a size 2/0 brush to add a white circle in the middle of the eye.

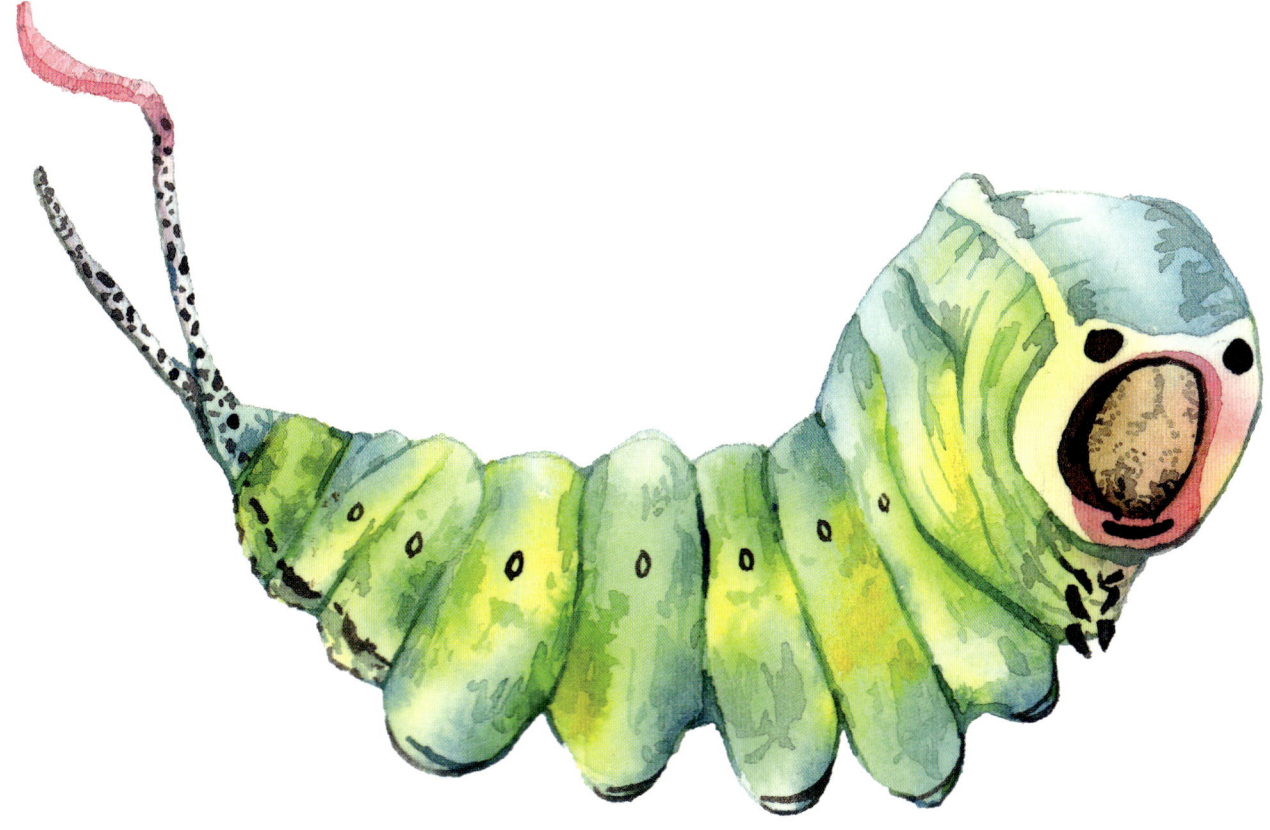

Puss Moth Caterpillar

Learn to paint the puss moth caterpillar, focusing on using a small brush for fine details and gradually adding funky, vibrant colors for a unique, eye-catching result.

Colors

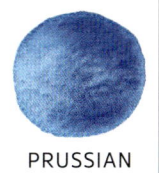

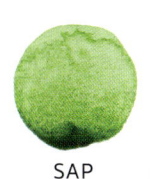

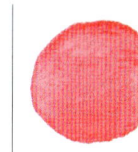

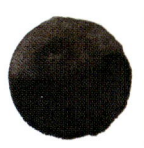

| PRUSSIAN BLUE | SAP GREEN | LEMON YELLOW | YELLOW OCHRE | PERMANENT ROSE | CADMIUM YELLOW HUE | LAMP BLACK | BURNT UMBER |

Brushes

Size 6 round brush

Size 3 round brush

Size 2/0 round brush for details

Paper

300 gsm cold-pressed

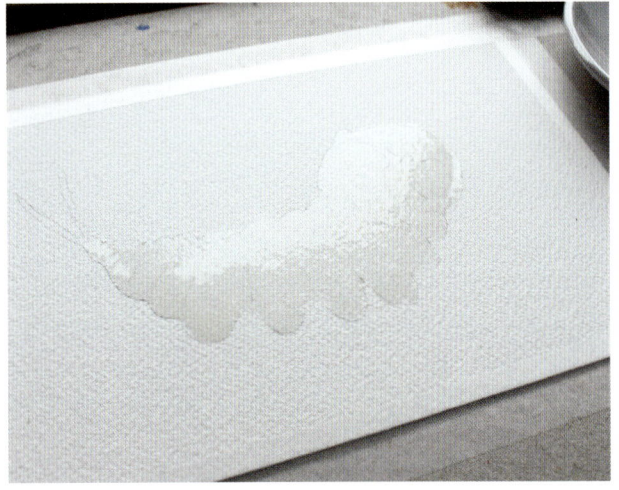

1. Apply an even layer of water to the whole body of the caterpillar using a size 3–6 brush. You can use a smaller brush to activate tricky areas with water (size 2/0).

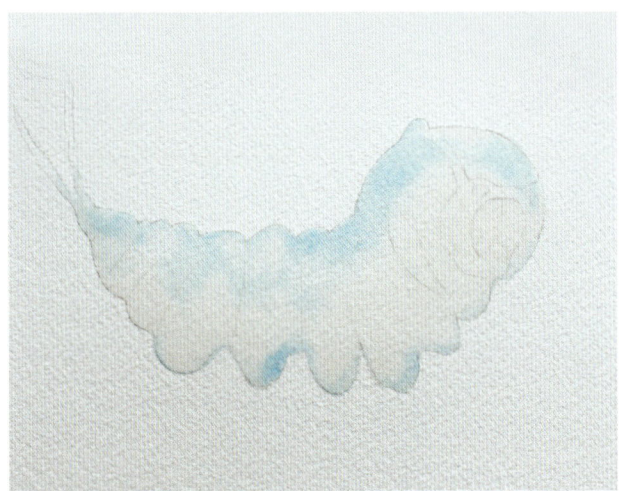

2. Once you have applied the water, use a size 6 brush to apply Prussian Blue (tea consistency) wet-on-wet, mainly on the edges.

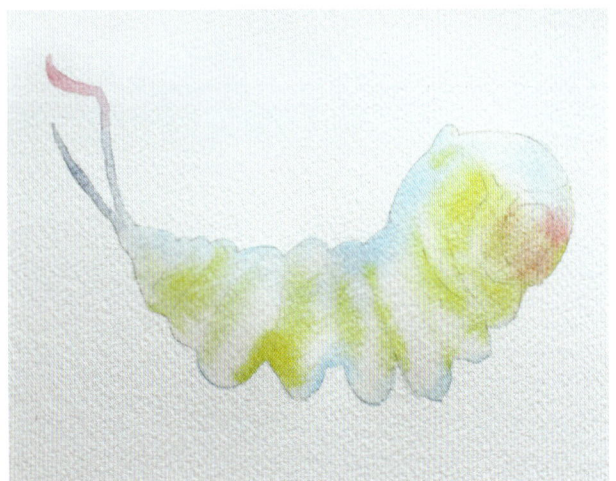

3. Then apply a mix of Sap Green and Lemon Yellow on the body and face and then Yellow Ochre (all tea consistency) with the same brush to add on the face. While the painting is still wet, add Permanent Rose (tea consistency) to the face and to the tail. Let it dry.

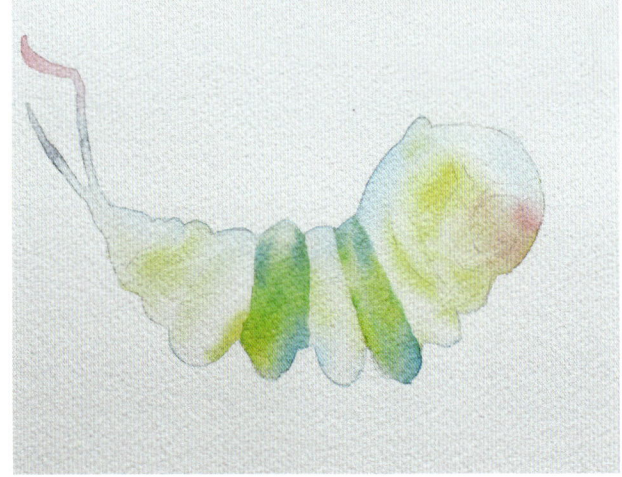

4. Start by activating with water separate parts on the caterpillar's body, making sure they are not situated next to each other to avoid merging. Now use a size 2/0 brush with Prussian Blue (milk consistency) and apply wet-on-wet on the parts where you applied water.

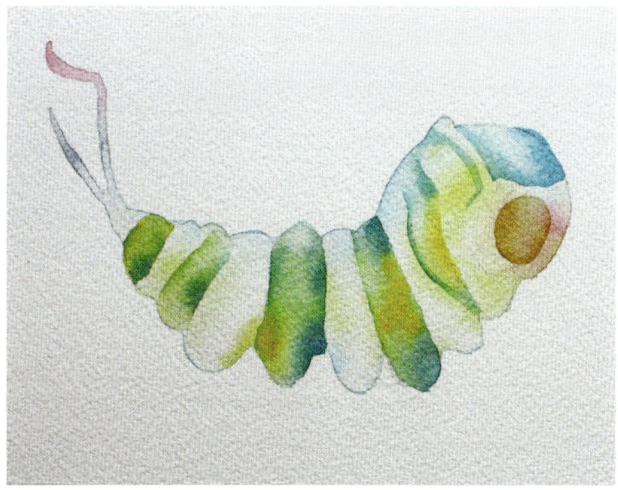

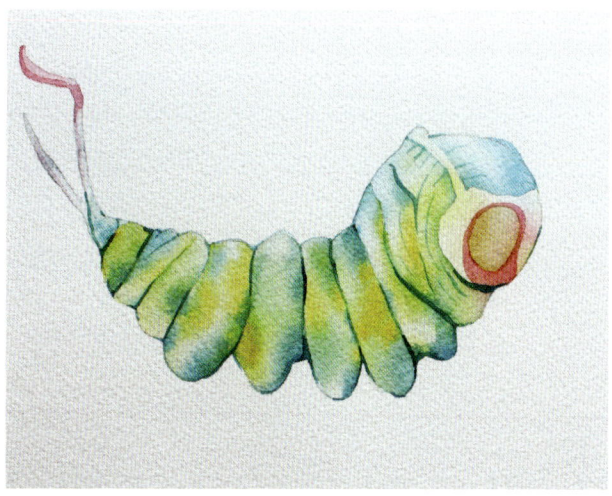

5. Apply another mix wet-on-wet: Sap Green and Lemon Yellow (milk consistency). Then, when they start to dry out, add Cadmium Yellow Hue (cream consistency). Allow to dry. Apply Yellow Ochre to paint the face of the caterpillar using a size 3 brush.

Also use more Prussian Blue wet-on-wet to saturate the head with color, leaving a highlight.

6. Activate the remaining segments on the caterpillar by applying an even layer of water using a size 3–6 brush. Apply Cadmium Yellow Hue (cream consistency) wet-on-wet using a size 2/0 brush. Then change the color to Prussian Blue and apply wet-on-wet mainly in the shadow areas between the segments. Lastly, mix Sap Green and Lemon Yellow to create an acidic green and apply wet-on-wet. Let it fully dry.

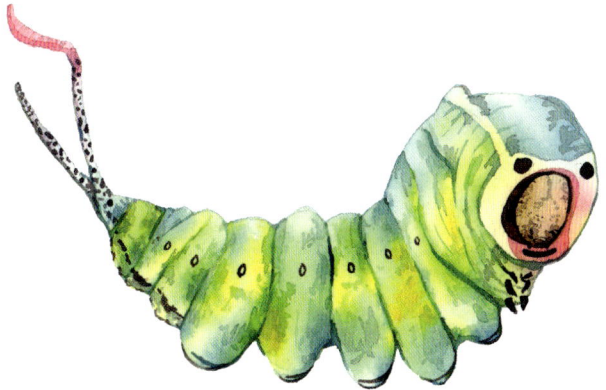

7. Apply a mix of Prussian Blue and Sap Green wet-on-dry to add shadows using a size 2/0 brush. Apply Permanent Rose wet-on-dry to paint a pink patch on the face and add shadows on the tail. Apply Lamp Black (cream consistency) wet-on-dry on the face, painting dots and a dark shadow. Using Burnt Umber, add dots to the face wet-on-dry using a size 2/0 brush. Apply Prussian Blue (tea consistency) wet-on-dry to add some wrinkles on the head.

Apply a mix of Burnt Umber and Lamp Black to paint dots across the body, leaving a space inside circles. Add dots to the tail and darken details at the front, adding the caterpillar's legs and a black line on the pink patch. Allow it to dry.

Apply a mix of Prussian Blue and Sap Green (tea consistency) wet-on-dry to add texture.

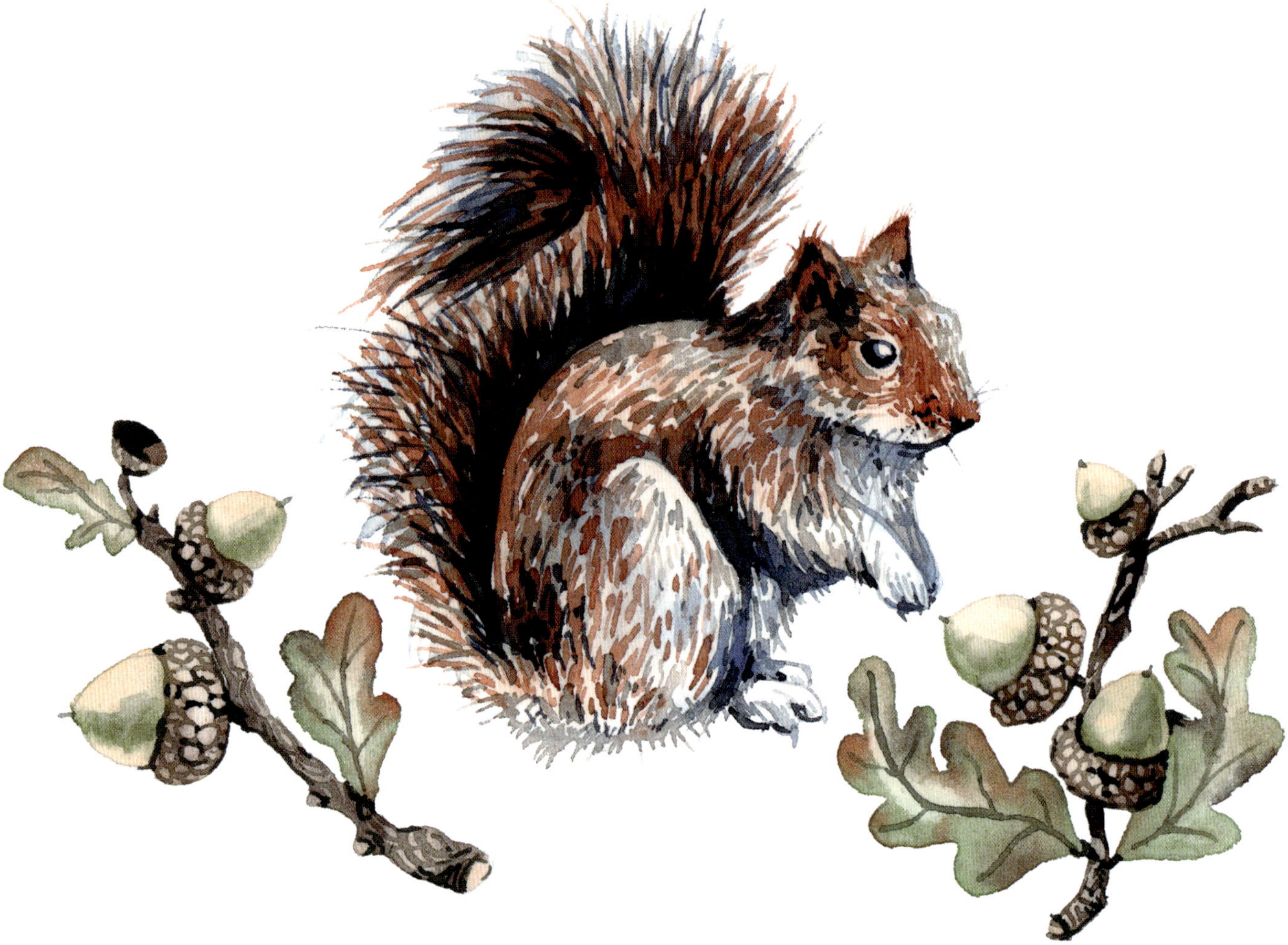

Red Squirrel with Acorns

A squirrel preparing for winter as the leaves turn brown and the acorns drop is a classic autumn scene. Practice creating animal shapes with brushstrokes that follow the natural curves of the landscape.

Colors

RAW UMBER

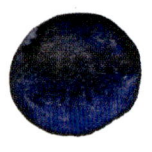
PAYNE'S GRAY

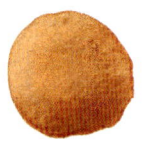
BURNT SIENNA

SAP GREEN

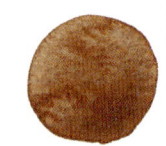
BURNT UMBER

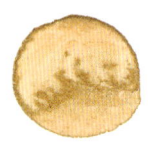
YELLOW OCHRE

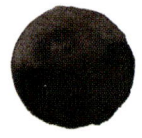
LAMP BLACK

Brushes

Size 6 round brush

Size 3 round brush

Size 2/0 round brush for details

Paper

300 gsm cold-pressed

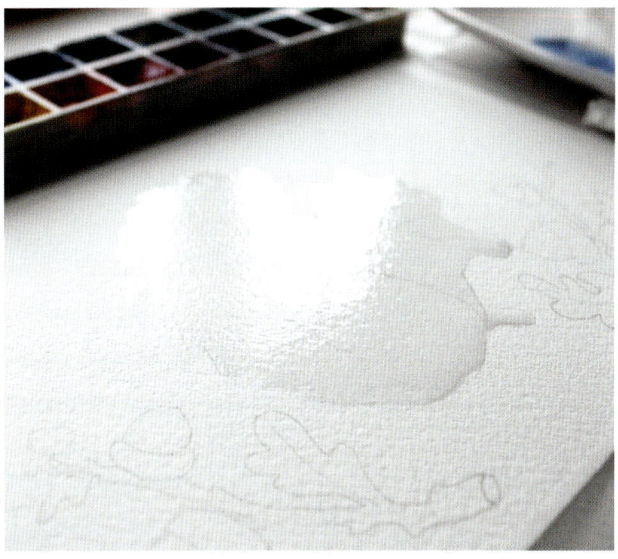

1. Apply an even, thick layer of water to the entire area of the squirrel using a size 6 brush.

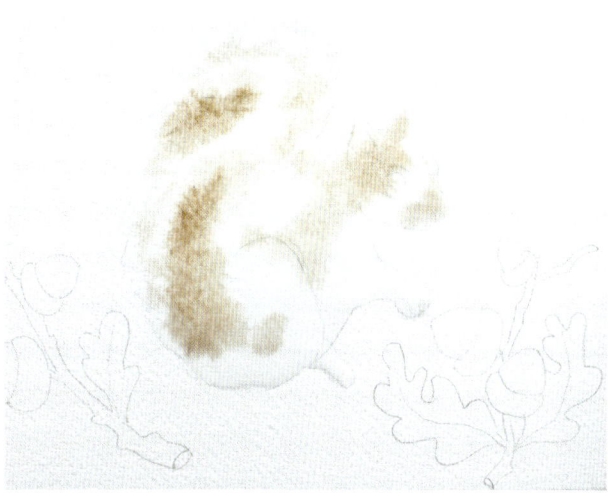

2. Apply Raw Umber (tea consistency) wet-on-wet using a size 6 brush.

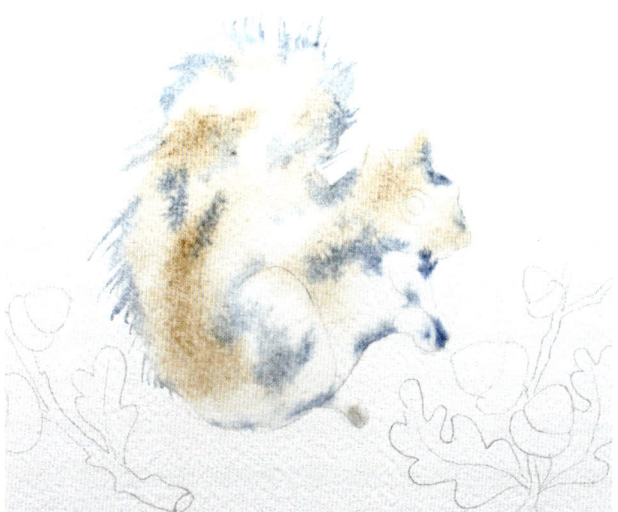

3. Now apply Payne's Gray wet-on-wet using a size 2/0 brush.

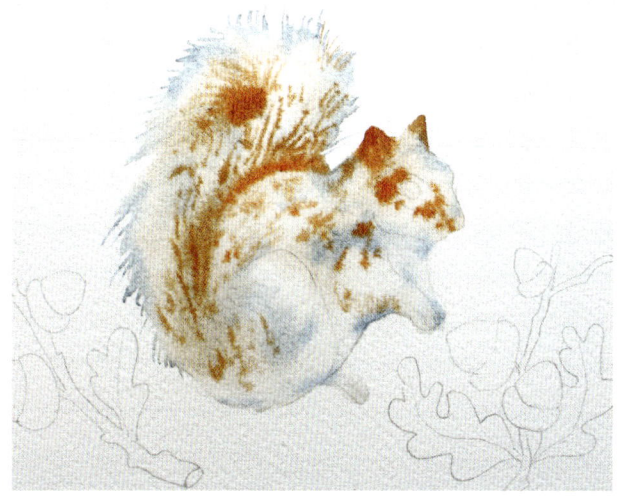

4. Mix Burnt Sienna (cream consistency) on your palette and apply wet-on-wet using a size 2/0 brush. Leave it to dry.

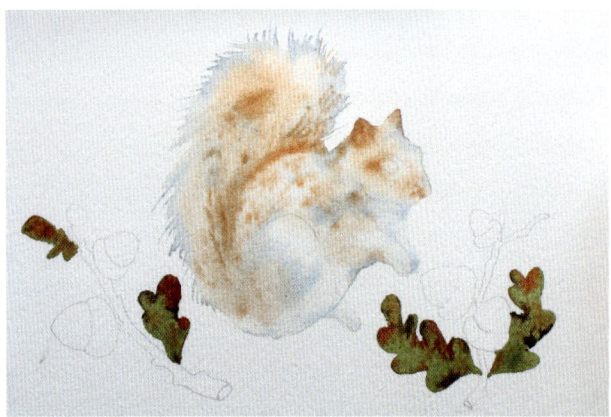

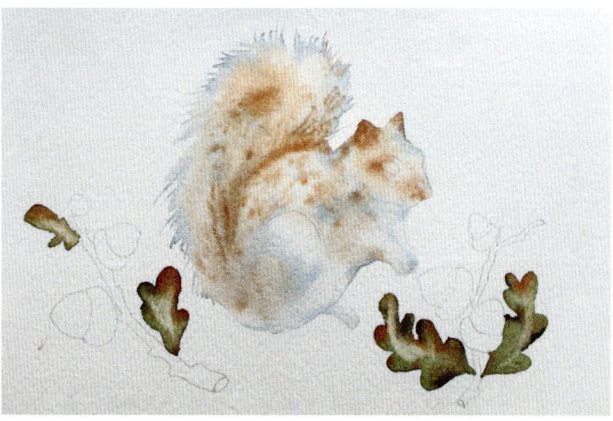

5. Mix Sap Green and Raw Umber (milk consistency) and paint all the leaves wet-on-dry using a size 3 brush.

Apply Burnt Sienna (cream consistency) wet-on-wet to some leaves.

Now apply Burnt Umber (cream consistency) wet-on-wet to the edges of the leaves. Leave it to dry.

6. While the leaves are still wet, dip a clean size 6 brush into water, then dry it against tissue paper so that it's damp.

Place the brush (with all the hairs) on the paper and, with light pressure, move it in the middle of the leaves to collect excess pigment, creating a lighter value in the center. Rinse and wipe your brush in between lifting the pigment to avoid bringing the paint back.

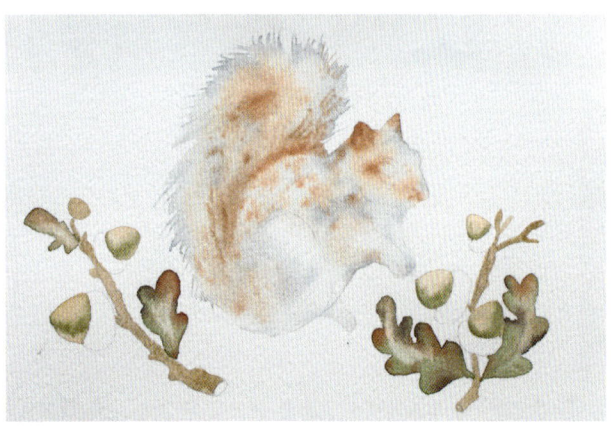

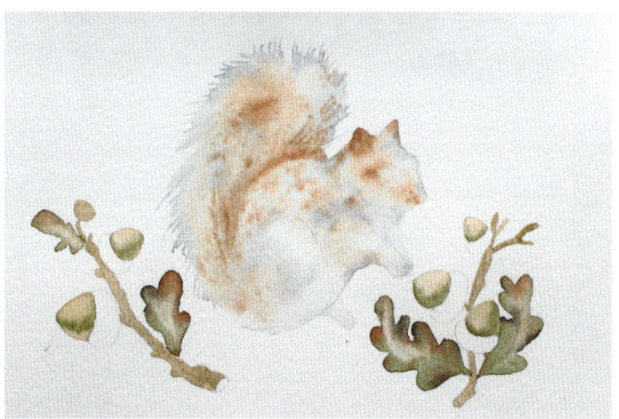

7. Apply Raw Umber and Yellow Ochre (tea consistency) to cover all the acorns, except for their caps, using a size 3 brush.

Apply Sap Green and Raw Umber (cream consistency) to the wet acorn, focusing on the middle to create a shadow, using a size 2/0 brush.

Control the spread with a size 3 brush, lifting pigment from the sides if the second mix travels too far. Leave it to dry.

8. Apply Payne's Gray (milk consistency) using a size 3 brush, then switch to a size 2/0 brush for smaller details. Work wet-on-dry to define the fur and add values to the squirrel.

Use Raw Umber to cover the branches with a light brown color. Apply Burnt Umber wet-on-wet to create darker values using a size 2/0 brush.

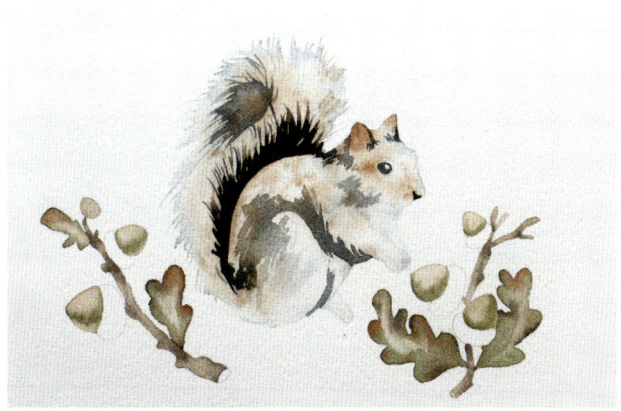

9. Now apply Lamp Black to the shadow area, separating the tail and the body, using a size 3 brush.

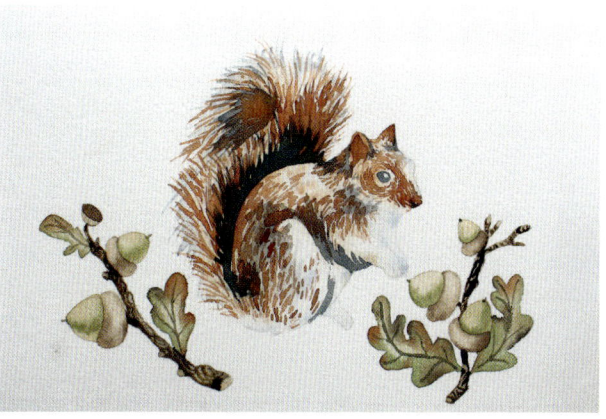

10. Apply Burnt Sienna wet-on-dry to refine the fur using a size 3 brush. Switch to a smaller brush to make tiny brushstrokes around the face.

Apply a mix of Burnt Umber and Raw Umber (milk) wet-on-dry for the bark.

Paint the caps of the acorns with Raw Umber wet-on-dry using a size 3 brush.

Apply Burnt Umber wet-on-wet to each acorn to create shadows. Apply a mix of Sap Green and Raw Umber wet-on-dry to paint veins on the leaves.

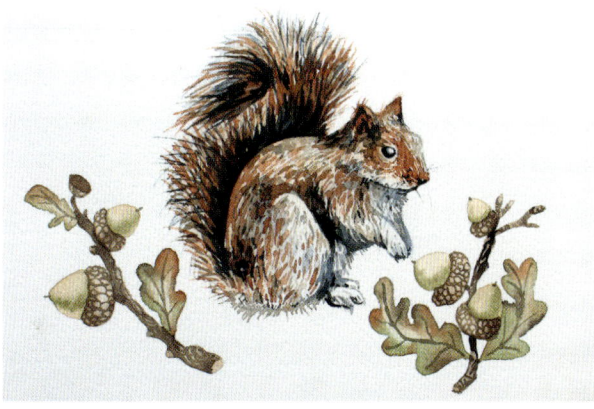

11. Use the Burnt Umber and Raw Umber mix to paint the details on the acorn caps with a size 2/0 brush. Use Raw Umber then Payne's Gray to paint lighter areas on the fur.

Apply Burnt Sienna using a size 2/0 brush. Paint a few hairs sticking out from the pencil lines to make them look more realistic. Use Payne's Gray to add more details.

Paint the eye with Lamp Black, leaving a little bit of Payne's Gray visible. Apply Lamp Black to add whiskers using a size 2/0 brush.

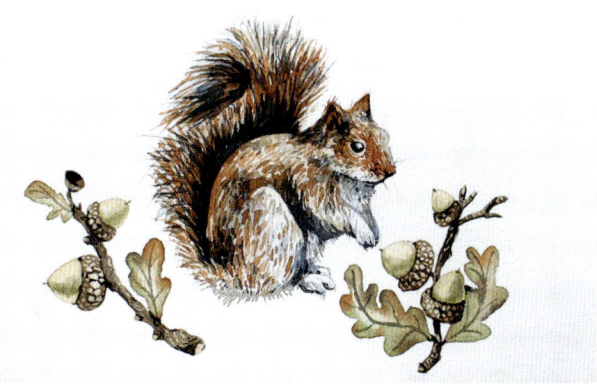

12. Mix Burnt Umber and Lamp Black to paint darker values on the branches and acorn caps.

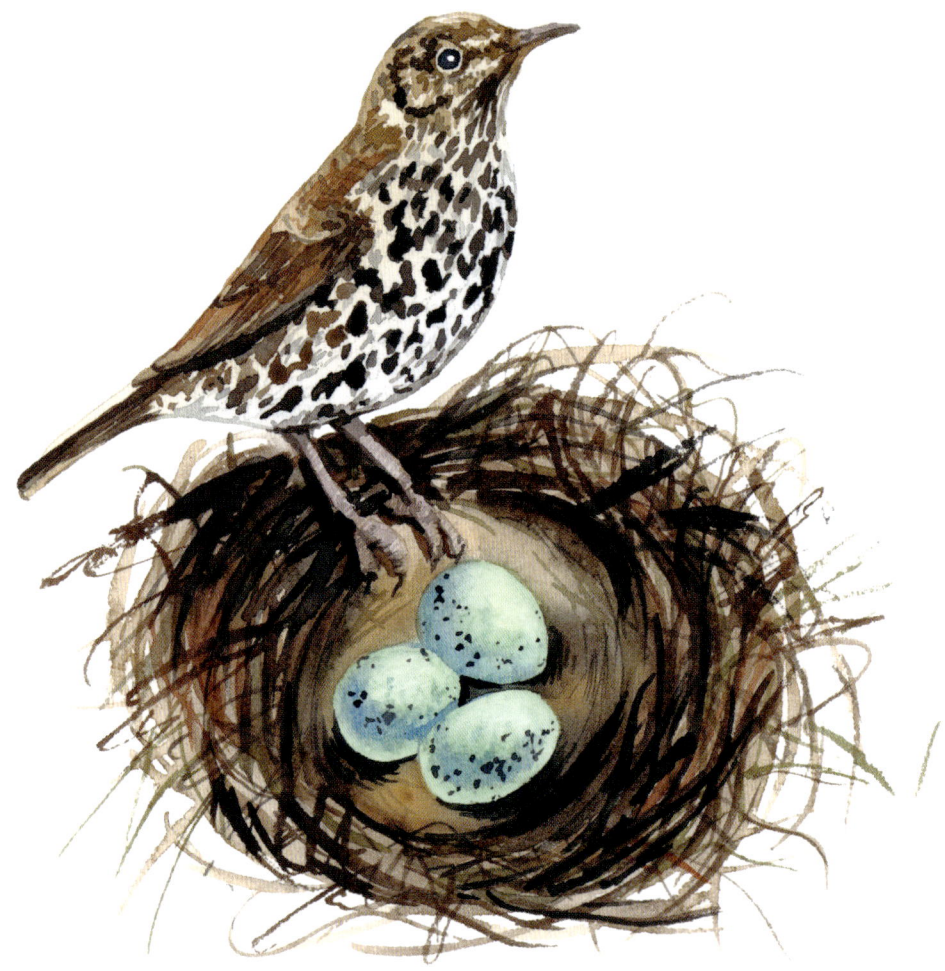

Thrush and Nest

Wouldn't you love to paint the iconic blue eggs laid by a thrush? In this lesson, you'll practice combining all the main watercolor techniques to create a beautiful springtime painting in your sketchbook.

Colors

  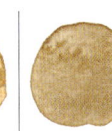 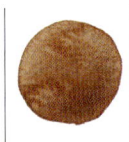 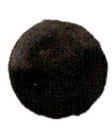 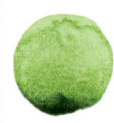 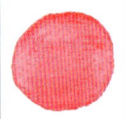  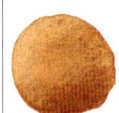 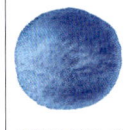

| ULTRAMA-RINE BLUE | YELLOW OCHRE | RAW UMBER | BURNT UMBER | LAMP BLACK | SAP GREEN | PERMANENT ROSE | LEMON YELLOW | BURNT SIENNA | PRUSSIAN BLUE |

Brushes

Size 8 round brush

Size 6 round brush

Size 3 round brush

Size 2/0 round brush for details

Old brush for applying masking fluid

Paper

300 gsm cold-pressed

Other

Masking fluid

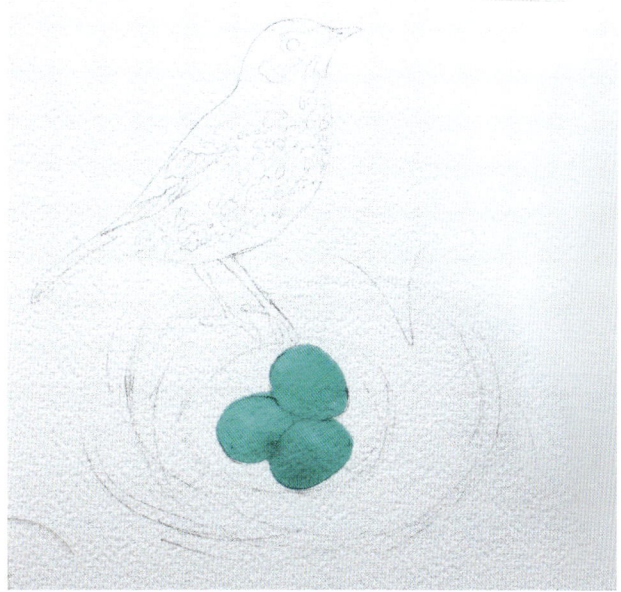

1. Apply masking fluid to block out all three eggs. Let it dry completely.

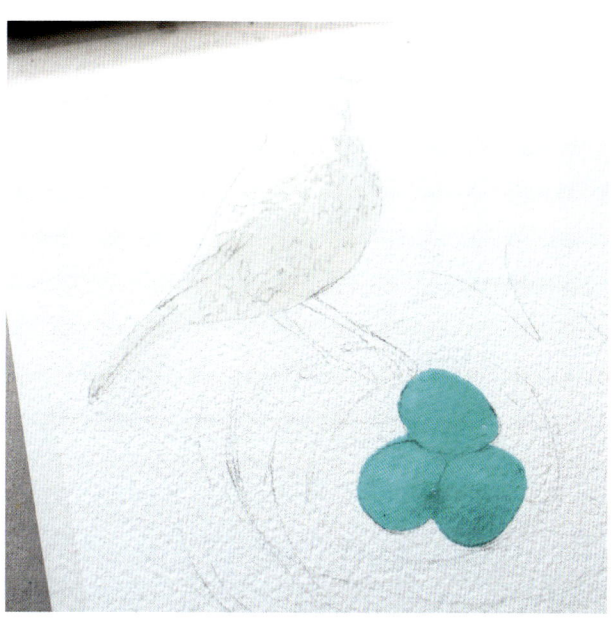

2. Apply an even layer of water to the entire area of the thrush using a size 3 brush.

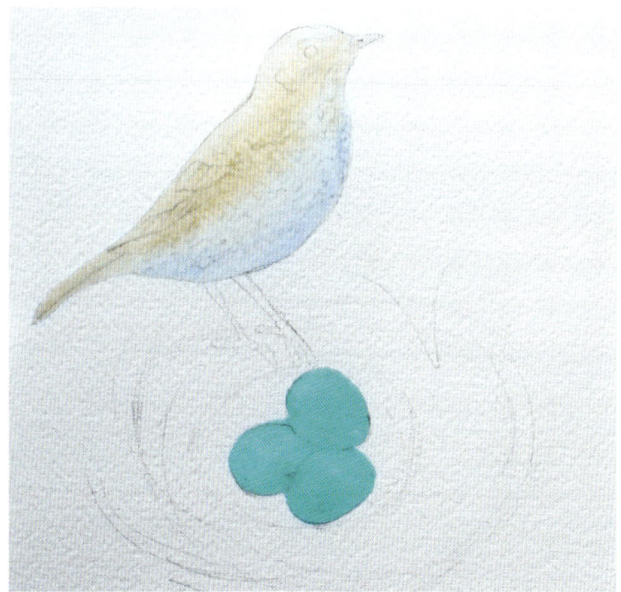

3. Apply Ultramarine Blue (tea consistency) wet-on-wet to the belly using a size 6 brush. Then, apply Yellow Ochre (tea consistency) to the back of the bird.

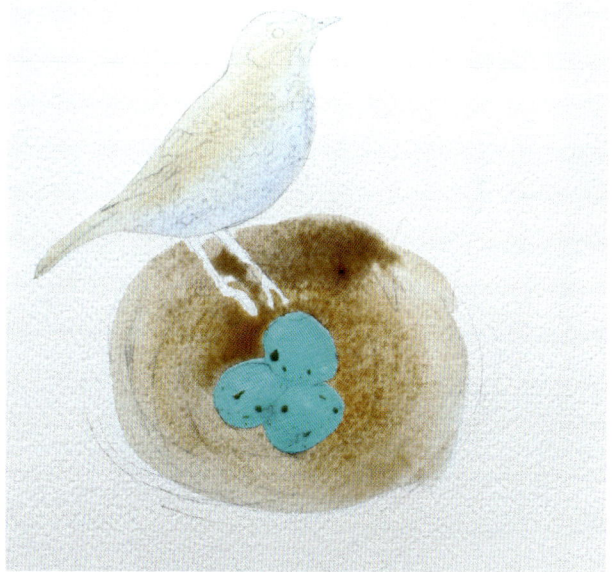

4. Apply a mix of Raw Umber and Yellow Ochre to the entire area of the nest using a size 8 brush. Add more Yellow Ochre to the center around the eggs. Make sure the masking fluid is fully dry.

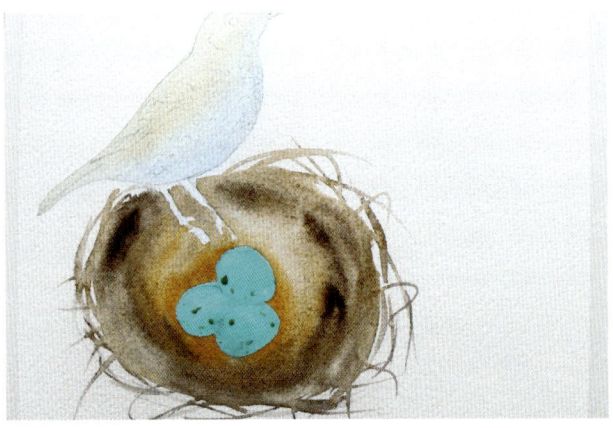

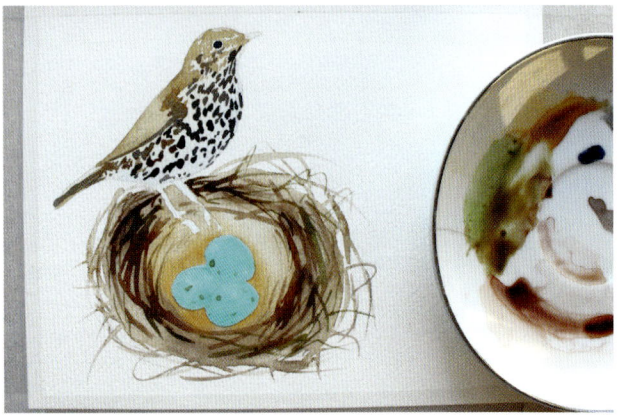

5. Apply Raw Umber to drag color and form bits of grass and twigs sticking out of the nest using a size 6 brush.

Apply Burnt Umber wet-on-wet to the middle of the nest using a size 3 brush. Let it dry fully.

6. Apply Raw Umber wet-on-dry to the back of the bird, wings, and tail using a size 3 brush.

Apply a mix of Lamp Black and Burnt Umber (milk consistency) to paint a darker brown on the back of the bird and a bit on the belly.

Apply Lamp Black (cream consistency) wet-on-dry to paint spots on the belly and the eye using a size 3 brush.

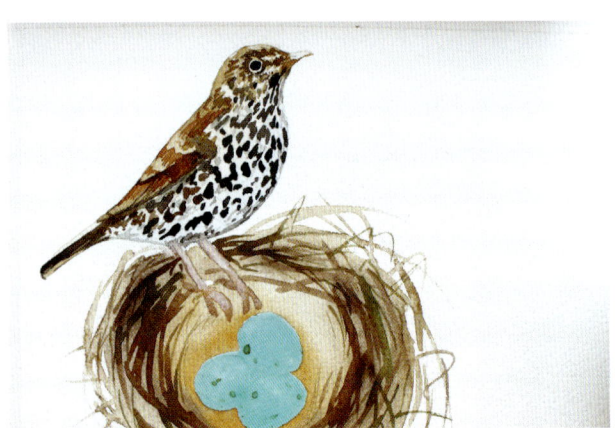

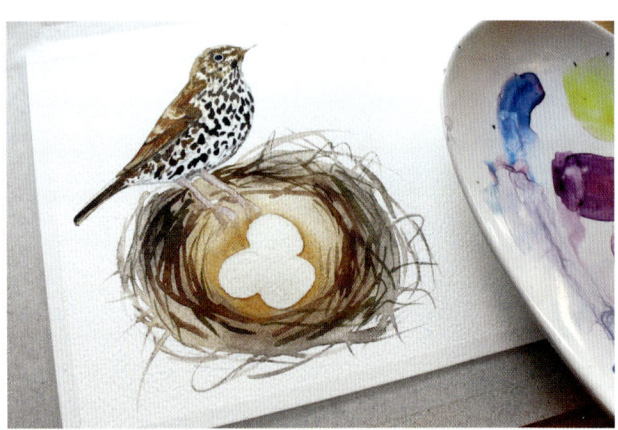

7. Prepare a mix of Sap Green and Burnt Umber, and paint grass wet-on-dry with a size 3 brush. Paint darker twigs and grass with Burnt Umber.

Apply Burnt Sienna and Raw Umber wet-on-dry around the beak and eye using a size 2/0 brush. Use this same mix to paint feathers around the face and back.

Apply a mix of Permanent Rose and Burnt Umber to the bird's legs using a size 2/0 brush. Lift some paint off to create a lighter value.

8. Gently peel off the masking fluid with your fingers.

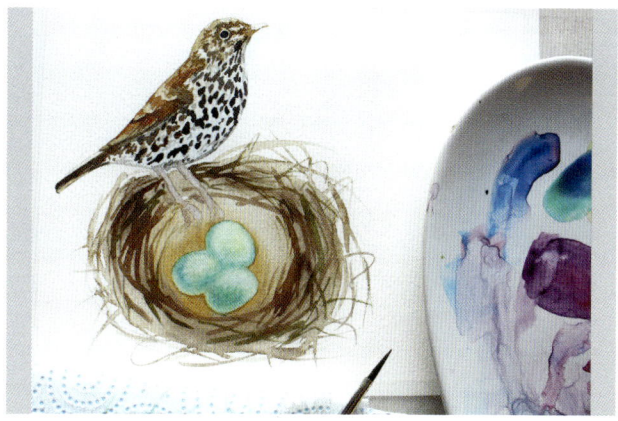

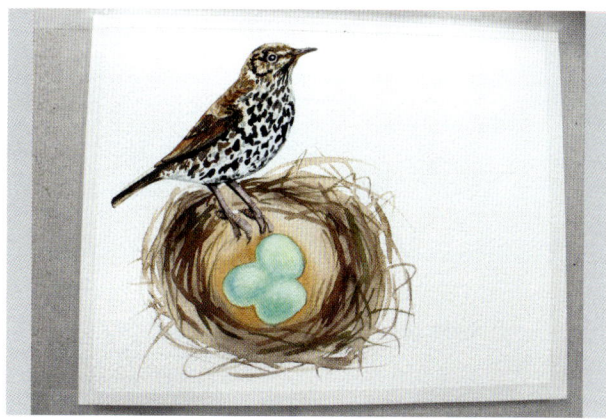

9. Apply water to all three eggs. Apply Lemon Yellow (tea) wet-on-wet using a size 3 brush, leaving the center of each untouched. Apply Prussian Blue and Lemon Yellow wet-on-wet using a size 2/0 brush, leaving the center untouched.

Mix Prussian Blue and Ultramarine Blue, then add a few touches to the shadow areas on the eggs, wet-on-wet. Use a size 3 brush to lift color from the center of each egg, then at the bottom of each egg.

10. Apply Permanent Rose and Burnt Umber to paint horizontal lines over the bird's feet using a size 2/0 brush. Apply Lamp Black (cream consistency) wet-on-dry to add the darkest values to the bird using a size 2/0 brush, painting shadows and darker feathers.

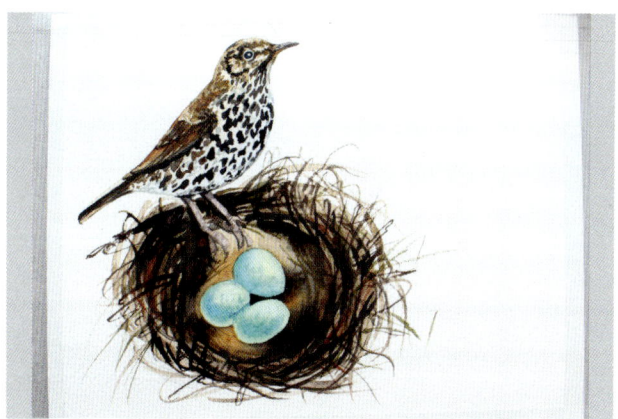

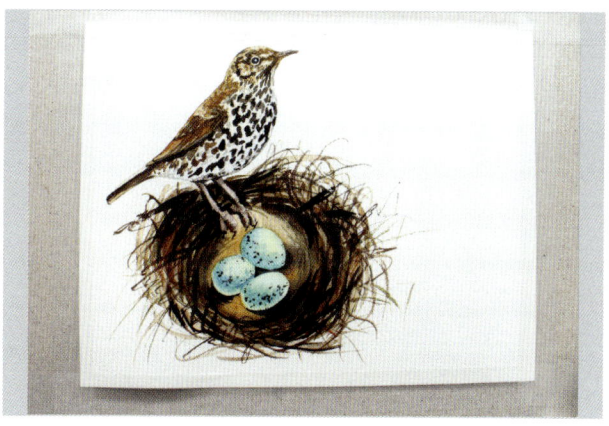

11. Activate the area around the eggs with water. Apply more colors wet-on-wet using a size 3 brush. Apply Yellow Ochre (cream) next to the eggs.

Mix Burnt Umber and Lamp Black and paint the shadow areas under the eggs, twigs, and grass. Apply a mix of Burnt Sienna and Sap Green to the nest in a few places with a size 2/0 brush for tiny details.

Apply a mix of Prussian Blue and Lemon Yellow (tea) wet-on-dry using a size 3 brush, dabbing on the eggs. Let it dry.

12. Paint black dots on the eggs wet-on-dry with Lamp Black using a size 2/0 brush. Make a few very dark twigs using Lamp Black and also paint a shadow under the bird, adding values to the eye.

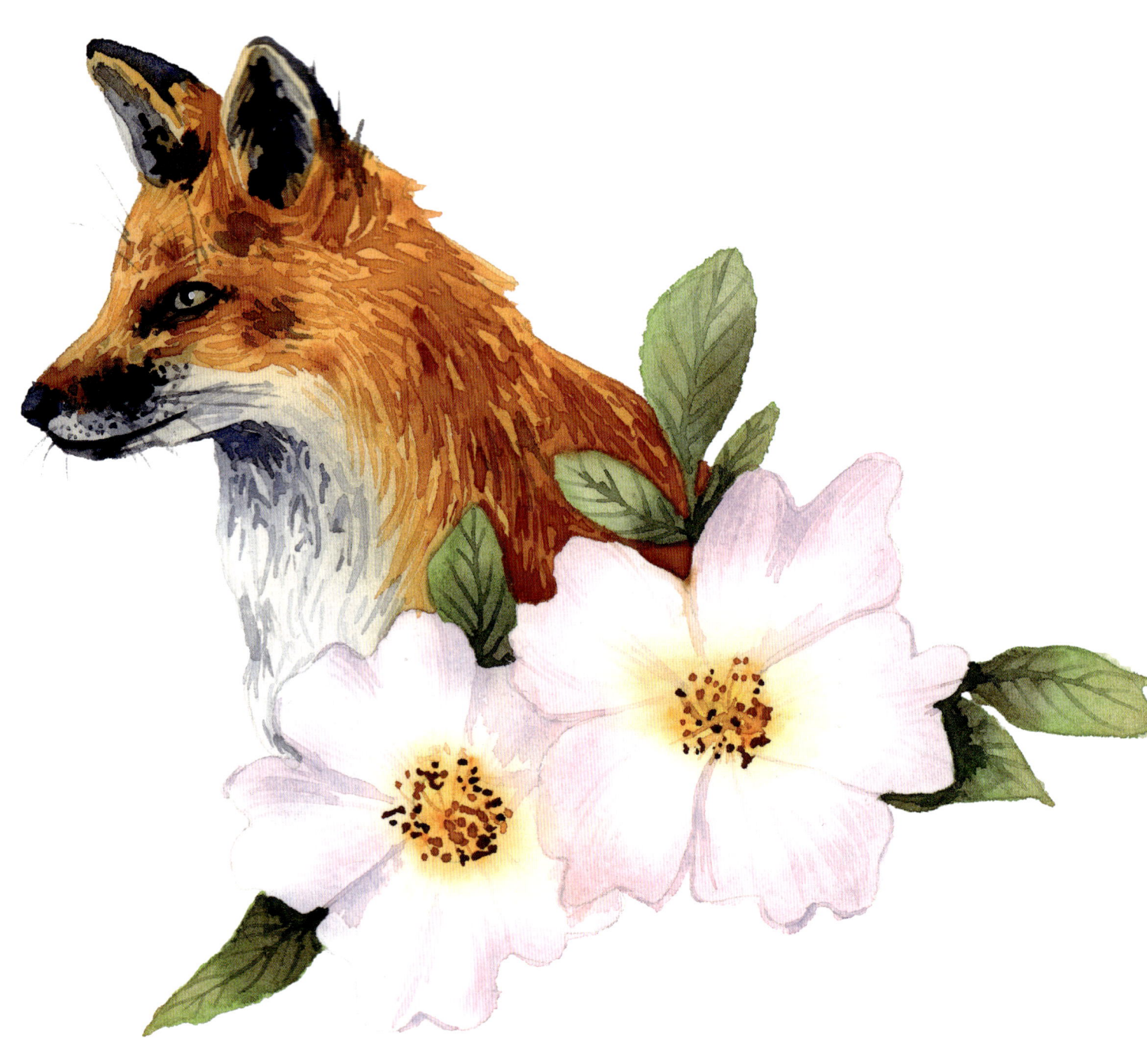

Red Fox and Dog Roses

A playful fox hides among some dog roses. This colorful scene will help you explore a variety of hues while practicing key watercolor techniques like wet-on-wet and wet-on-dry.

Colors

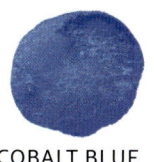 COBALT BLUE

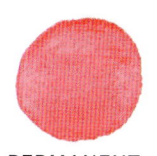 PERMANENT ROSE

 PAYNE'S GRAY

 CADMIUM YELLOW HUE

 RAW UMBER

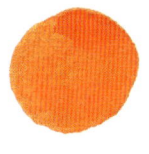 CADMIUM ORANGE HUE

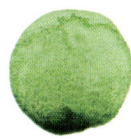 SAP GREEN

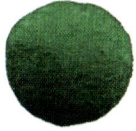 HOOKER'S GREEN

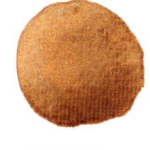 BURNT SIENNA

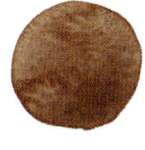 BURNT UMBER

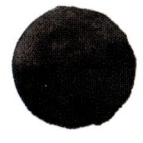 LAMP BLACK

 WHITE GOUACHE

Brushes

Size 6 round brush

Size 3 round brush

Size 2/0 round brush for details

Paper

300 gsm cold-pressed

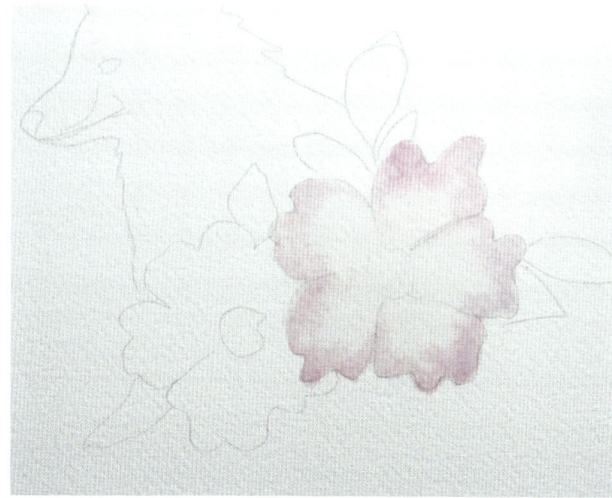

1. Apply an even layer of water to one of the flowers. Apply a mix of Cobalt Blue and Permanent Rose (tea consistency) mainly to the edges of each petal on the watered flower using a size 2/0 brush. Let it dry.

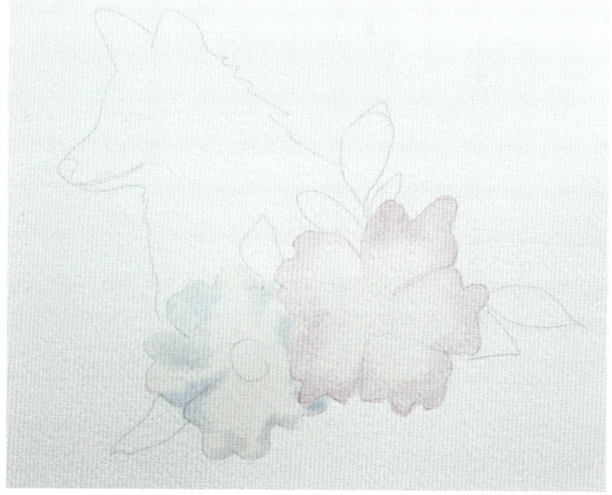

2. Repeat the process with the other flower by first wetting it, then using a mix of Cobalt Blue and Payne's Gray (tea consistency) to add to the edges, making that flower slightly gray. Then use a little bit of Permanent Rose and apply it wet-on-wet on some petals.

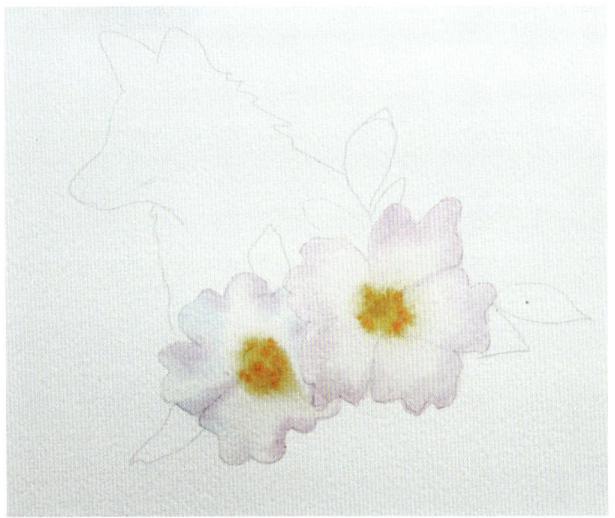

3. Use Cadmium Yellow Hue and then Raw Umber to apply dots in the center of both flowers. Follow with Cadmium Orange Hue to make the dots brighter. Let it dry.

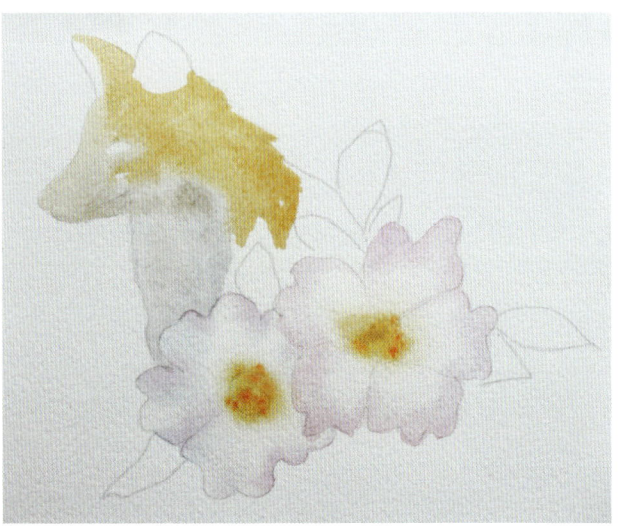

4. Prepare a mix of Raw Umber and Payne's Gray (tea consistency) on your palette. Use a size 6 brush to apply water to the white chest of the fox, then apply the Raw Umber and Payne's Gray mix.

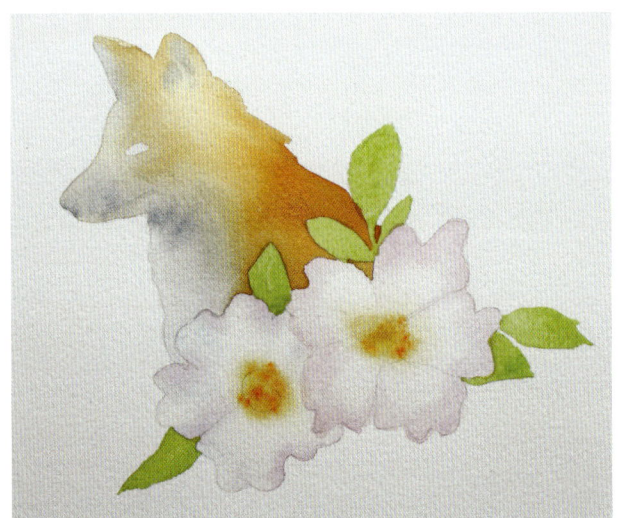

5. Apply just Raw Umber to the nose and then use Cadmium Orange Hue (tea consistency) to paint orange areas on the fox using a size 3–6 brush. Use more orange on the back of the fox. Apply Payne's Gray wet-on-dry on the face area, under the chin, and inside the ears using a size 3 brush.

Apply Sap Green (milk consistency) wet-on-dry to all leaves using a size 3 brush.

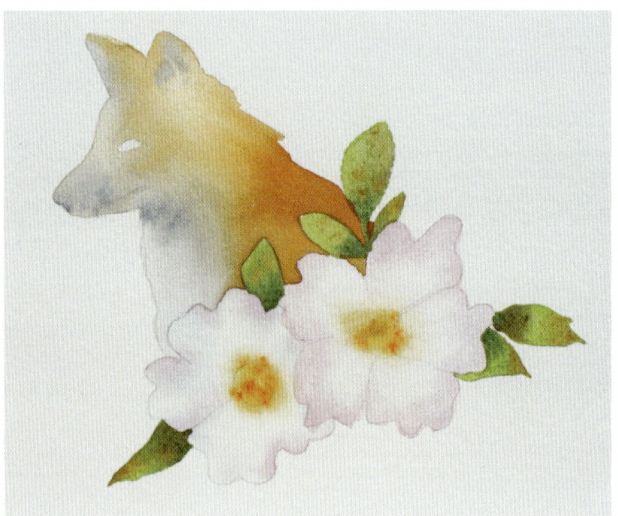

6. While the leaves are still wet, apply a mix of Hooker's Green and Raw Umber (milk consistency) to the bottom of each leaf to add shade and value using a size 3 brush. Change to Burnt Sienna and add a few dots to the wet leaves. Let it dry.

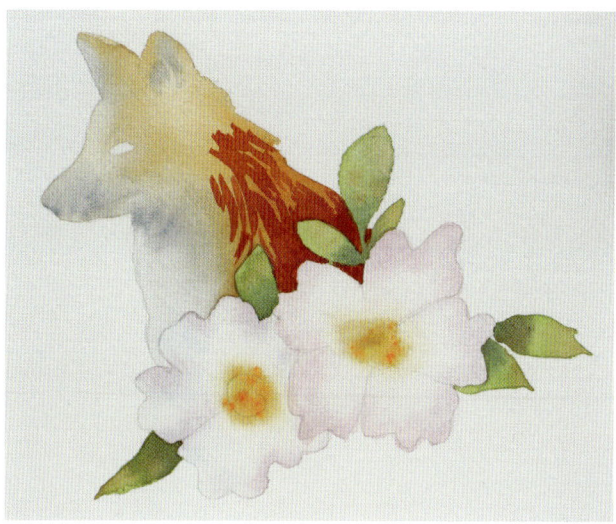

7. Apply a mix of Burnt Sienna and Cadmium Orange Hue (milk consistency) wet-on-dry to the back of the fox to imitate fur.

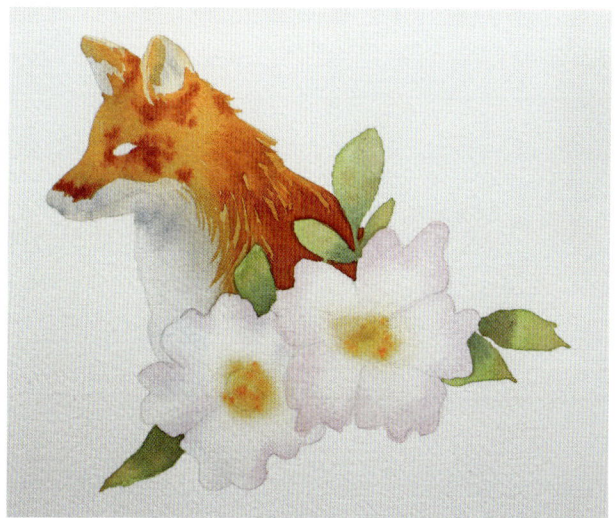

8. Activate the remaining area of orange fur with a wet size 3 brush, then add the Burnt Sienna and Cadmium Orange Hue mix wet-on-wet to darken some patches of fur using a size 2/0 brush.

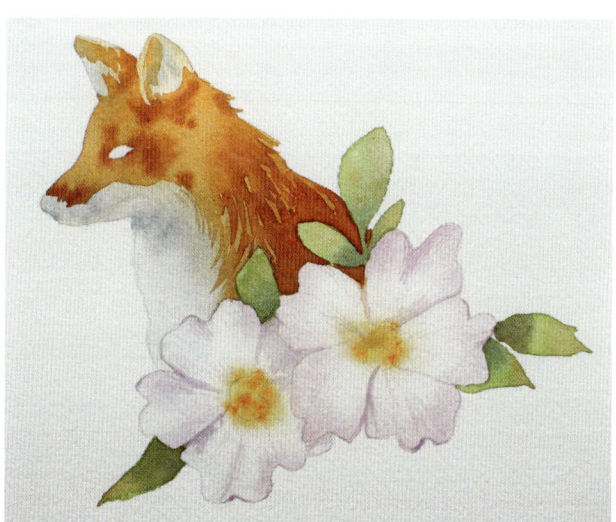

9. Mix Cobalt Blue and Permanent Rose (tea consistency) and use light transparent brushstrokes on the petals of a dog rose.

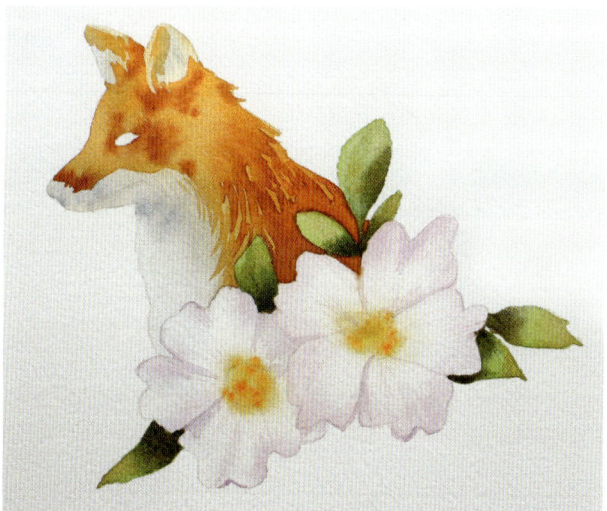

10. Make dots with Burnt Umber wet-on-dry in the middle of the flower using a size 2/0 brush. Change to the Burnt Sienna and Cadmium Orange Hue mix and make more dots with different colors, applying them randomly. Use Cadmium Orange Hue to paint the filaments.

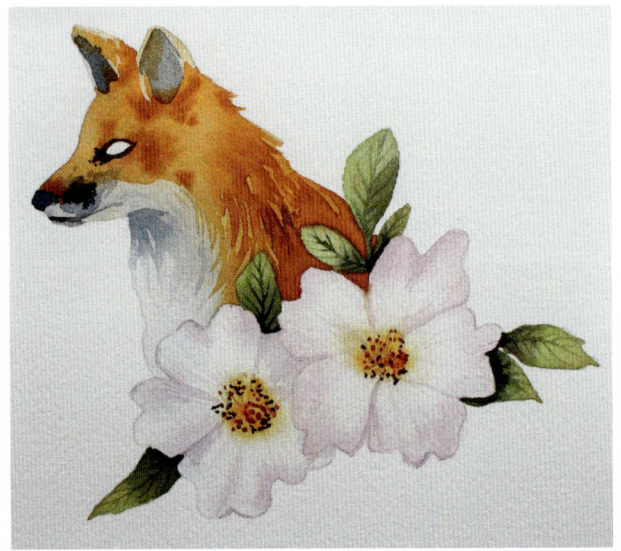

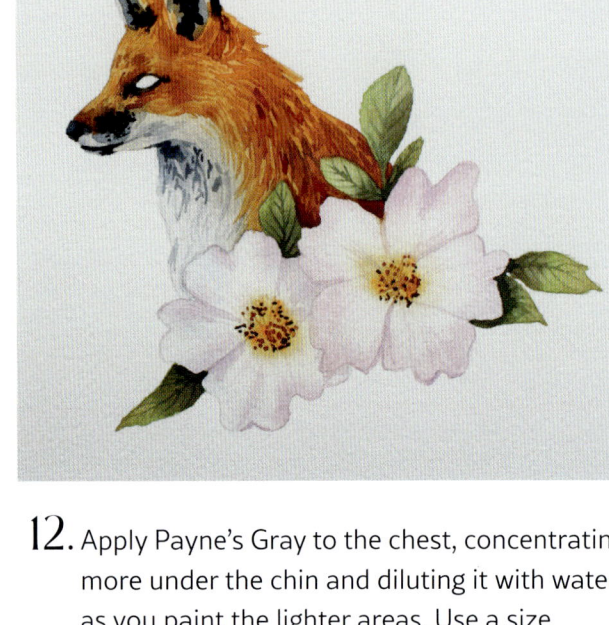

11. Apply a mix of Raw Umber and Hooker's Green wet-on-dry to paint veins on leaves using a size 2/0 brush. Apply Payne's Gray wet-on-dry to add black details on the fox's face using a size 2/0 brush.

12. Apply Payne's Gray to the chest, concentrating more under the chin and diluting it with water as you paint the lighter areas. Use a size 2/0 brush to paint fur and follow the fur's directions on the back with the Burnt Sienna and Cadmium Orange Hue mix and on the face. Add black dots to the darker patch near the nose and add more depth to the mouth, nose, and tops of the ears.

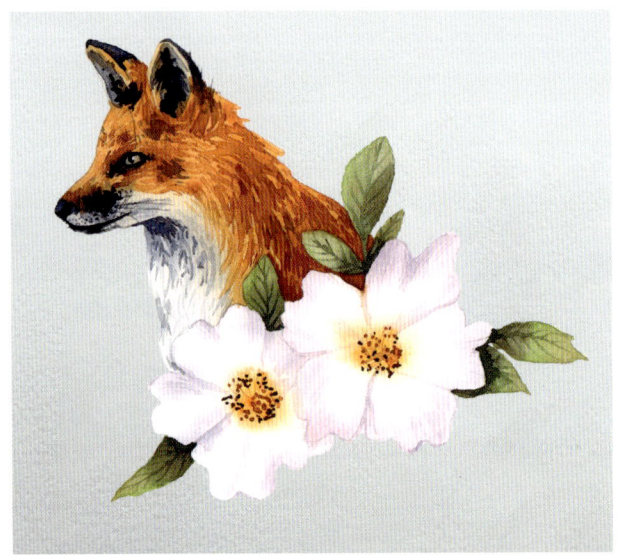

13. Use the tiniest size 2/0 brush to paint whiskers. Color the inside of the fox's eye with a mix of Sap Green and Burnt Sienna, let it dry, then make a pupil with Lamp Black. Let it dry and then come back with white gouache to add a highlight.

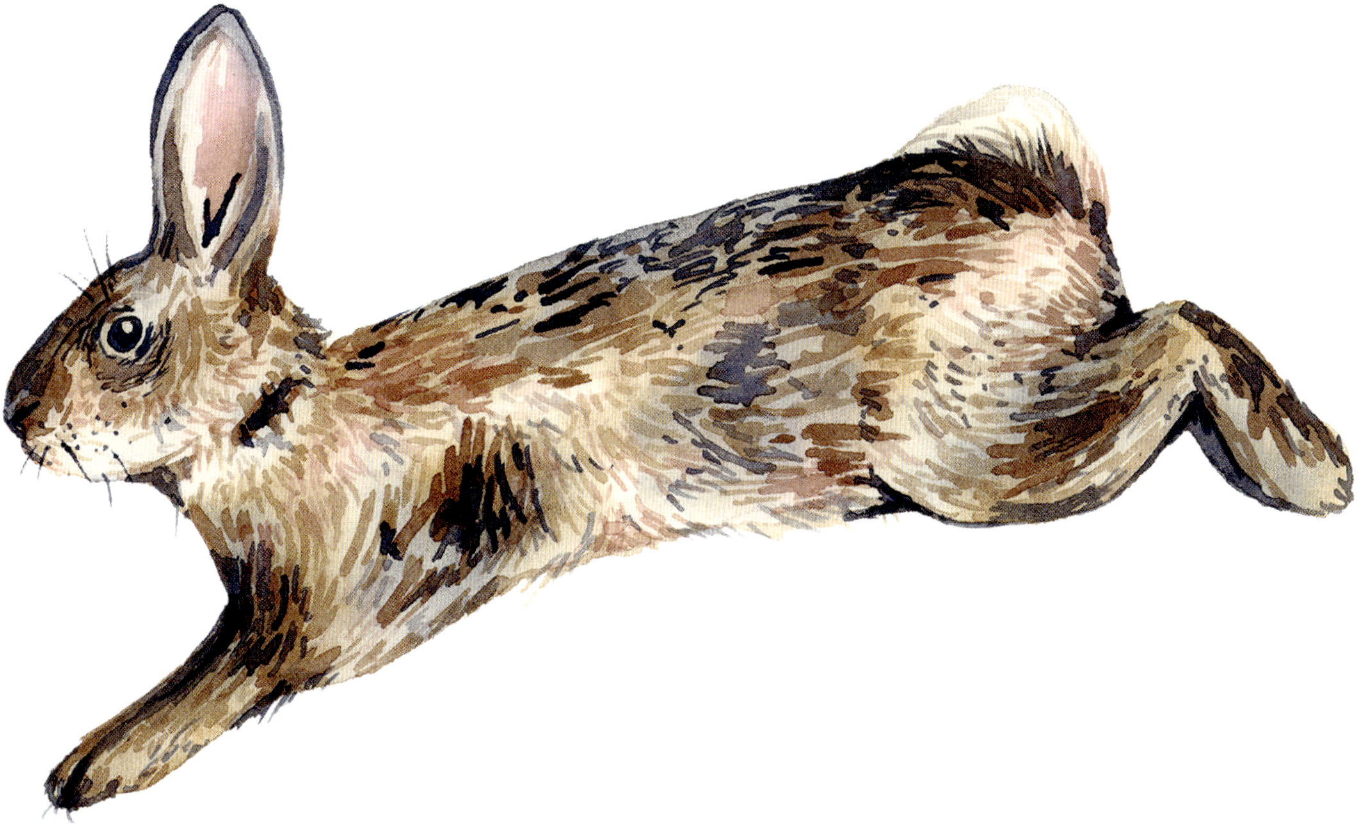

Brown Hare

Who wouldn't want to capture an image of a young hare running through the fields? In this lesson, you'll practice wet-on-wet and wet-on-dry techniques to create depth and detail, while also learning to depict the movement and dynamics of an animal's fur.

Colors

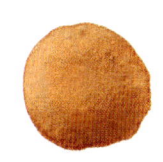
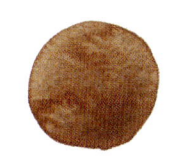
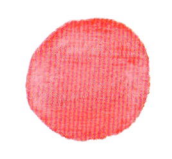

| RAW UMBER | BURNT SIENNA | BURNT UMBER | PERMANENT ROSE | PAYNE'S GRAY |

Brushes

Size 6 round brush

Size 3 round brush

Size 2/0 round brush for details

Paper

300 gsm cold-pressed

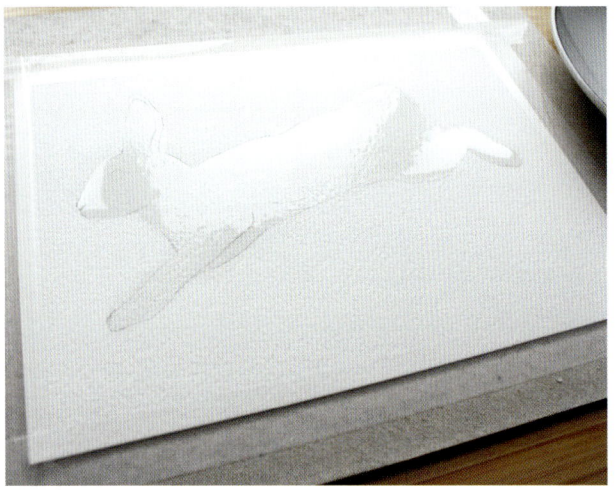

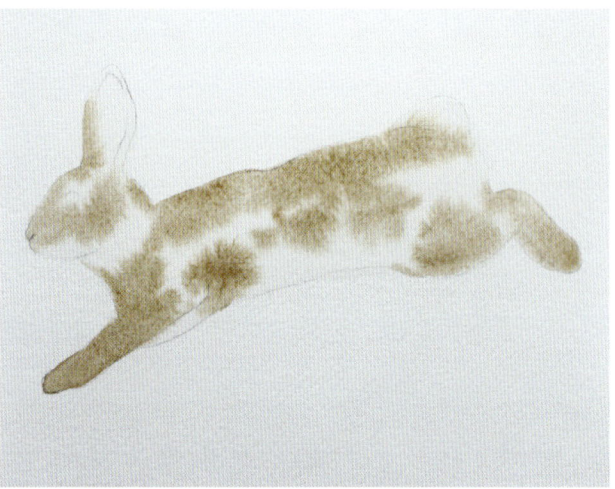

1. Apply a thick layer of water using a size 6 brush to the entire area of the hare. Spread the water evenly, making sure to cover all corners up to the pencil marks. The surface should be evenly glistening, with no large puddles of water.

2. Prepare the following colors on a ceramic palette in the order they will be applied: Raw Umber, Burnt Sienna, Permanent Rose, and Payne's Gray. Each color should be mixed to a tea consistency. Apply these colors wet-on-wet using a size 2/0 brush and starting with the Raw Umber.

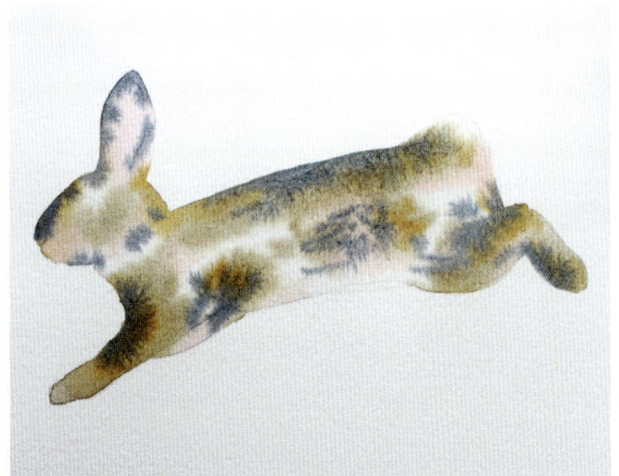

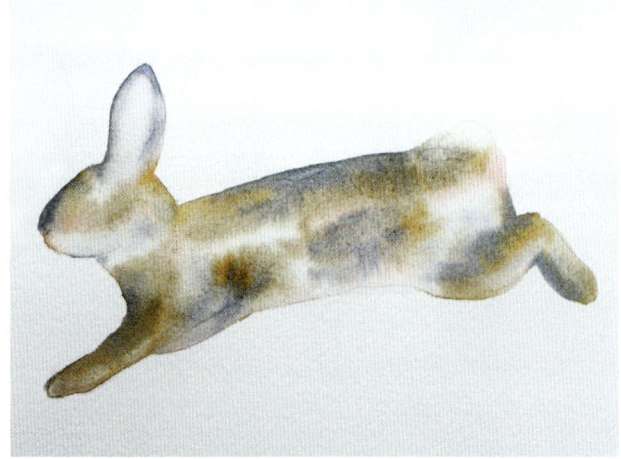

3. Apply the rest of the colors in the order listed above. The wet-on-wet technique will create soft edges between the colors.

4. If you notice too much pigment has been applied, use a size 6 brush to lift off excess color with the lifting technique. Let it dry completely.

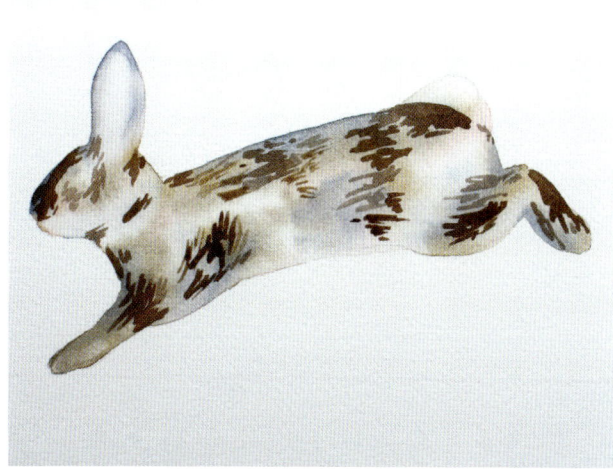

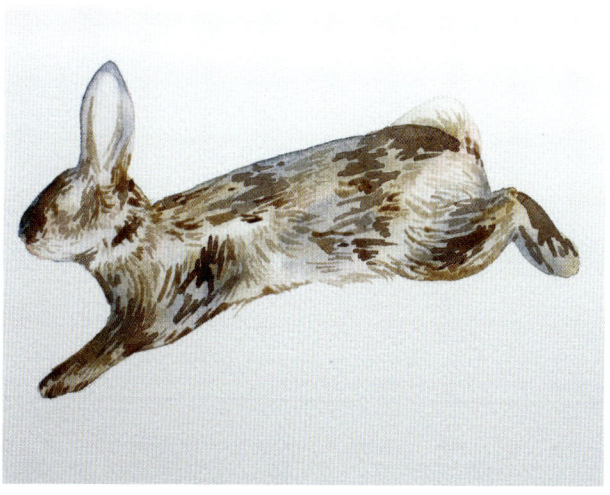

5. Apply a mix of Burnt Umber and Raw Umber (milk consistency) wet-on-dry using a size 3 brush. Pay attention to the direction of your brushstrokes, as they should follow the animal's anatomy and movement on the body.

6. Apply a mix of Permanent Rose and Raw Umber (milk consistency) wet-on-dry using a size 3 brush.

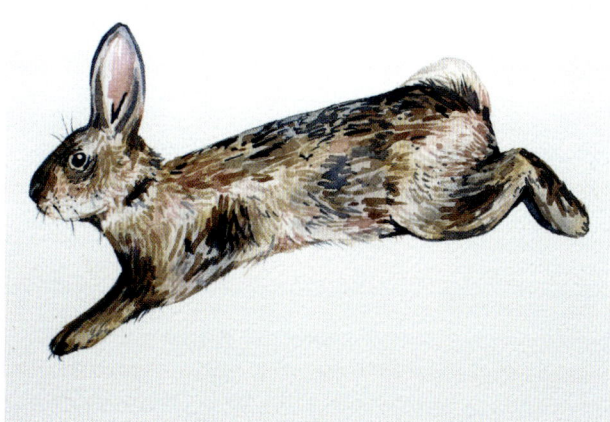

7. Next, switch to a size 2/0 brush and use Payne's Gray (milk consistency) to paint the darkest values. Focus on painting the darker fur areas, eyes, edges of the ears, and dark hair on the back of the hare.

   Vary your brushstrokes: Some should be longer, while others should be short and dotted, to capture the texture and direction of the fur.

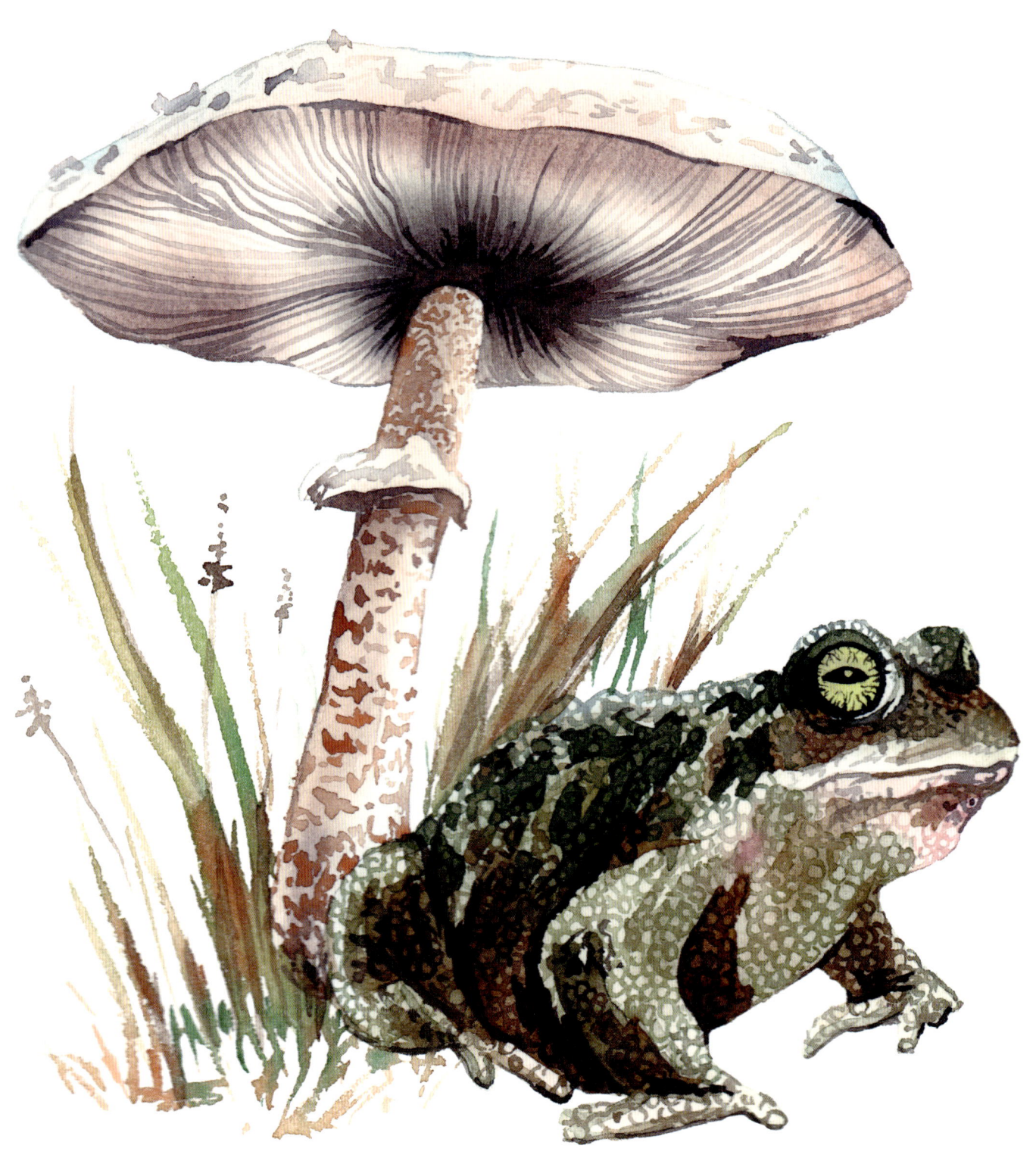

Parasol Mushroom and Common Toad

A traveling toad rests under the huge cap of a field mushroom, creating a whimsical scene that's a true watercolor masterpiece. This more complex tutorial will help you practice painting details, blending colors, and applying wet-on-wet techniques.

Colors

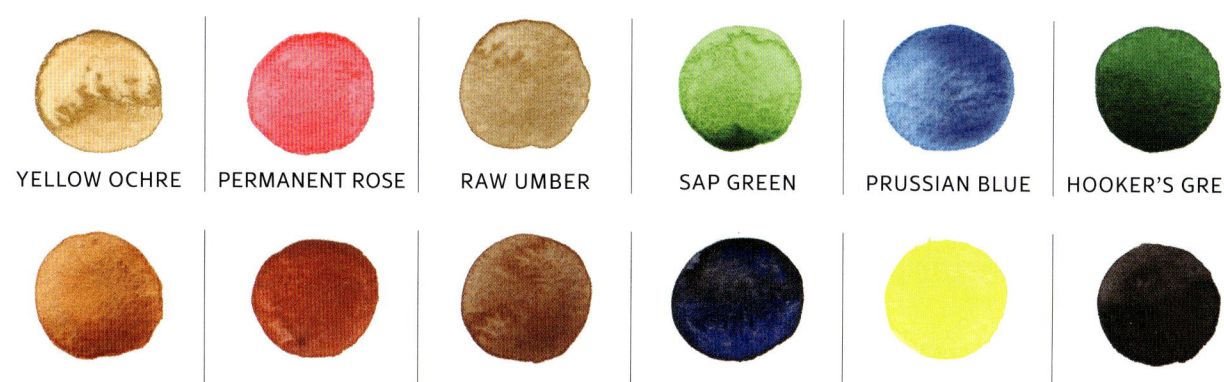

YELLOW OCHRE PERMANENT ROSE RAW UMBER SAP GREEN PRUSSIAN BLUE HOOKER'S GREEN

BURNT SIENNA LIGHT RED BURNT UMBER PAYNE'S GRAY LEMON YELLOW LAMP BLACK

Brushes

Size 8 round brush

Size 6 round brush

Size 3 round brush

Size 2/0 round brush for details

Paper

300 gsm cold-pressed

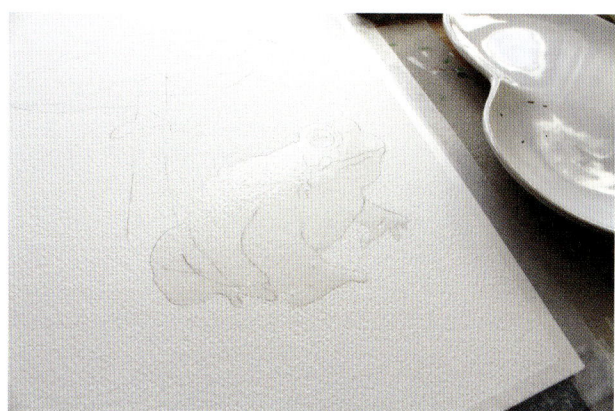

1. Apply a thick layer of water to the entire area of the toad using a size 6 brush.

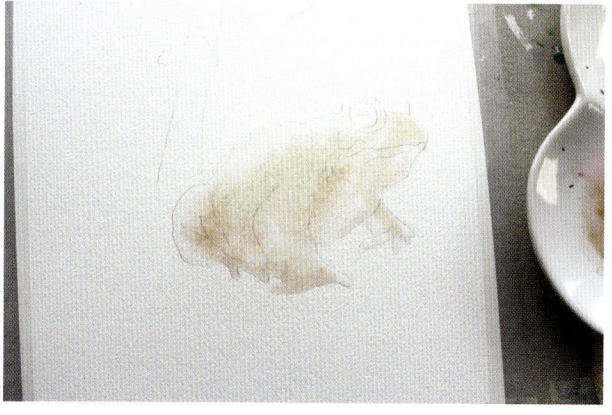

2. Apply a mix of Yellow Ochre and Permanent Rose (tea consistency) wet-on-wet using a size 6 brush.

Apply a mix of Raw Umber and Sap Green wet-on-wet above the first one.

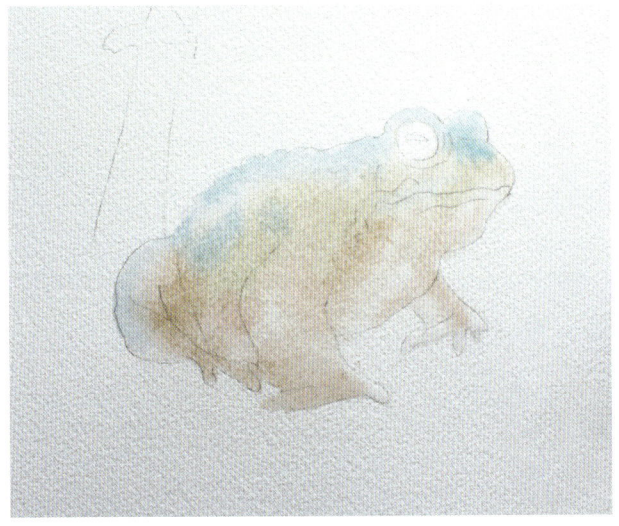

3. Apply Prussian Blue (tea consistency) wet-on-wet.

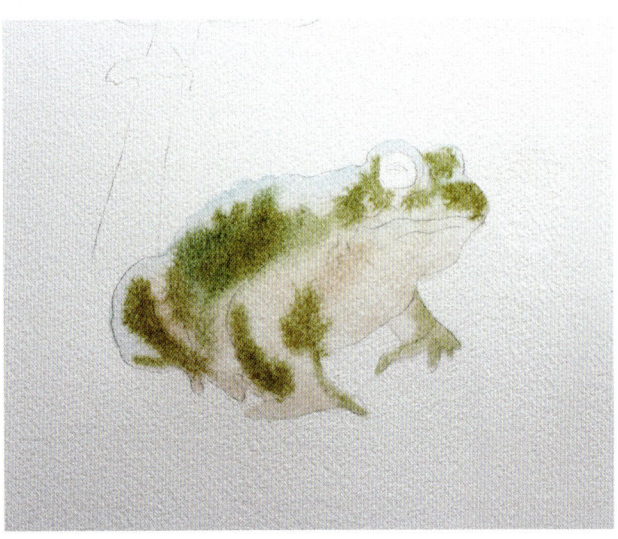

4. Apply a mix of Hooker's Green and Burnt Sienna (cream consistency) wet-on-wet using a size 6 brush. Leave it to dry.

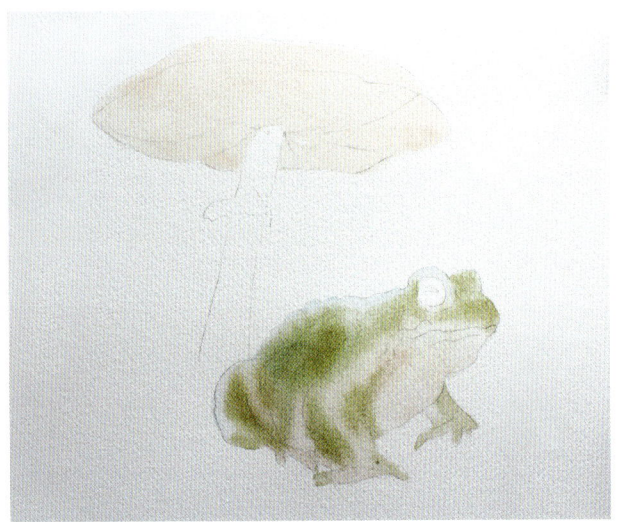

5. Apply a mix of Yellow Ochre and Permanent Rose (tea consistency) wet-on-dry using a size 8 brush to the cap of the mushroom, avoiding the stalk.

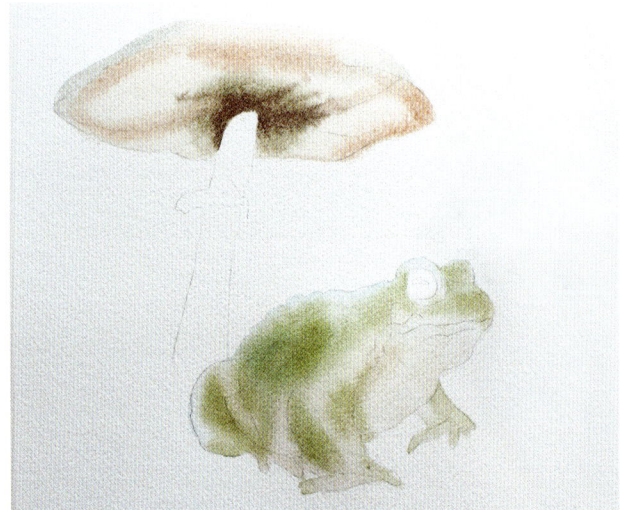

6. Immediately mix Hooker's Green and Light Red and apply wet-on-wet to the area around the stalk using a size 3 brush, making it dark brown with a hint of green.

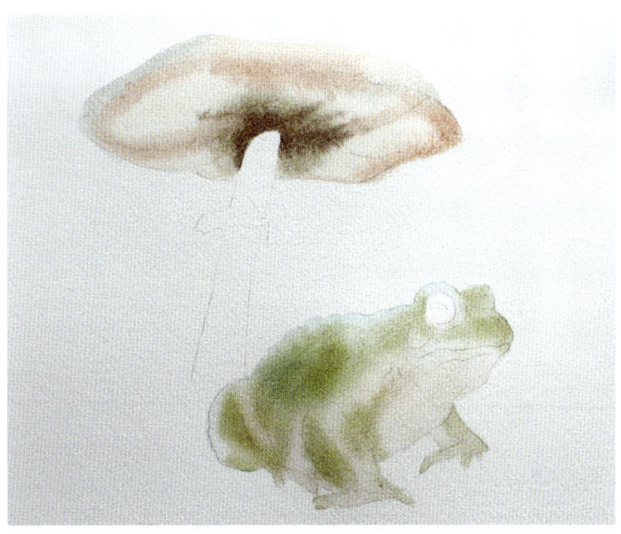

7. Apply a mix of Prussian Blue and Light Red (tea consistency) to the top of the mushroom, making it slightly lighter on the right-hand side.

Add a layer of Light Red (tea consistency) wet-on-wet around the cap using a size 3 brush. Let it dry.

Apply water to the stalk using a size 6 brush. Apply a mix of Raw Umber and Prussian Blue (tea consistency) wet-on-wet to the middle of the stalk.

Use Light Red and Burnt Umber to go over that area again.

Wash your brush and apply a little bit of Prussian Blue wet-on-wet to the right-hand side using a size 2/0 brush.

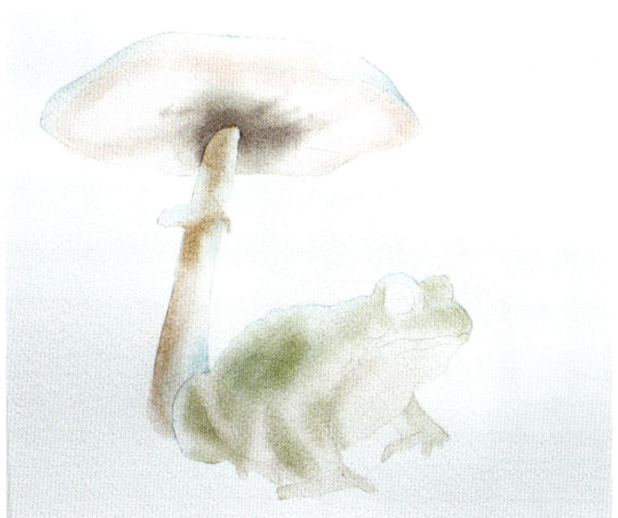

8. Mix Light Red and Payne's Gray (cream consistency) and wet the area under the cap using a size 6 brush.

Apply this mix around the edges wet-on-wet using a size 3 brush. Then use more to paint the area where the cap joins the stalk. Let it dry.

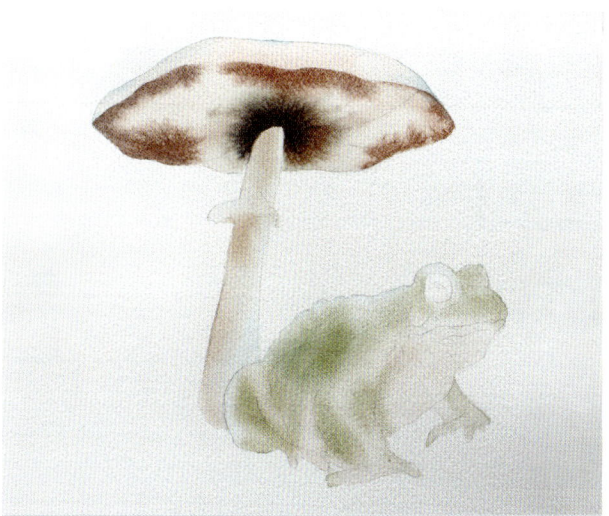

9. Apply the same mix of Light Red and Payne's Gray (cream consistency) wet-on-dry to paint darker values on the stalk using a size 3 brush.

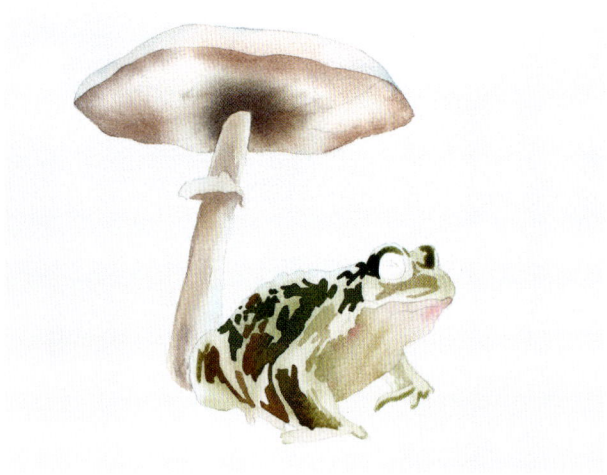

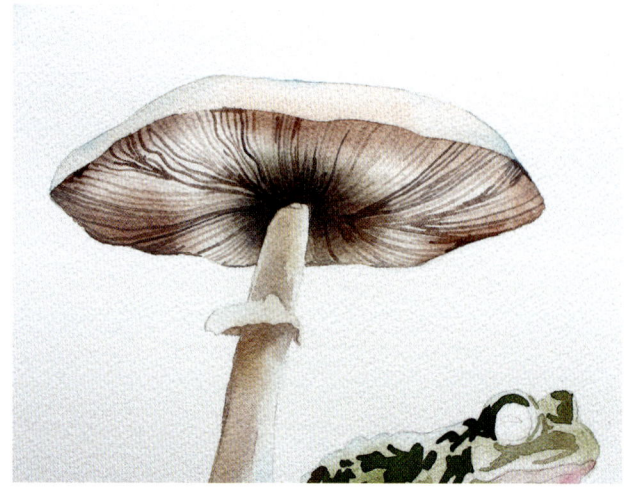

10. Prepare two mixes: Hooker's Green and Burnt Umber, and Yellow Ochre and Raw Umber. Apply patches of different shades on the toad wet-on-dry using a size 3 brush.

Activate the belly with water and apply the Yellow Ochre and Raw Umber mix. Add Permanent Rose wet-on-wet in a few spots using a size 3 brush.

11. Apply a mix of Light Red and Payne's Gray to paint lines under the mushroom's cap using a size 2/0 brush.

Paint more lines over the darker ones close to the stalk, adding more Payne's Gray to the mix.

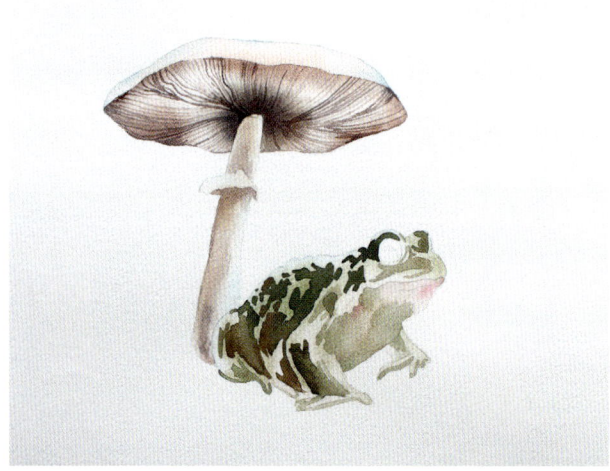

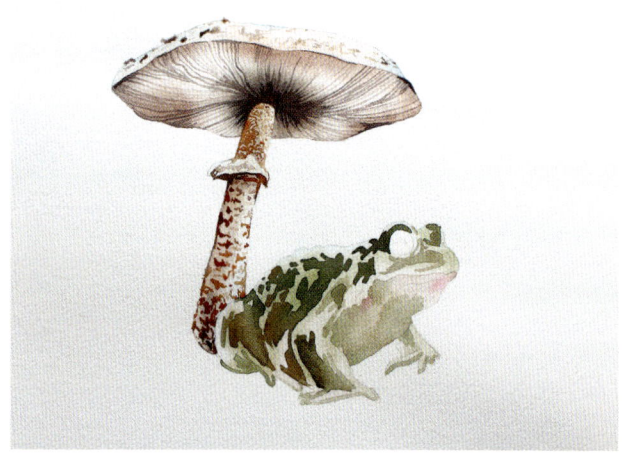

12. Apply a mix of Burnt Sienna and Light Red wet-on-dry to the stalk using a size 2/0 brush.

Mix Burnt Sienna and Burnt Umber and paint darker spots on the stalk, both wet-on-dry and wet-on-wet.

Apply a mix of Payne's Gray and Light Red wet-on-dry to paint flakes on the cap.

Add darker values between the top of the cap and underneath using the Payne's Gray and Light Red mix.

13. Use a mix of Raw Umber and Burnt Sienna to add darker brown values wet-on-dry using a size 3 brush. Let it dry.

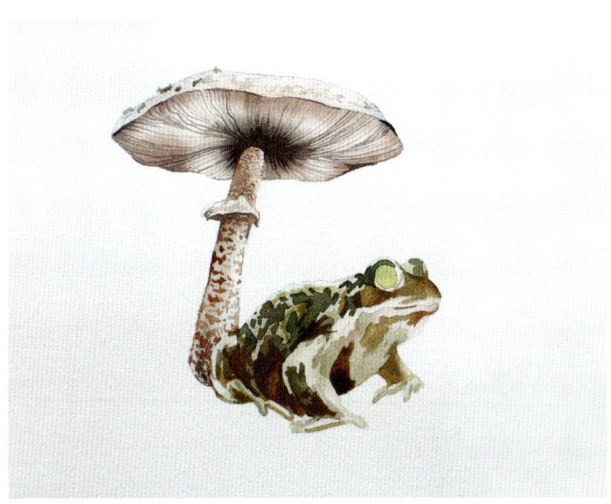

14. Apply Lemon Yellow to paint the toad's eye using a size 3 brush.

Prepare mixes to paint little circles all over the toad's body:

- Raw Umber and Burnt Sienna to paint over medium brown areas
- Hooker's Green and Burnt Umber to paint over dark green areas
- Prussian Blue and Sap Green to paint on top of the toad
- Permanent Rose and Raw Umber for the belly area
- Sap Green and Raw Umber to paint light green areas

Apply them wet-on-dry using a size 2/0 brush. Let it dry.

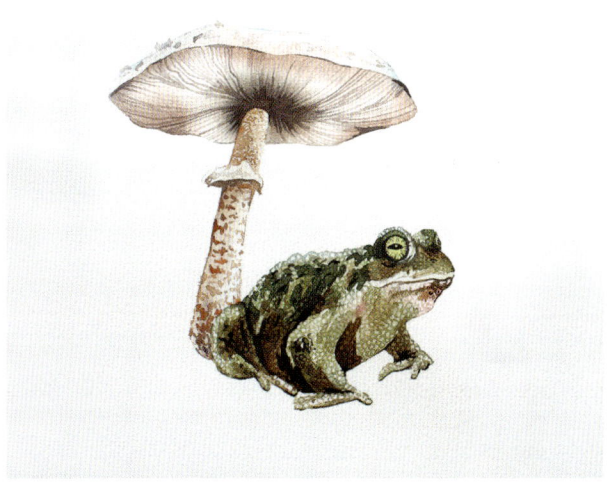

15. Use a mix of Burnt Umber and Hooker's Green to paint the darkest values on the toad's body.

Apply Lamp Black wet-on-dry to paint the pupil and black veins inside the eye using a size 2/0 brush.

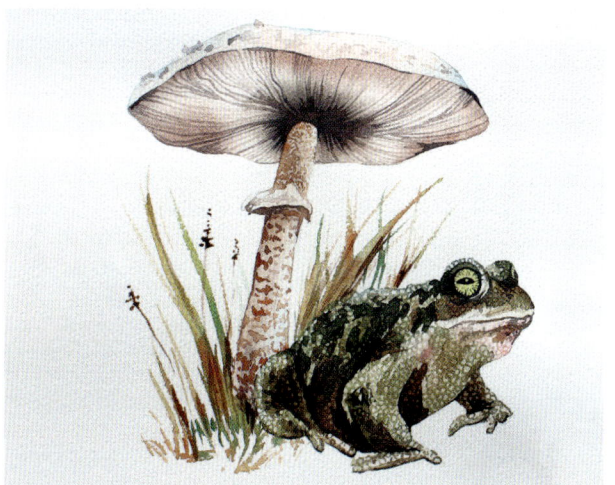

16. Paint grass behind the toad using a size 3 brush with a mix of Raw Umber and Sap Green (tea consistency). Paint the grass from the bottom up to ensure pointy ends.

Use Burnt Sienna to paint a few blades of grass, then Hooker's Green.

Finish the grass by using Burnt Umber to paint a few seed heads.

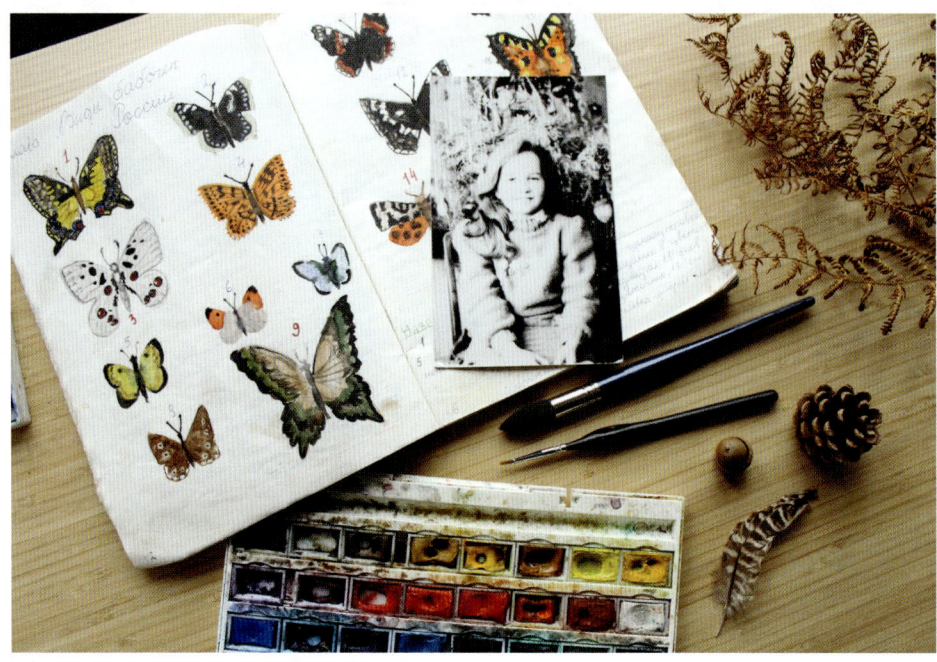

Young Rita and the nature journal she kept as a child.

About the Author

Rita Gould, also known as Margarita Galkina, is a Russian-born watercolor artist from Voronezh, currently residing in Staffordshire, UK. Her illustrations are characterized by intricate details, vibrant colors, and rich textures. Rita channels her passion into creating nature-themed stationery products, including calendars, notepads, postcards, greeting cards, stickers, and art prints.

Rita's love for the natural world began in childhood, spending summers at a *dacha*, or country house, surrounded by nature. She spent her days observing butterflies, frogs, and other creatures, which sparked her fascination with insects, particularly butterflies and moths. At age ten, she began a journal documenting local species, complete with illustrations.

Rita attended art school for five years, exploring various artistic mediums, including watercolor, composition, and ceramics. However, she initially pursued a degree in journalism and then transitioned into design. Rita worked in the publishing industry, IT sector, and web design, creating designs and illustrations for various clients. After a decade in digital design, she sought greater fulfillment in traditional art forms.

After moving to the UK and welcoming her son, Rita shifted her focus to watercolor and gouache. This pivotal change allowed her to find joy in painting nature, regardless of her exhaustion from motherhood. Over the years, she developed a unique style that blends loose watercolor techniques with detailed brushwork, focusing on subjects like insects, plants, and woodland creatures.

In recent years, Rita has expanded her artistic pursuits to include teaching watercolor skills both online and in-person, offering a variety of workshops in her local community. She runs an online watercolor education platform on Patreon, where she shares essential techniques and insights for aspiring artists, helping beginners gain confidence in their artistic journeys.

When she's not painting, Rita enjoys spending time with her family; gardening; walking in the woods; caring for her chickens, gecko, dog, and cat; or visiting museums, historical houses, and vintage markets.

Index